LOOKING 4 AZTLAN

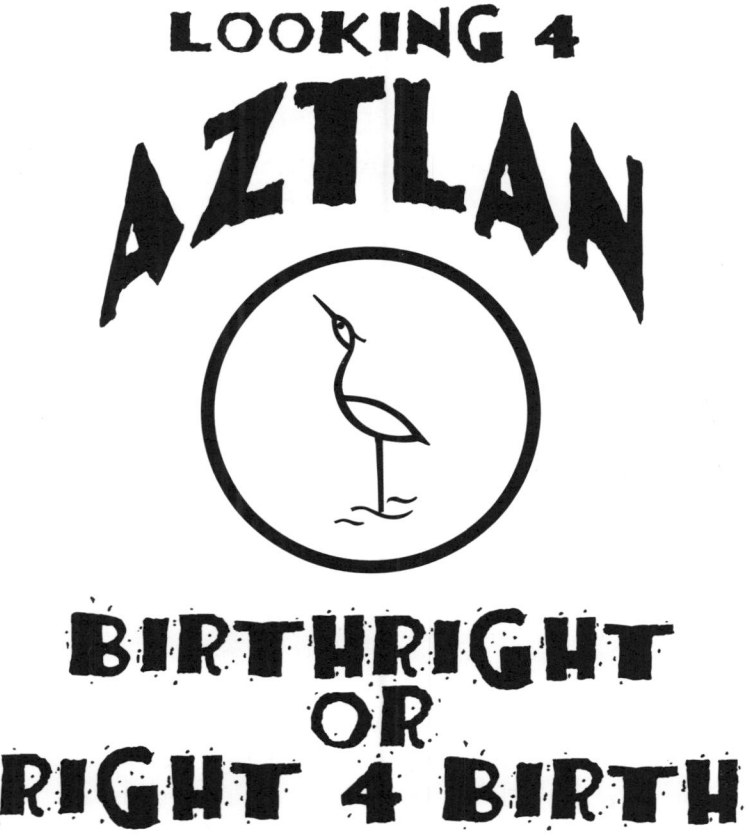

BIRTHRIGHT OR RIGHT 4 BIRTH

BY
APAXU MAIZ

Sun Dog Press

LOOKING 4 AZTLÁN
BIRTHRIGHT OR RIGHT 4 BIRTH

©2004 Apaxu Maiz

All rights reserved. No part of this manuscript may be used or reproduced in any manner without written permission, except in the case of brief quotations embodied in critical articles and reviews. For information, contact the author at:

info@xicanonationalism.com

www.xicanonationalism.com

Cover and interior design and layout by Danny Layne, JSRI
Cover Artwork provided by Tizoc Xita Garcia

This publication was privately funded by the author. The contents and views expressed herein are solely those of the author and may not necessarily reflect those of JSRI or Michigan State University.

DEDICATION

This Book is dedicated to my wife, Tonatzin. Because, it was she who had the foresight, insight, courage, persistence, resilience, and commitment to initially force-feed me the concept of "MI CASA PRIMERO, PRIMERO MI CASA."

Thank you, Koya

To Maria Kresta, a girl with a #Still, yo telephone not, must you find my Kez, book y[...]

ACKNOWLEDGEMENTS

The researching and compiling of this book gives credence to the principle: "No man is an island." Many individuals contributed both knowingly and unknowingly, directly and indirectly. Though I take complete personal responsibility for the tone, the grammar, the directions, and the conclusions of this writing there were many people who contributed interlocking bits, pieces, at times even chunks. I was humbled by their contributions and I hope this final product gives them pride to see their names associated with it. Thank you all.

To Diana Rivera who at the time I began my research was head of the M.S.U. map library. She presently serves as a Xicano studies bibliographer. Her assistance led me to the maps of Alexander Von Humboldt.

To Kathleen Wessies who replaced Diana at the map library. Ms. Wessies directed me to the map library's archives in the basement and the monumental classic titled, *Mapping the Transmississippi West* by Carl I. Wheat.

To Daniel Osuna who sent me the copied portion of the Disturnell Map of 1847 that inspired me to go looking 4 Aztlán.

To Ernesto Vigil who sent me a newspaper article on the 1847 Disturnell map and Aztlán that provided the vivid illustration of what this map means to Xicanos and how it is being promoted nationally.

To Roberto Rodriguez and Patricia Gonzales who took the pioneering initiative to make the 1847 Disturnell map available to the populous by reproducing and distributing it on a large scale. This map has provided La Raza with a benchmark for debates, pro and con.

To Ted, Annette, Arianna, and "Redikalus" Nicolas Alfaro for providing me with shelter, food, jobs, and love.

To Tizóc Xita García who did the artwork for the book's cover and unknowingly served as my spiritual advisor over the years.

To Huakín Puma García who provided me with shelter, food, jobs, money, and medical treatment.

To Hercules Cimorreli who contributed food, shelter and friendship.

A special thanks to Julian Samara Research Institute (JSRI) at Michigan State University. JSRI assertively opened its doors and provided me the forum to be a voice on a national level. To Dr. Israel Cuellar, its courageous director, who took a personal yet impartial interest in my right to be heard. To JSRI staff who trusted Dr. Israel Cuellar's judgment and intentions. To Danny Layne who provided his time, expertise and effort in the book's layout. And, to Dr. Saturnino "Nino" Rodriguez who challenged me and encouraged me.

Ultimately, I want to thank a person who must remain a silhouette. Unfortunately, it is a shame, but this person cannot be acknowledged by name. Because, even though this country supposedly prides its dedication to the constitutional principles of "freedom of speech" and "freedom of association," the reality is you can speak and associate freely as long as people are not listening or following. I expect that there will be persons out there in readership land who will listen and react accordingly to what I have written and suggested. Consequently, I myself expect to eventually be a target of Americans in general and Xicanos in particular. Therefore, I cannot publicly acknowledge this person.

Apaxu Maiz

TABLE OF CONTENTS

Preface i
Introduction..v

Part One: The Chronological Metamorphosis of Aztlán, The Place

I.   The Mexica go Looking 4 Aztlán 2
      1433: History a la Carte 3
      A Special Note on Codices 6
      1493: Official Birth of Las Indias 8
      The European Doctrine of Conquest and Discovery 9

II.   1519: The Spaniards go Looking 4 Aztlán 12
      A Special Note about Maps...14
      1520: The Origin of the Place Name California.......................17
      1528: The Golden Age of Chisme 19
      1530: Follow the Yellow Brick Road 20
      1536: De Spies Missionaries 21

III. 1538: Chicomoztoc Another Name 4 Aztlán 23

IV. 1539: Cibola: Yet Another Name 4 Aztlán is Born....................25
      Play It Again, Sam..26
      Cibola Maps: 1541, 1578, 1597 27

V.   1540: Gran Quivira is Born, Yet Another Name 4 Aztlán 32

VI. 1556: Monkey See, Monkey Do:
      Cartographers Go Looking 4 Aztlán..36

VII. 1565: Copala: Another Name 4 Aztlán......................................38
      1570 39
      1577: The First Map Showing the Name, Aztlán 40
      1578: The Cibola Fantasy Continues 41
      1581, 1582, 1583, 1587 The Mysterious Large Lake of Gold 42
      1598: Oñate Returns to Find the Mysterious Lake of Gold................43

VIII.	1604-05: Sante Fe: Base Camp in Looking 4 Aztlán	44
	1650	46
	1652: Quien Sabe?	47
IX.	1678: Teguayo, Another Name 4 Aztlán	48
	Lake Copala	50
	Sierra Azul	51
	1686: Teguayo vs. Gran Quivira, a Cartographic Divorce	53
X.	France Wants to go Looking 4 Aztlán	54
	1694: Kino Discovers and and Names Casa Grande	55
	1724-26: The Legend of Teguayo Continues to Grow on Paper	59
XI.	1727: The MOTHER Map, First Map to Show 3 Aztec Stops	60
	1727: Barreiro Creates the Mother Map or Cartographic DNA	61
	Rescates and Bondos	64
	1736-1743: Codice Boturini	68
XII.	1765: Rivera Secretly Goes Looking 4 Aztlán	70
	1768: Don Copycat	72
XIII.	1774: Missionaries Continue Looking 4 Aztlán	74
	1774: Mythical Rio Timpanogos	76
XIV.	1776: Dominguez-Escalante Expedition	
	Go Looking 4 Aztlán	77
	Ruins	82
	Aztec Ruins	85
	The Great Salt Lake	86
	Green River	88
XV.	Timpanogos: Still Another Name 4 Aztlán	89
	Where did the Hispanized Name *Timpanogos* Come From?	91
XVI.	1803: Alexander the Great Goes Looking 4 Aztlán	96
XVII.	The DAUGHTER Map	98
	1829: Anahuac in the Northwest U.S.A.	110

XVIII.	1847: "Antigua Residencia de los Aztecas" or Stop Number One	111
	Ruinas de las Casas Aztecas or Stop Number Two	121
	The Confluence of Confusion	123
	1850: The Name Teguayo Fades Away	127
XIX.	1870: Gringo Scholars Go Looking 4 Aztlán: The Resurrection of Aztlán	128
	1880: Quien Sabe II	133
XX.	1885: Gringo Politicos Go Looking 4 Aztlán	134
	1933: Aztlán in Wisconsin?	140
	1969: Xicano Resurrection of Aztlán	141
XXI.	Aztlánahuac: *Xicanos Go Looking 4 Aztlán*	142

Part Two: The Making of Aztlán, the Concept

I.	Birthright: *Natural Inheritance or Descent and Distribution*	150
II.	Identity: The Doorway to *Natural Inheritance* (Indian - Pre-American - Chichimeca - Xicano)	159
III.	Extinction and Absorption (Detribalization/Denationalization) or the Same Difference	178
	From Chichimeca to Chichimecos to Mecos	183
IV.	Right 4 Birth: *Nation Building (Doorway to Power)*	191
V.	Nation or State	197

Endnotes	199
Bibliography	204

PREFACE

If I had to reduce the description of this book to one sentence, it would read:

STOP PIMPING THE AZTECS AND START NATION-BUILDING.

I say this because in my decade plus of Looking 4 Aztlán, I came to realize the crippling effects the fascination of Aztecs and Aztlán have had on Xicanos. My greatest fear is that this obsession of finding Aztlán and myopically and parasitically using the historical Aztecs will continue to cripple our community through the phenomenon of continual intergenerational transmission.

Unfortunately, Aztecs and Aztlán have become the centerpiece and keystone of our attention, goals, modern identity, and even existence. The Aztecs and Aztlán are but a microscopic component of what contribute to the make-up of the modern day Xicano community. We have evolved from multiple eras, regions, nations, and events. Still many Xicanos have concentrated solely on the Aztecs and Aztlán disregarding all other aspects of our mosaic make-up.

Throughout the book, I give examples of this parasitic relationship. Here are some examples: I have never encountered a Xicano who graduated from or participated in Xicano Studies that has converted his or her Romanized name to an Aztec name or any other indigenous western hemispheric name. I also find it odd that so many organizations, programs, groups, institutes and publishers, etc are represented by Aztec names, logos and other symbolism yet they themselves have not discarded and replaced their Romanized names. We complain of externally and forcefully imposed identities upon us but the simplest, safest and yet most important identity, our individual names we have over looked and continue to frightfully embrace.

On a national (Xicano/Mexicano) level, an example is the annual calendar date of Noche Triste that continues to be recognized as a tragedy historically. On this day Cortez's invading genocidal Spaniards marched through Mexico-Tenochtitlan murdering thousands of indigenous Indians (Aztec). Fleeing in panic, 800 of these Spaniards fell to their death in battle or drowned in Lake Texcoco because of overloading their backpacks with stolen gold. It would seem that the people of Mexico and Xicanos, as proud Aztec descendants, who praise and elevate the Aztec today would properly relabel this as a holiday of celebration and rename it "Noche Alegre." Yet as Aztec descendants, we continue to filter monumental events such as this through the eyes and hearts of the descendants of the colonizers rather than ourselves.

The colonizers have stolen the indigenous significance of these events and unilaterally redefined their significance. This is what happened with the battle of the Alamo. An American cadre of settlers infiltrated Texas with the secret intent of eventually overthrowing the Mexican government. The American "terrorist" rebels were slaughtered by the Mexican government's army. Their battle cry then became "Remember the Alamo." You would think because we don't celebrate these two victories that indigenous peoples lost these battles. We talk a good revolution but it's all talk. The root word of revolution is revolve which means to turn or to change.

There is no more classic example of this parasitic relationship with Aztecs, Aztlán and Xicanos than the notation "Antigua Residencia de Los Aztecas" on the 1847 Disturnell map. In other words, give me the benefits of identifying with the Aztecs but not the responsibility. We do not want their names, their religion, their language or to recognize the disturbing fact that they were imperialistic (Rome at Home). What we selectively want from them, by embracing and identifying with them, is the land base (Aztlán) it supposedly gives us, the Indianess and the indigenous status. Since we insist that Aztlán is somewhere in the United States the present European American colonizer must knight us as indigenous. Once, we are knighted by the true foreigners, we expect many wonderful things will happen. However, let me caution you that in reality, enrolled Indians (federally recognized) whose indigenous status is not questioned in this country live in the most severe poverty in this hemisphere.

A more vivid example is the black man that has been scientifically established (for the moment) as the first and original race on earth. Yet, throughout the world they live in agonizing poverty and suffer from exploitation and oppression. My point is that being first and indigenous does not mandate equality, freedom, respect, wealth, or power. In other words, we don't need to be Aztecs or to be in Aztlán, to be proud and free, we need to be powerful. We don't need to find Aztlán; we need to build it.

Because of the obsessive preoccupation, tunnel vision and fictitious relationship with the Aztecs we have distorted our reality and are preventing our progress. We need to enter the real world to expand and explore our perspectives and possibilities. Nationalism has not been on the Xicano radar screen. The pied pipers of our intellectual aristocracy have instead led us with delicious sounds and smells of Aztec artistry, fancy, and fiction.

We need to listen to and explore the real and vivid sounds of nationalism. There is no greater power on earth than the congregation of people. Nationalism gives the congregation of people boundaries of rigidness. You are able to read this preface only because you have been nationalized. The standardization of English reading and writing is a component of nationalism, in this case Americanism. If the word or concept of nationalism shocks or frightens you then you do not know its' definition and elasticity. But don't listen to me, I am not a pied piper, find out for yourself.

In the book, I expose the inaccuracies of the 1847 Disturnell map. I also broadcast questions that Xicanos are not answering or even posing, such as: Why are Xicanos only looking in the United States for Aztlán, when it has been hypothesized that it could possibly be in Mexico, Argentina, mythical Atlantis or even China? If historical Aztlán is an itty-bitty island then how did it become the entire southwest? Some Xicanos call the land area taken by expansionist young America in the Mexican-American War in 1846-1848 or the southwest, Aztlán. Was Mexico acting as an incubator for Xicanos and Aztlán? What do we tell other indigenous Indians of the southwest, that Aztlán is *our* homeland? Is this our version of Xicano Manifest Destiny? The original Aztecs were genetically exactly the same as all other pre-Columbian nations around them separated only by language, religion, culture, customs, politics and boundaries. If race can be genetically transmitted, but not culture (which is learned behavior) and Xicanos don't embrace and practice Aztec culture, then how can we say that we are related specifically and only to the Aztecs?

If what you have just read angers you or insults you then DO NOT READ THIS BOOK! This book is meant to analyze, criticize, and revolutionize, even at the risk of being accused of betraying the interests of our Xicano community.

MI CASA PRIMERO
PRIMERO MI CASA

INTRODUCTION

This book is divided into two major discussions: 1) Aztlán the Place; Discusses the history of how, for over 550 years, different people for different reasons have been Looking 4 Aztlán. What all these explorers for Aztlán, had or have in common is the belief that its discovery will automatically yield "magical" benefits. The many names that Aztlán has been called are revealed. It is a book about maps, mapmaking, mapmakers, and map worshippers. I examine the evolution of how particular notations are given birth on maps and how these notations become gospel truth because they are on maps. I also discuss the Xicano resurrection of the search for Aztlán the Place, its elusiveness, and its dangers. The keystone of this research and discussion is the 1847 Disturnell map notation "Antigua Residencia de los Aztecas." This particular notation on the Disturnell map is growing day by day in its artificial importance to the Xicano community. Unfortunately, it is being promoted as a *birth certificate* for many Xicanos. In the section titled, "Aztlánahuac, Xicanos Go Looking 4 Aztlán," I reveal these facts along with the dangers of viewing this map as our birth certificate. Later in the book, I explain the shallowness and danger of Xicanos myopically making the Aztecs (Mexica) exclusively their beginning and their end in terms of ancestry over the centuries and the shortcomings of this fact in our present day identities.

My cartographical journey, as you will see, brought me to the conclusion and reality that the 1847 Disturnell map is grossly inaccurate, and as grossly disrespected in the eyes of history, politics, and cartography. On the other hand, the white European, the true foreigner, embraces a different sort of map to harness and secure his power and position of supremacy over all indigenous people. That map is the doctrine of *Conquest and Discovery,* which is discussed in detail.

2) Aztlán the Concept; Explains, elaborates, and discusses the concept of birthright which I call *natural inheritance.* That which is rightfully ours because it was handed down to us by our birth and the death of our blood ancestors. The original source of natural inheritance is from *the Creator* and not from man. As Thomas Paine, author of

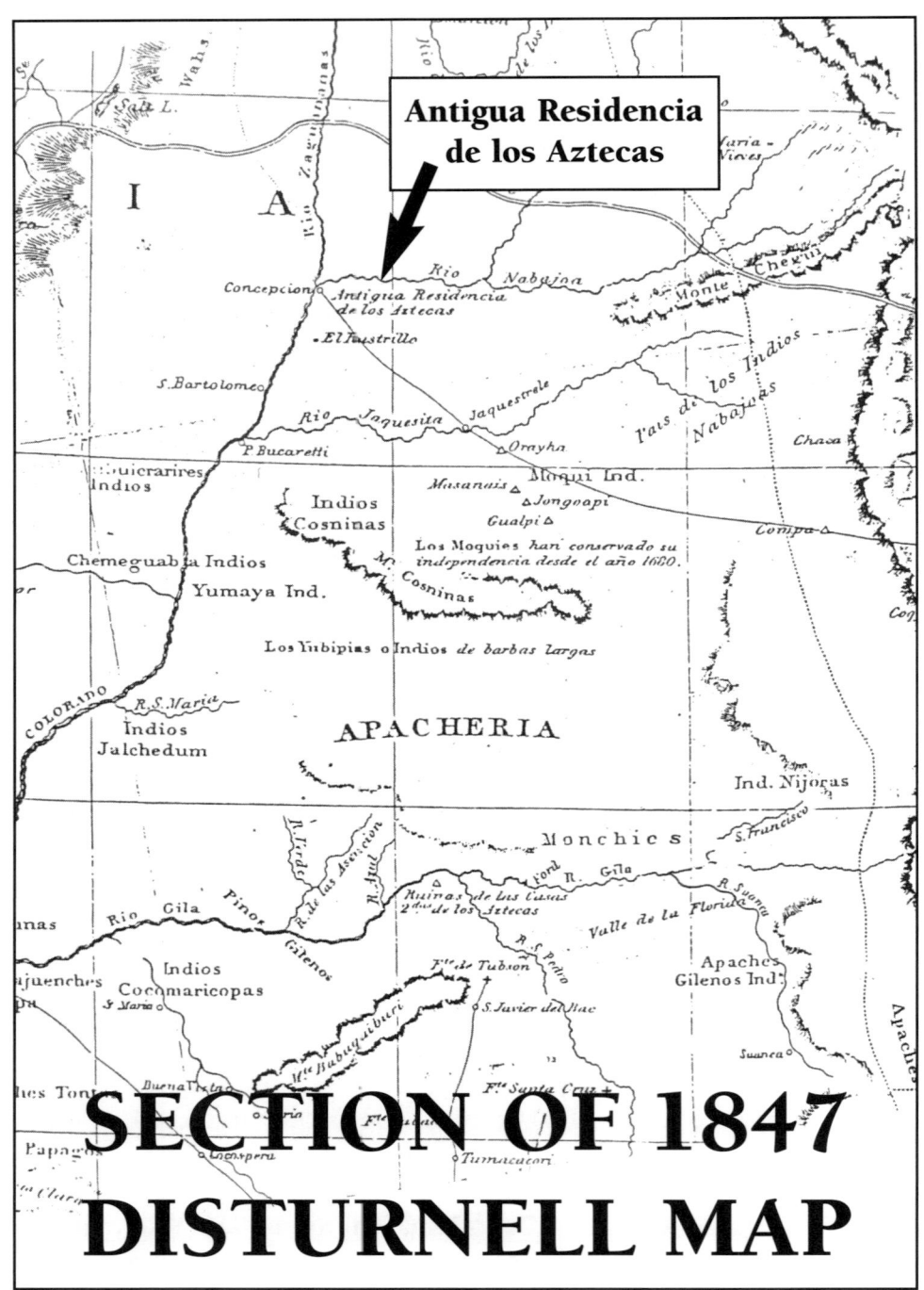

Common Sense, and the concept of natural rights, states: "Natural rights are those which apertain to man in right of his existence. Of this kind, are all intellectual rights, or rights of the mind, and also all those rights that are not injurious to the rights of others." It is the belief and intent of Xicanos to cash in this birth certificate for values such as respect from others, self-respect, glory, and especially being granted indigenous status within the boundaries of this country. As stated by Thomas Paine, "An inquiry into the origin of rights will demonstrate to us that rights are not gifts from one man to another nor from one class of men to another; for who is he who could be the first giver, or by what principle or on what authority could he possess the right of giving?" The principle of natural rights is the bedrock of this country's constitution and Declaration of Independence.

The *doorway* to our natural inheritance is our identity and/or identities. That doorway, has been sealed shut because of how the European invader of yesteryear and white America of today have unilaterally and selfishly taken the initiative to define us with their benefits in mind, not ours. I explain how we ourselves must deconstruct their selfish identities of us and reconstruct our own identities in our favor to reentitle us in our minds and in our hearts to our stolen natural inheritance. I speak of the mechanism we must closely examine and very possibly utilize in order to reclaim our natural inheritance and that mechanism is nationalism. The disintegration of the Xicano movement of the 1960's and 70's failed in my opinion, not because of infiltration and sabotage by America's law enforcement entirely, but because of our national leaders omission of nation building principles or inability to disseminate it's properties and consolidate its framework within the Xicano community.

If I were to return to college, I would not enroll in a Xicano Studies program, but a Jewish studies program. Why? Because, the real issue in all this is power. The vehicle to harness people power is nationalism. There is no better documented evidence of nation-building than that of Jews who resurrected themselves from the ashes of ancient conquest and world diaspora. Xicano Studies on the other hand cannot point to case studies in nation-building and concentrates more on contributions made to this country. As we know, this country does not reward ethics and contributions, only power.

We can no longer hide behind poems, songs, dance, talk, articles, fantasy, and maps. The concept of Aztlán as it stands among Xicanos today is frivolous fantasy. It is time to graduate to real solutions and real actions. This proposed notion and map could become a death certificate.

Finally, I believe the challenge is not the discovery of Aztlán and the birthright it magically would give us, but the challenge of building Aztlán, because it is Right 4 Birth.

About the title and White Crane symbol. We can consume ourselves in Looking for Aztlán and using it as a birthright. Or, we can get to the point and begin building Aztlán for it is Right 4 Birth.

The Name <u>AZTLAN</u>

By using the literal linguistic translation of Aztlán; the original home land of the Azteca, scholars have attempted to extract hints of where this island or homeland might have been. Of course like with the exact translation of Chicomoztoc, this is yet another controversial term; the actual meaning of Aztlán, a Nahuatl word.

In his book, *Montezuma*, C.A. Burland writes, "At first they claimed that they came from a place called Aztlán, which seems in fact to have been called Aztatlan (beside the white heron). Their warriors usually wore two heron feather in their headband as a crest, which serves to hint at the real name of the homeland". Later in his book he again makes reference to the white crane feathers, "each year in the summer there were festivals for the warriors, when the boys, dressed in cloaks of cotton netting and the crane feathers..."

In the Mexican text *Diccionaria de Aztequismos* it further supports this claim. Aztlán – Az-tlan, sinopa eufonica de **Azta-tlan**: **aztatl**, garza; **tlan**, junto a: "Junto a las Garzas." (p. 68)

In a lecture I heard given by a Mexican elder and historian (Tlakaelel) he gave this description. The word Aztatlan, he said, means an abundance of crane for food. He further stated that a hieroglyph for the word Aztatlan would show the diagram of a standing crane showing a mouth with teeth at its long legs and feet as if it was eating the crane.

We stereotypically think of nations, clans or other groupings of identifying with such birds as eagles or hawks because of their great courage and hunting skills. After reading of cranes in general I found they shared these admirable and comparable qualities that human groups may want to identify with. Cranes are very territorial and ferocious when defending their territory. These types of birds live in family units instead of large flocks. The male and female couple are faithful to each other and will stay together for life. Only when one of the pair dies will the other search for a mate. The work of raising a family is shared by crane couples. Edward Benton-Banai author of *The Mishomis Book, the Voice of the Ojibway* writes of the great respect given to the crane in his history of the crane system. "But the Creator remembered how the earth's people had suffered in the past. He decided that the earth's second people needed a system – a framework of government to give them strength and order. To do this he gave them the o-do-i-daym-i-wan' (clan system). There were seven original o-do-i-daym-i-wug (clans). The first clan was the Ah-ji-jawk or crane. Each of these clans was given a function to serve the people."

"The Crane and the Loon clans were given the power of chieftainship. They were given to people with natural qualities and abilities for leadership. Each of these two clans gave the people a balanced government with each serving as a check for the other." Some experts believe the crane to be the oldest kind of bird having existed on earth with dinosaurs over 60 million years ago. In other words, this makes it a symbol of courage, love, fidelity, family, organization and indigenous longevity with great survival skills. It is also a bird of the *waters or marshlands* representing great poise and beauty. After all, wasn't Aztlán an island on a lake? I now understand the pride and power of its symbolism – and why some nation, tribe or tribelet would embrace it as their own symbol.

I have yet to see Xicanos anywhere to use the white crane as their symbol of Aztlán. This symbol I think would be most appropriate, unless of course Aztlán has a different meaning and history.

This is why I chose the crane to be on the cover of my book and to represent it. I hope someday it will serve as the symbol for the Xicano flag.

THE CHRONOLOGICAL METAMORPHOSIS OF AZTLAN

THE PLACE

THE MEXICA
GO LOOKING 4 AZTLÁN

For at least the last 550 years, different people for different reasons have been looking 4 Aztlán. "The quest to find the original Aztlán was actually begun by the Emperor Motecuhzoma I, probably during the 1440's. By that time the *location* of Aztlán had become a mythic memory, but as the Mexica Empire expanded and its rulers became actively engaged in building a sense of national identity, the notion of finding their place of origin assumed special significance."[1]

According to the story told to Fray Diego Duran, a 16th century Spanish historian, an expedition of 60 wise men sent to find Aztlán, found Aztlán and even encountered the mother of Huitzilopochtli, their central deity. They were scolded for living a "soft and luxurious life in Tenochtitlan" and warned, "…with a dire prophesy to the effect that they would be conquered one day just as they had conquered others." (loc. cit.)

Therefore, the Mexicas' purpose in looking 4 Aztlán was to locate, if possible, Aztlán and to give its citizenry in central Mexico, but especially Mexico-Tenochtitlan, a sense of identity and origin. For the Mexica, to realize that they came from such primitive beginnings while now enjoying a most advanced civilization would no doubt contribute to the psyche of this already proud people.

But did the Mexica actually locate Aztlán? Speaking for myself, I would say no. The stories told to the Spanish historian sound incredible and even cartoon like. For example, the 60 wise men after leaving, encountered a supernatural being who transformed them into birds allowing them to fly to Aztlán where they were then transformed back to humans. After finishing their visit in Aztlán, they were transformed back into birds to enable them to return to Mexico-Tenochtitlan and upon arrival transformed back into human beings.

The more important point is this. Even, if the Mexica did locate the original homeland of Aztlán, then either their documentation of its location was lost, destroyed by the Spaniards, or incorrectly interpreted over the centuries.

1433
HISTORY A LA CARTE

"It seems that in 1433, shortly after the Aztecs had consolidated their victory over the Tepanecas of Azcapotzalco and began their rise to power they burned their picture books and rewrote their history," writes Michael Pina in "The Archaic, Historical and Mystified Dimensions of Aztlán."[2]

"Under the direction of Tlacaél, counselor to rulers of Tenochtitlan, both the Aztec and Tepaneca books were destroyed. A new history more fitting to the new imperial power of Anahuac was composed."[3] Michael Pina further cautions researchers when they interpret documents of the past. "This revelation implies that many documentary sources that have survived into the present-day contain embellished versions of the Aztec past. Modern researchers struggling to make sense of a distant cultural world must consider this knowledge into their research." (p. 30). Xicanos who seek to find Aztlán and or the history of the Mexica (Aztecs) must recognize this essential fact. However, the fact is that Xicanos today like the Aztecs of the past practice what I call "history a la carte." By this, I mean we are guilty of picking and choosing what we like as our history while discarding or ignoring that which we find negative, unattractive, or unproductive in supporting our goals.

The author Soustelle in *Daily Life of the Aztecs* explains how the Aztecs wanted the best of both worlds historically speaking. The best of the ancient past, which was uncivilized, rugged, masculine, and yet pure; and the best of the present, which was civilized, noble and highly accomplished.

"The central Mexicans were very much aware of the value of their culture and its superiority to that of other Indian peoples. On the other hand, they held that certain tribes were backward and barbarous. They knew perfectly well that their own nation, which had only recently settled in the central valley had also lived a barbarian kind of life until not long ago: but they thought of themselves as the heirs of the civilized men who had colonized the plateau and built their great towns there long before them."[4]

"To these two extremes, the barbarian and the civilized man, answer two conceptions made up of combined history and myth – the *CHICHIMECA* and the *TOLTECA*." (loc. cit.) The Chichimeca being the generic, northern primitive and nomadic superior hunters who were therefore excellent potential for warriors. And the Tolteca who were highly civilized, sedentary and culturally refined. In fact, many historians believe the word Tolteca means *craftsman*. The elements of *Chichimeca* and *Tolteca* were carefully woven historically by Mexica historians to create a magnificent people.

Who, what, where and why are always considerations that must be strictly dissected when attempting to accurately retrace and reconstruct history as it may have happened. Michael Pina classifies the sources available to researchers into seven major categories:"[5] Where possible I have attempted in my own words to expand upon the authors' descriptions.

1) "Pre-Hispanic" or stories told by Indians through underdeveloped writing styles with oral tradition serving as the final authority. As most Xicanos, I want to believe *our* histories as indigenous peoples told by *our* indigenous ancestors are more accurate. However, when these histories are eroded by time, endless intergenerational evolution and suffer from contradictions by other indigenous sources, then we need to examine and filter the facts and maybe even on occasion accept the fact that we may never know the truth.

2) "Post Hispanic" - which the invading Spaniards commissioned while others were written independently. "They primarily deal with pre-Hispanic historic and cosmological traditions." The minute the European colonizers set foot on *our* hemisphere history and documentation and interpretations of who or what we are was at the mercy of the white invaders. As we have read, heard, seen, and experienced, they have no mercy.

3) "Transitional Prose Documents" - "Early post conquest documents, written in Nahautl, Spanish or French..."

4) "Mestizo Sources" – "Authored by the descendants of the pre-conquest royalty..." The fact that Mestizos wrote history does not guarantee accuracy. History like everything else indigenous was also colonized.

5) "<u>Spanish letters and description</u>" – "eyewitness accounts of Aztec events, society and culture." It must always be kept in mind that we were seen, described, and evaluated through the eyes of conquistadors. It is a lot easier for your conscience to conquer that which you demonize.

6) "<u>Priestly writings</u>" – missionaries who unlike the common Spaniard were well schooled in literacy who however were there to destroy indigenous religions and to replace them with their own. As Richard Ricard in *Spiritual Conquest of Mexico* repeatedly demonstrates, the religious were the most invasive, destructive, and controlling of all segments of Spanish society.

7) "<u>Archaeological evidence</u>" – which uses artifacts and other forms of physical evidence to reconstruct past societies. *White archaeology reconstructs and interprets in such vague eras using just as vague interpretations of synthetic cultures with synthetic names that often they are of little value to Xicanos, especially in Looking 4 Aztlán.*

History a la carte actually was a methodology utilized also by the Romans as described here in Albert A. Trever's History of Ancient Civilization, Volume II, The Roman World. He writes "The historian of early Rome is faced with a very baffling task. The oldest extant histories of the kingdom and early republic were not written until the close of the pre-christian era or later, yet they tell their story of Roman beginning in greatest detail, and with apparent exact knowledge. It is, in reality, largely an uncritical texture of legend and patriotic imagination, of value chiefly as revealing what the mature Romans believed about their past. The writers drew uncritically from earlier annalists of the third and second century B.C. who were also centuries removed from Roman origins. . . The earliest Roman written tradition from the third and second century annalists is fragmentary, and was warped by a patriotic national pride in victorious Rome... Greek legends, institutions, and heroes were appropriated to embellish the Roman story; public documents, ancestral records, and funeral eulogies were fabricated; contemporary institutions, conditions, and events were read back into the remote past and adorned with a wealth of detail to teach the Roman youth good citizenship and national patriotism." [page 9]

The twin brothers Romulus and Remus were said to have been raised in the wild by a wolf. If you can believe this then you can believe the Mexica who turned themselves into birds then back to humans.

To make a point, at one of my lectures, I waved and offered $100 to the person who could name the first person to discover America. Immediately there were yells of "Columbus." Why? Because we are victims of white American supremacy history, a la carte. Are we to uncritically absorb and embrace Xicano history a la carte?

A SPECIAL NOTE ON CODICES

When you read or hear of someone who establishes the reliability, credibility, and authority of their information by pointing out that it comes from a codex you tend to surrender any resistance or challenge you may have originally posed. I know that was my individual response initially. However, since studying its definition and historical use I do not surrender so quickly anymore.

In the Thorndike-Barnhart dictionary, it gives this explanation. *Codices* are the plural form for *codex*. "Codex. 1. a manuscript volume, especially one of the scriptures or of a classical author. 2. *obsolete*. Code [<Latin *códex*, variant of *caudex* tree trunk, block of wood split into flat tablets for writing; book."

In fact, in my study of early maps, I found that they were often made on thin slices of wood trunks. Finally, a codice can be as simple as a minor document or as complex or important as Codex Juris Canonici, which is "the official statement of cannon law by the Roman Catholic Church made in 1918 and since then effective." (Barnhart-Thorndike) However, it is not something, which because of it being a codice should be given a special authority.

The most famous of Mexica history codices is probably Codex Boturini. "One of the most indispensable documents in the reconstruction of the mythic narrative surrounding Aztlán is known as Códice Boturini. This document is considered to reflect in style, content, and format the traditional pictoral manuscript of pre-conquest times, composed during the sixteenth century outside the accepted bounds of Spanish patronage, it is fortunate it did not fall prey to the zealous flames of colonial proselytization." What does it mean or say that it's incredible that this document was not destroyed or negatively influenced by the invasionary Spaniards? It may say this is quite accurate, but the others are contaminated! Contrary to the common belief of many Xicanos the codice as we see was not composed by indigenous people nor was it pre-Hispanic. The author continues, "It became a part of a collection of Mexican Indian documents gathered by Lorenzo Boturini Benaduci during the years 1736-1743. This codex portrays… their exit from Aztlán until their arrival at the hill of Chapultepec and subjugation by the Culhuacanos." Because of this codex, indigenous oral tradition is heavily anchored by its historical description as is stated here. "A series of glyphs, ideographs, and phonetic symbols such as this one, *assisted* the indigenous story tellers *memories*. Although produced after the conquest, this text evidences the retention of historical consciousness and identity among the indigenous population."[6] It seems the Indian served the function as informant, while the European acted as the final historian.

Richard F. Townsend in his book shows a drawing that evidently accompanies Codex Boturini. Below the drawing he writes: "The Aztec migration begins from the legendary island of Aztlán (left), led by a priest carrying an effigy of the deified hero Huitzilopochtili (right)." Three others follow the lead priest. The drawing he describes to the "left" as the island of Aztlán struck me as odd. The reason is the island has within it a drawing of a pyramid-like structure. The original Aztecs were not pyramid builders, yet one is shown here. Construction of pyramids, temples, and other higher forms of architecture were not learned until the Azteca successfully entered and were stabilized in the central valley of Mexico. Why would it show what seems to be a pyramid? To show that there was an exodus from the island an Indian is shown in a canoe leaving it. In my studies of the indigenous cultures of the southwest, I have not come across any drawings, photographs, or descriptions, which would indicate a canoe like artifact such as in the codice here.

1493
OFFICIAL BIRTH OF LAS INDIAS

It is often unknown by indigenous peoples of the western hemisphere that this vast area in its entirety was called Las Indias. "Based on the discoveries of Columbus, the papal line of demarcation of 1493, and the Treaty of Tordesillas with Portugal in 1494, Spain claimed all the western hemisphere except the bulge of South America – Brazil."[7]

These newly discovered lands were called *Las Indias*. The indigenous habitants of the newly discovered hemisphere were generally referred to as Indios (Indians). The Concilio De Las Indias who enforced the legal code, Las Leyes de las Indias, which applied specifically to Indios, governed them separately.

In 1494, "Spain and Portugal sign the Treaty of Tordesillas, agreeing to divide newly discovered lands in America and Asia."[8] This begins to explain the extreme secrecy Spain used in documenting discoveries and maps of the new world. Spain had every intention of keeping the new world to itself and hurried to conquer, rape, and control Las Indias under Europeans watchful eyes.

It is critical to point out that Spain like its European brethren took lands from the Indians by force without the use of maps. There was never, at any time, a notation on maps of the western hemisphere stating: *"Antigua Residencia de Los Gringos."* A recent unrealistic phenomenon implemented by modern Xicanos is the use of maps to gain respect and acceptance from our exploiters and colonizers; self respect for ourselves; and even for some a tool for regaining our stolen lands. In contrast, white Europeans and white Americans have used power to gain control of lands; Xicanos on the other hand attempt to use *"wower."* By this, I mean showing white America that we have maps to prove our indigenous status. White America is expected to respond, "Wow, we didn't know that! We are really sorry, amigo. Here is your land, your indigenous status and your self respect." Pity is not a source of power; it is a luxury of power if it so chooses to use it.

THE EUROPEAN DOCTRINE OF
CONQUEST AND DISCOVERY

Originally referred to as the doctrine of conquest and discovery it has been euphemistically changed to the doctrine of discovery. "The national celebrations of European arrival in the Western Hemisphere cause resentment among many Native Americans who are aware of the so-called "doctrine of discovery." This doctrine is the European-invented legal theory upon which all claims to, and acquisition of, Indian lands in North America is ultimately founded.

During the discovery era's fierce international competition for new lands, a need arose for some commonly acknowledged principles by which rights – as between European nations - could be established. The main purpose for developing such principles was to avoid war over conflicting claims and settlements.

In the earliest years, the competing powers relied on grants from the Pope. The prevailing belief, stated by King Duarte of Portugal, was "whatever is possessed by the authority and permission of [the Pope] is understood to be held in a special way and with the permission of almighty God" (Williams 1990, p. 70). But the Pope's international authority was lessening with the growing Protestant movement and other world developments. A new system had to be adopted.

Over time, and through many agreements, grants, charters, and even skirmishes, the European nations established the principle that initial *discovery* of lands gave title therein unto the government whose subjects, or by whose authority, the discovery was made. This title, ignoring the Native peoples, was good against all other European or civilized (i.e. Christian) governments. *It could be secured by possession of the land through the continued presence of the government's citizens or representatives somewhere within the bounds of the claimed area.**

**This is why Spanish missionization of Indians throughout the Americas was so important. Primarily, they were to pacify the militarily conquered Indians and or to "citizenize" the now converted Spanish-speaking Indians of the Spanish crown within the discovered and possessed New Spanish lands.*

The United States officially embraced the discovery doctrine in 1823 through the Supreme Court case of *Johnson v. McIntosh*. The following paragraphs, which conclude this opening section of the book, are excerpts from that precedent-setting case in federal Indian law. They begin by addressing the proclaimed superior right of Euro-American governments to sell Indian lands-despite the fact that Indians might claim and be living on them. The last paragraph leaves no doubt as to the U.S. view of the legal effect of European discovery.

While the different nations of Europe respected the right of the Natives, as occupants, they asserted the ultimate dominion to be in themselves; and claimed and exercised, as a consequence of this ultimate dominion, a power to grant the soil, while yet in possession of the Natives. These grants have been understood by all, to convey a title to the grantees, subject only to the Indian right of occupancy. [For which some form of compensation was usually paid.]

No one of the powers of Europe gave its full assent to this principle, more unequivocally than England. The documents upon this subject are ample and complete.

Thus, all the nations of Europe, who have acquired territory on this continent, have asserted in themselves, and have recognized in others, the exclusive right of the discoverer to appropriate the lands occupied by the Indians. Have the American States rejected or adopted this principle?

By the treaty which concluded the war of our revolution, Great Britain relinquished all claim, not only to the government, but to the "property and territorial rights of the United States," ...*By this treaty, the powers of government, and the right to the soil, which had previously been in Great Britain, passed definitely to these States.*

The United States, then, have unequivocally acceded to that great and broad rule by which its civilized inhabitants now hold this country. They hold, and assert in themselves, the title by which it was acquired. They maintain, as all others have maintained, *that discovery gave an exclusive right to extinguish the*

Indian title of occupancy, either by purchase or by conquest; and gave also a right to such a degree of sovereignty [over Indians and their land], as the circumstances of the people [of the U.S.] would allow them to exercise."[9][italics added]

As I am sure you noticed, after having read the above, there is no mention of maps, just a lot of white military power and coexisting agreements between European nations. The excerpt, *"They maintain, as all others have maintained, that discovery gave an exclusive right to extinguish the Indian title of occupancy,* (hold on it gets even better) *either by purchase or by conquest."* (loc. cit.) First white America and its government cannot distance themselves from their disgusting conquering ancestors as they always attempt to. The reason here is they (white America) through the courts still embrace and implement these principles without shame. Secondly, and just as importantly it shows conquered people that *reentitlement* can only come from *reconquest*! Map that, my fellow Xicano citizens! This document of conquest and discovery is the document we should be circulating throughout our communities and not a map. However, the reverse is true. The 1847 Disturnell map that notates Antigua Residencia de Los Aztecas has become the Xicano *Holy Grail*.

1519
THE SPANIARDS
GO LOOKING 4 AZTLÁN

After the initial 1519, Cortez invasion and 1521 dismantling of Mexico-Tenochtitlan (the heart of its empire) the Spaniards responded to the indigenous stories of Aztlán with an insatiable desire themselves to find it. The Spaniards were quick and eager to tell Indians, "We suffer from a disease of the heart that only gold can cure."

However, they were not really interested in Aztlán. They believed Aztlán would lead them somewhere else. That somewhere else was Chicomoztoc. In other words as we shall see along the historical and present trail Aztlán is being used to achieve something else. It was the belief of what finding Aztlán would bring these selfish researchers, and not the finding of Aztlán as an end in itself.

The Aztecs after leaving Aztlán sojourned at Chicomoztoc on their way to the valley of now central Mexico. But why Chicomoztoc? Because Chicomoztoc in the twisted and greedy minds of the Spaniards was believed to be the mythical seven cities of gold where the streets were paved with gold. For the Aztecs it was simply the birthplace of all mankind.

In mythology, the Aztecs were said to have emerged from the mountain called *Chicomoztoc* and migrated southward to what was eventually to become Mexico-Tenochtitlan. When the time came to leave Aztlán they stopped at *Chicomoztoc* after leaving for their 100 years plus long migration. This would indicate to the Spaniards that Chicomoztoc, since it was a stopping place on the way to the valley of Mexico, was within range of the homeland Aztlán. In other words, *find Aztlán and you will find Chicomoztoc or the seven cities of gold* – nearby. To do this, the gold thirsty Spaniards had to carefully examine the myths, legends and histories of Aztlán as told to them by the central Mexican Indians.

But why would the Spaniards believe that Chicomoztoc had seven cities of gold?

"Strangely enough, the Spaniards brought this myth of the seven cities with them from Europe. The story went that in the eighth century, a bishop fearing the approach of the Arabs, fled from Lisbon westward across the sea to a land where he founded seven flourishing cities. This tale was paralleled by a possibly old Indian legend from Mexico and Central America, a story of "seven caves," from which a number of tribes derived their origin. In one of the numerous early "histories," the word "Chicomotoque" occurs. It is from the Náhuatl word *Chicomoztoc*, which means approximately "seven caves." These two myths became a detailed narrative and ultimately merged into what seemed to be an authentic account. Somewhere in the north it should be possible to find the cities."[10]

A SPECIAL NOTE ABOUT
MAPS

Just a few important notes about maps and map-making. Because maps present a visual image of something they take on a vivid importance for people who use them, whether it is for research, recreation, curiosity, or navigation. However, in the 3 to 3.5 centuries after the arrival of the Spaniards maps left a lot to be desired in their accurate depiction of the "New World" in general and North America in particular. Because of the limited and incremental explorations of the New World, North America maps slowly became more accurate. Technology also saw a slow but positive progression. The earlier maps, however, were more artistry than accurate and fantasy than fact. But even after improved technology, research, education and resources some maps continued to transmit old map mistakes. The 1847 Disturnell map is one of these maps.

Slowly, but surely most of these cartographic errors were corrected. That is if governments wanted accuracy and fact, for maps were excellent ways of motivating the masses to immigrate into or to emigrate out of particular regions. Iceland was initially and supposedly named such, to create the image of extreme ice and cold to persuade people to stay away. While, allowing its discoverers and other select groups to enjoy its beauty. Greenland on the other hand was not as attractive as Iceland, but its name gave the image of greenery and beauty, when actually it was a lot of snow, ice, and cold. However, its name motivated people to migrate there, which was the intent of those that named it. In other words, some times maps are political tools.

Maps do not die easily though because like the dictionary or the Bible they are considered documents of ultimate authority.

In his book *Down to Earth: Mapping for Everybody,* author David Greenwood comments on some very basic principles about the power of maps on individuals, groups, and even nations.

(1) Because of their scientific nature and guiding power, maps impress people as being of high authority; (2) History makes maps and they in turn make history; (3)…maps may be correct for a certain period; (4) maps are supposed to give information, but they can also put up an argument. This argument will appear so convincing that only another map can successfully refute it; (5) <u>People are plain suckers if they never question the reliability of maps</u>; (6) No matter how much you may like maps *they might get you into trouble* if you look at them with an uncritical eye.[11] (I can speak personally to 5 and 6 with experience.)

In other words at least in the beginning, maps of North America should have been labeled with the logo that depicts a skull and cross bones as certain poisons do today to warn of "*danger*", this is not a reliable map. I will pinpoint certain maps as I go along because maps also reflect thinking for the time period of the map made and used. Also, maps especially earlier maps served as stepping-stones to later maps.

David Greenwood gave examples of how maps are purposely designed and publicly distributed to give *disinformation* as well as accurate information. He states: "This great power of maps is quickly seized upon by propagandists for swaying and often misleading the public. The wily demagogue in the pretense of doing something "educational", or of showing "scientific proof", will issue falsified maps, or maps with alluring devises for deception or maps may be correct for a certain period or a special purpose but in his hands are as wrong and dangerous as an altered crossroads sign." He further states, "Frederick the Great had some maps of Silesia printed with uncorrected mistakes, so as to mislead his enemies."[12]

Here is a more local and recent example.

"In 1901, a bold project was finished. A 50-mile irrigation canal was dug from the Colorado River at Yuma to the Salton Sink. Because the sink is far below the river, water flowed through the canal.

The canal builders wanted to attract settlers. But it would be hard to sell a scorching desert. So they called it "The Imperial Valley." The settlers came [page 80].*

---

*<u>The Colorado, Mover of Mountains</u> by Alexander Crosby; Garrard Publishing Company ; Champaign, Illinois, copyright 1961.

When Spain invaded the western hemisphere, it outlawed individuals or groups in commercial dealings or for personal gain to engage with non-Spanish countries without the knowledge and approval of the Spanish government. Maps made by Spain were carefully distributed and guarded to prevent non-Spanish countries to gain from their explorations and cartography. Therefore, non-Spanish countries were many times "*guessing*" when they made their maps of North America. Also, the *earliest* maps made by Spain were based on fewer than a dozen voyages of exploration. To show the power of maps, Greenhood gives two outstanding examples: "For instance, a map-maker once put down the name of the wrong explorer as being the one to name a region after and the name stuck, even after the map-maker himself and the public must have recognized the mistake. That region was the New World and the name was America! History makes maps, and they in turn make history!" (loc. cit.) The other outstanding example is: "Shut in one cold, rainy day in Scotland, a young man and a boy amused themselves by painting pictures. The young man, more boy-like than his companion, drew a map of an island, one which he had never seen or heard of. But the longer he looked at it the more real it became. Its story unfolded in his mind: Treasure Island! Stevenson's first novel was inspired by a map."[13] As we have begun to see and will continue to see in this book, stories make documents, documents make maps, and maps in the end make truth.

I have attempted to carefully select dates, stories, and documents, maps that serve as benchmarks, and finally bring us to the map of the 1847 Disturnell map. Why? Because it is this map that Xicanos are carelessly waving before the public as *proof* that the Aztecs originated in the southwest and therefore *proves* Xicanos and Mexicanos are indigenous to the southwest.

1520
THE ORIGIN OF THE PLACE-NAME
CALIFORNIA

"Northward from Acapulco on Mexico's west coast, they had discovered what they considered to be a great island, which they named Santa Cruz. Later, the name was changed to California, from a story in the novel *Las Sergas de Esplandian*. According to the story, "... on the right hand of the Indies there is an island called California very close to terrestrial paradise; and it was peopled by black women without any men among them, for they lived in the fashion of Amazons*... their arms (weapons) were all gold and so was the harness of the wild beasts which they tamed to ride for in the whole island there was not metal! But gold." The ruler of this mythical island was said to be Queen Calafía."[14]

California as we now know was not, is not an island as once believed. Nor did Amazon women people it. The explorers, however, who read the book or heard the story of the Amazon women thought or at least hoped it was and named it as though it was. Maps of the "mysterious north" therefore began to show the place-name California and California as an island. It would take a law from the Spanish King himself to force cartographers to conform and inform in their map-making the truth that California was not an island.

Wilfred Funk, Litt. D., gives an interesting origin of the word, amazon in his book *Word Origins and their Romantic Stories*:

> AMAZONS: *they had only one breast*. The *Amazons* were a race of female warriors who were alleged by the Greek historian Herodotus to live in Scythia. These man-like women fought many battles with the Greeks and the famous hero. Achilles was presumed to have slain their queen Penthesilea when the *Amazons* were trying to help the besieged Trojans. These mythical women were said to have cut off their right breasts so they could

---

*The Amazon River was named so because one of its earliest European explorers was said to have seen "Amazon" women along the river banks.

draw their bows more easily. The Greeks invented this fable to connect the word Amazon with *a*, "without," and *mazos*, "breast." These Scythian women were responsible for the name of our South American river, the *Amazon*. This river was called by its discoverer Rio Santa Maria de la Mar Dulce. But when the Spanish explorer Orellana made the first descent of the river from the Andes to the sea, he was engaged in battle by a savage tribe in which he believed that women fought beside the men and it is the accepted story that he then rechristened the mighty river *Amazonas*. So when we call a modern woman an *amazon*, we mean that she is masculine, powerful, and inclined to give battle.[15]

You begin to see the pattern of how European fantasy after fantasy seemed to quickly find homes in the western hemisphere. And, so it was with map-making.

1528
THE GOLDEN AGE OF CHISME

"The stage had been set for the great Coronado expedition several years earlier, in 1528 when an exploring party was shipwrecked off the coast of Florida. Using makeshift rafts, the survivors tried to make their way back to New Spain by following the gulf shore of today's United States. They were wrecked again, this time on the west coast."[16]

The local Indians would then take captives the four shipwrecked Spaniards. Most critical and famous among the names of these four survivors are Cabeza de Vaca and the Black slave Estevan. "They spent the next eight years walking across the wilderness of today's Texas and northern Mexico." (loc.cit.)

Certain dates are landmark or benchmark dates for history. 1492 was the date for the discovery of the American hemisphere. After the white establishments' catching of so much hell from indigenous peoples for this obviously racist claim and the discovered truths of this murderous savage and the government he represented the claim has now become euphemistically revised. Now it is officially called the date for the *Age of Discovery*.

1776 is another date that is monumental and needs little description when expressed. This is the year that a group of oppressed white colonies who were colonized by white Europeans took the initiative to declare themselves to have the natural right to *independently*, of their oppressors, wipe out and replace our indigenous ancestors.

The year 1528 should have the same monumental significance for our indigenous minds and hearts because this is the year when fantasy started to become fact in the minds of the Spaniards. The stories told to them by the Indians along the way and over the years on their way back to central New Spain were validation (in their own minds) that golden Aztlán was for real. It was an earlier philosopher who once said "opinion unlike truth needs no passport to travel the world!"

These shipwrecked survivors would spread the chisme of golden cities creating an avalanche of conquistadors, missionaries, settlers and recently conquered Indians (of Mexico) throughout the American southwest. This domino effect would be felt for centuries to come.

1530
FOLLOW THE YELLOW BRICK ROAD...

John E. Chavez writes in his chapter titled *Aztlán, Cibola and Frontier New Spain:* "In 1530, about four hundred miles northwest of Mexico City, the conquistador Nuño de Guzmán encountered a place called Aztatlán, whose name and environment resembled those of the legendary Aztlán. Though the evidence indicated (and still indicates) that Aztatlan and Aztlán were one and the same place, it must have seemed too mundane a location for a land that had been idealized to the point of a paradise on earth."[17] Seeming to support my suspicion that it was Chicomoztoc and not Aztlán the greedy Spaniards were seeking Chavez continues: "Furthermore, storytellers had recounted that in Aztlán there were caves, specifically the seven caves, the Totemic shrines of the Aztec clans. Since these caves, had not been found in Aztatlan, the Spanish decided Aztlán must be farther to the north." (loc. cit.)

Again, they were not looking for Aztlán. Aztlán simply served as a landmark for Chicomoztoc. Eventually it would not even be called Chicomoztoc but any name and any place that suggested the immense presence of gold. The Aztecs had become synonymous with gold and Aztlán was synonymous with the Aztecs. Then Chicomoztoc had become synonymous with Aztlán and therefore with gold. The place-names Aztlán and Chicomoztoc soon became interchangeable and confusing. It evolved quickly in to the "chicken or the egg syndrome." Eventually, the multitude of place-names did not matter only the gold itself. The Spaniards simply were following the *yellow brick road*.

1536
De SPIES MISSIONARIES

In 1536, they (Estevan and Cabeza de Vaca) made it into Culiacan, Sinaloa. "Taken before Viceroy Antoñio Mendoza, de Vaca unraveled a tale of great cities. He hadn't seen them, but he had heard stories from the natives of the existence of seven cities of gold."[18] Emphasis must be given to the fact that "he hadn't seen them, but he had heard stories..."

Mendoza in response selected "Francisco de Coronado to lead the Quest." In the meantime a Franciscan Padre, Fray Marcos de Niza, and Estevan the black slave survivor preceded Coronado "north on a reconnaissance mission to verify the existence of the golden cities." The year they departed was 1539.

It was not unusual for *Padres or Missionaries* to serve as reconnoiters for conquistadores. Since, they were schooled in and served as military intelligence gatherers and cartographers while posing as innocent harmless individuals dressed in black robes carrying a cross in the wilderness out to save Indian souls in the name of the King and Queen of Spain and Almighty God. The fact is they also served primarily as government SPIES, pacification agents, and the fifth column.

For Mendoza the missionary of his choice had some especially attractive qualifications as indicated by Luis F. Hernandez in his book "Aztlán: The Southwest and its Peoples." He writes, "Fray Marcos had been with Pizarro and had written of the conquest of Peru. Mendoza anxious for success felt that here was a man who could lead the expedition that would find the seven cities. When he approached the religious brother with the idea, Fray Marcos accepted most eagerly. Immediately, a group was organized with Fray Marcos... A full escort of Indians and Esteban, who would serve the important position of interpreter and guide."[19]

Author Hernandez further writes: "As Esteban waited, in the short period of six years (1536-1542), seven expeditions ventured northward seeking the seven caves of *Aztlán*. Three of the expeditions were by sea, four by land." (loc. cit.)

Mr. Hernandez provides us with a modern example of how Aztlán and Chicomoztoc were and are often confused and therefore often *fused* as one and the same. Here he speaks of "The seven caves of Aztlán." Instead, of the seven caves of Chicomoztoc. The reality is that Aztlán was an *itty bitty* island someplace and Chicomoztoc with its mythical caves were located elsewhere. The Aztecs, or Chichimeca or Mexica or by whatever name they went by sojourned at Chicomoztoc on their 100 year journey into today's central Mexico where they founded the island of Mexico-Tenochtitlan.

More fascinating is how the *itty-bitty* island of Aztlán will geographically metamorphisize into the entire southwestern United States. A kind of Xicano manifest destiny.

1538
CHICOMOZTOC:
ANOTHER NAME FOR AZTLÁN

"As a consequence, in 1538 Juan de La Ascunción and Pedro Nadal, two Franciscan friars, set out in search of Chicomoztoc, another name for Aztlán meaning "place of the seven caves." Together with their Indian porters, these explorers marched west from Mexico City to the coast, then to the distant north, possibly as far as the Colorado River, which today forms the boundary between Arizona and California. If they actually went that far, they may have been the first formal expedition to reach the southwest by land. *In any case they were the first to seek Aztlán in that vicinity, and their search would lead to the centuries-old myth that Aztlán was in the southwest...* While friars found no signs of the seven caves, on their return they reported hearing word from the Indians of great cities farther north – thus keeping alive the myth of the southwest as a land of golden promise."[20] This date is critical in establishing the birth date and birthplace and belief of Aztlán in the southwest. That is at lease in terms of the Spaniards seeking Aztlán. Again, we see an example in this section of how it is not Aztlán they are interested in but the 7 caves of Chicomoztoc.

The Spanish started out seeking Aztlán just northwest of Mexico-Tenochtitlan, and then northwest Mexico, and then the southwest, and eventually even northwest of the southwest. As they went along, whenever the Spaniards were not successful in finding Aztlán or Chicomoztoc they would conclude, "It must be further north." Had the Spaniards not been driven out of New Spain by dirt poor Mexican Indians by now they would be claiming "Aztlán must be further north in Canada" or even the North Pole.

For the Mexica (Azteca) Chicomoztoc has a very different significance. From the document Historia *Tolteca-Chichimeca*, author Richard Townsend extracts this information: "The migration legend describes a route of travel leading to two important places: *Culhuacan*, "curved mountain," and *Chicomoztoc*, "seven caves." The exact location of these sites remain unclear, ... the scholar Paul Kirchoff argued effectively that the seven caves (Chicomoztoc) were actually a feature of the curved mountain Culhuacan. Chicomoztoc-Culhuacan was also known by ten other names..."[21]

Townsend continues, "The manuscript Historia Tolteca-Chichimeca records that earlier migratory groups had abided here, before continuing to settle in Puebla-Tlaxcala. A famous page from the manuscript depicts Culhuacan-Chicomoztoc as a mountain with womb-like caves, representing the ancient notion of the mountain as a procreative entity. The manuscript portrays a Chichimec priest enacting a creation myth, symbolically bringing forth the tribes from earth as a sign of their passage from hunting and gathering in search for a new place of agriculture. The importance of this consecrated site was a place of religious renewal, where a course of action might be sanctioned, or a people "reborn" with a connection to the primordial forces of life, or where new leaders might be installed in office through a rite of passage. The wandering Mexica portrayed themselves as stopping at this ancient shrine and if indeed they did so, they surely undertook similar rites of regeneration and collective rededication of purpose." (loc.cit.)

1539
CIBOLA:
YET ANOTHER NAME 4 AZTLÁN IS BORN

While going north with their entourage acting as reconnoiters for Coronado, Estevan the black Spaniard would separate from Caveza de Vaca heading even further north in advance of Fray Marcos de Niza.

Marshall Trimble in *Arizona; a Cavalcade of History* writes: "A few weeks later Esteban was killed by natives at the Pueblo Indian village of Hawikuh, near today's Zuni, New Mexico. Fray Marcos de Niza responded by fleeing back to Mexico City. "The further he got from Hawikuh the more his imagination began conjuring tales of great wealth in the new lands. In his fertile mind the tiny, mud and wattle village of Hawikuh grew into a city larger than Mexico City with buildings ten stories high where natives wore pearls, gold beads and emeralds, ate their meals out of gold and silver utensils, and decorated their door with turquoise. When de Niza finished his tale, all Mexico City went into a gold-crazed frenzy."[22]

Why did de Niza make such claims? "Esteban moved ahead of the main expedition and sent reports and direction back to Fray Marcos. At one point Esteban reported that he had news from the Indians of "the greatest thing in the world." He reported that ahead of him was a city called "Cibola" (Bison) – the first of seven cities. Thus, a southwestern Indian conception of a local homeland was joined to the Spanish and Aztec image of the seven cities of Cibola."[23]

Fray Marcos continued north until he learned of Esteban's death in the first of the probable seven cities. Marcos fearing for his own life never went into Cibola, but immediately headed south to Mexico City claiming he did and making fantastic claims based on his information from Estevan. Marcos also feared the wrath of his Viceroy but as much as that from the assassins of Esteban. But Fray Marcos was no dummy and he gave this rationale to the viceroy Mendoza when he arrived in Culiacan to speak with Coronado while writing the viceroy Mendoza of his findings. "It is situated on a level stretch on the brow of a roundish hill.

It appears to be a very beautiful city, the best that I have seen in these parts... the town is bigger than the city of Mexico. At times I was tempted to go to it, because I knew I risked nothing but my life, which I offered to God the day I commenced the journey; finally I feared to do so, considering my danger and that if I died, I would not be able to give an account of this country, which seems to me to be the greatest and best of discoveries."[24] This guy would have made a great modern white American historian!

Ol' *pah-drey* didn't waste his trip to the southwest for he also invested in land for his Spanish empire. "Building a large pile of stones with a cross on top, he formally laid claims to Hawikuh and the other cities of Cibola in the names of the viceroy of Nueva España and the emperor of the empire. He included the regions Totonteaciacus and Marata and called the land the *new kingdom of Saint Francis*. (loc.cit.) Now, wasn't that the *good ole days* when you could stick a cross in the ground and take someone else's land?

PLAY IT AGAIN, SAM

"Hence, these four starved, ragged unshaven castaways from one of Spain's many fiascos, making contact with their own civilization after eight rigorous years of untold hardships, also brought to Mexico – or New Spain, as it was known in 1536 – the story, rumor, or legend of seven rich communities lying somewhere to the north. Each time the story was repeated the seven cities became a little larger and a little wealthier.

This imaginary tale happened to coincide almost exactly with one of the myths of the Spanish Empire, the story of the seven lost cities of the Antilles. The story was born of wishful thinking and was nurtured on hope. There wasn't one jot of truth in it. It came out of the Middle Ages and never died; it was something everyone wanted to believe; it was too good not to be true.

In essence, it was this: In 1150, the Moors captured the Spanish city of Merida. Seven bishops of the Catholic Church, each with a group of followers, fled to avoid death at the hands of the Mohammedans. They carried all their valuables and sailed west across the "Sea of Darkness" and established a new civilization in a new land. Each bishop founded a city and each city grew to fabulous wealth. Streets were paved with gold, houses were made of silver and studded with rubies and emeralds. The ignorant masses believed this childish story, and many of the educated people accepted it as well. The thing to do was to find these seven rich cities and make them forever Spain's. And where were they? Somewhere in the New World.

It was thought that Columbus would find them. He didn't. It was thought that Balboa, or Pizarro, or Ponce de Leon, or Cortes would find them. They didn't.

And then, in 1536, from the mouths of the four who might have died came the story of the existence of seven great cities farther to the north. The Indian word for them was Cibola (pronounced see-bo-la with the accent on the "see") and there was little doubt in the public mind that these Seven Cities of Cibola were the long-lost Spanish treasure trove.

Don Antonio de Mendoza in Mexico City was the viceroy for Charles V. He was a man of great acumen, ability, and cupidity, and he loved luxury. He had sixty servants to jump to his bidding and he never went anywhere without a bodyguard of twenty-five men. He wanted to serve his king well, and he did so, but most of all he wanted to have the credit of discovering Cibola – if it existed."[25]

CIBOLA MAPS: 1541, 1578, 1597

Originally, I thought the name Cibola was brought from Spain with the legend. But as indicated here the word is hispanized but indigenous in origin. "Cibola", may be the earliest New Mexico place name to appear on a map since it is shown on Castillo's Map in 1541. It appears as "La Ciudad de Cibola", and is shown with towers and walls, on a somewhat smaller scale than those of "La Ciudad de Mexico," farther south and east. After Friar Marcos de Niza described Cibola as a very beautiful city (the smallest of seven cities like it) with terraced houses all of stone, and bigger than Mexico City, the entire northern region was sometimes spoken of as Cibola, the seven cities of Cibola, and men were willing to hazard all for its reputed wealth. Frederick Webb Hodge points out that Fray Marcos learned the name in the language of one of the Piman tribes of northern Sonora or southern Arizona and he ventures the suggestion that *Cibola* may be a transliteration of *Shiwina*, the Zuñi name for their tribal range. Fray Escobar, in his diary of the Oñate expedition to California, 1605, says the Spaniards called the Zuñi Pueblo of Hawikuh by the name of Scibola. This place name was transferred in Spanish to the great animal native to the region, the buffalo (bison Americans). Casteñada describes the seven little villages... all within four leagues... together they are called the kingdom of Cibola. Cleve Hanenbeck in his translation, *The Journey of Fray Marcos* (1949) at page 8 states that the Isleta Indians have a word *si – bu – la – da* meaning "buffalo", that may have been learned from the Aztec term for the animal. Hallenbeck believes Fray Marcos was acquainted with the word and its meaning before he ever started on his journey."[26]

As it turns out Fray Marcos in fact had not seen much if any of the village of Cibola yet was able to give this fantastic detailed description of how it looked by claiming he did see it. This event will be revisited later. What is important to note is this phenomenon. First, the Spaniards hear "stories." If these stories sound similar in anyway to some of their own stories they become "documented" and the Spaniards were very detailed and even very guilty of *red tape*,* in fact the phrase is from Spain. Once these stories become documented, they become "mapped" as is the case of Cibola. Once they become mapped, they become "fact" at least until proven otherwise and sometimes they remain fact even when proven otherwise. But documents and maps often came before thorough research. This cycle will be utilized throughout the Spanish occupation of the colony of New Spain. In the book *Down to Earth*, the author cautions readers with this phrase: "History makes maps and maps in turn make history."[27] Although Cibola did not exist, it now existed on a map and that in the minds of the unknowing, made it a fact.

By revealing to you this excerpt from *The Place Names of New Mexico*, it is not my intent to further confuse you but to show you the state of confusion that existed during the Spanish occupation of the southwest and the pursuit of Aztlán.

---

*Marshall Trimble describes the origin of the phrase "red tape" as coming from Spain. Because of the vastness of the Spanish Empire in the New World and the slow movement of transportation and communication from Spain all official sanctions and order or documents came very slowly and wrapped with a "red ribbon or tape" to show "official decisions or orders".

CIBOLA (general). Pronounced SEE-bo-lah. Like the mythic cities it once named, *Cibola* has been one of the most elusive terms in NM history. Almost everyone agrees it's derived from an Indian word for "buffalo," but it is unclear as to how the Spanish explorers first heard it and applied it to the fabled golden cities they sought so hopefully in NM. In medieval Europe a popular legend told of the Seven Cities of Antilia, located across the Atlantic Ocean. When the Spanish sailed to the New World, it was natural that they try to find the legendary cities, particularly as some Aztec and Incan cities had indeed approached the legend in golden riches. The legend certainly came to their minds when vague reports reached Mexico City hinting of fabulously wealthy cities in the unexplored territory to the N, in what is now NM, and when the Spanish journeyed northward they somehow linked the legend with the word *cíbola*, thus creating the Seven Cities of Cibola.

Some scholars have suggested that *cíbola* comes from a Comanche word and that Nuñez Cabeza de Vaca and his three companions might have heard it from the Plains Indians as they made their long trek across SW Texas in 1529-36; instead of translating it as "buffalo plains" as the Indians meant, the four castaways interpreted it to refer to the wealthy empire-another Mexico, another Peru-that Spaniards wanted to believe lay in the interior of North America. Others have suggested that Fray Marcos de Niza heard it from the Pima tribes of northern Sonora or southern Arizona as he traveled northward in 1539 seeking the cities reported by Cabeza de Vaca; he certainly was using the term be-fore he arrived at the Zuni villages that his guides said were Cibola, and he used the term later when he described the Zuni village he thought was Cibola as a magnificent city -- the smallest of seven.

The debunking of Fray Marcos's report by Coronado's expedition of 1540-41 did not dissolve the myth; *Cibola simply retreated farther into the interior.* When Domingo de Castillo's map of the W coast of Mexico appeared in 1541, the only place he bothered to label in the interior of the continent was La Ciudada de Cibora; it was the first place in NM to appear on a map. Similarly, on an untitled 1578 map of North America by Joan Martínes, *Civola* is the map's most conspicuous feature; Martínes sketched the individual cities, complete with towers, gates, battlements, and heraldic banners; no other feature in the interior appears. A 1597 map prepared by Cornelius van Wytfliet shows seven cities surrounding a lake; the Zunis in 1582 had told Antonio de Espejo the lake was ringed with gold.

Eventually, however, successive disappointing expeditions forced the Spanish to accept that Cibola was *a place name without a place,* and the world began to revert to its original meaning. Fray Alonso de Posada, writing around 1660 about the Pecos River, said, "The latter flows into the interior of the Plains of Cibola... due to the river's attractions there are many wild cows called Cibola." Ciboleros was a term used later in the colonial period for hardy New Mexicans who ventured onto the plains to hunt buffalo."[28] (italics/emphasis added).

Like the mystical Aztlán, Cibola, its' other place-name, "simply retreated farther into the interior" or "further north" when it was realized that it had not been found. In reality, Cibola never existed except in the minds and hearts of greedy Spaniards. Could this be true of Aztlán today, and its Mexicano and Xicano explorers?

"In the same year, two other men were stirred into action, Hernando de Soto and Pedro de Alvarado. When Hernando de Soto heard of Cabeza de Vacas journey he got official approval to conquer the land north of Ciba. DeSoto and his men landed near Tampa Bay on the west coast of Florida, where they found Juan Ortiz, a survivor of Narvaéz expedition in which Cabeza de Vaca, Esteban, and other had figured. Juan Ortíz had been living among the Indians for ten years and had heard that gold was to be found somewhere in land to the north. Using Ortiz as a guide and interpreter, de Soto and his men began a march which lasted for three years."[29]

When the Spanish Conquistadores left for *Cibola*, they were intent on war, conquest and gold. Author Luis F. Hernandez writes, "In 1539 viceroy Mendoza launched his plan for the conquest of the seven cities of Cibola. He ordered the *alcalde* (mayor) of Culiacan, Melchoir Diaz, to gather information about the route traveled by Fray Marcos, and he requested that Hernando de Alarcón command three supply ships. These ships were to sail up the Gulf of California and offer support to the main expedition, which was to follow the overland route." (p. 17).

Simultaneously, yet another Spaniard is equipped with an army and seeking to find Cibola. "Ulloa had sailed north from Acapulco in July 1539 hoping to reach the seven cities by sea. He did not succeed of course! He did prove, though, that California was not a mythical island ruled by Queen Calafia but was actually an extension of the mainland, partly a peninsula.* Ullua's party had sailed north to the head of the Gulf of California and sailed up the Pacific side to Cedros Island, where they put in for the winter months. In April 1540, one ship was sent back to Acapulco with news that Ulloa was continuing to sail up the Pacific coast. This was the last that was ever heard from him or his men. In all likelihood, they were dashed to pieces on the rocky coast of California." (p.15).

The Cibola maps of 1541, 1578, and 1597 showed the extent of cartographers' artistic imagination and gullibility. These maps were not based on personal observations or scientific calculations. The cartographers of this era had also gotten caught up in the gold craze.

---

*Map makers and explorers continued for at least another century to notate and speak of California as an island. It took a decree by the King of Spain making it illegal to map or speak of California as an island before it was finally accepted as a part of the continential mainland.

1540

GRAN QUIVIRA IS BORN, YET ANOTHER NAME FOR AZTLÁN

Finally in 1540, Francisco Vasquez de Coronado with 300 horsemen and foot soldiers supported by over 1,000 Indian auxiliaries and black slaves left for the region they called the "Northern Mystery."[30]

Learning what the invading and intimidating Spaniards were looking for (and the golden disease they suffered from), many natives and native villages reacted to the invading forces with more stories. "The natives quickly learned that the best way to rid themselves of the pesky Spaniards was to tell them of the treasures sought could be found elsewhere. Seven cities existed, they said, some distance to the northwest. (loc. cit.) Early Spanish cartographers responded to these stories at times by placing these rich and luxurious villages or regions on their maps without first hand knowledge relying completely on native stories or even Spanish guesses. Whenever and wherever Coronado went and was told of golden cities, Coronado would send yet another sub-expedition to investigate stories. When told of a river that Coronado thought might be the mythical "northwest passage," Coronado did not hesitate. "Another expedition of 25 horsemen led by Captain de Cardenas set out to find the river" (p. 58).

The naval arm of the Coronado expedition was led by Hernando Alarcón who was sailing the Gulf of Mexico, unable to penetrate by ship the mouth of the Colorado to rendezvous with Coronado, Alarcón turned back and returned to Mexico. "He did however leave proof of earlier presence in the form of his letters buried at the base of a marked tree. A short time later these letters were found by still another arm of the expedition led by Capt. Melchoir. Diaz and 25 soldiers had been sent in a northwesterly direction by Coronado in hopes of finding Alarcón" (p. 59).

Still unsuccessful but still unsatisfied Coronado turned eastward toward the Rio Grande. "He made his camp at Tiguex, a pueblo near today's, Bernalillo (a few miles north of Albuquerque)." (loc.cit.) They stayed here for the next two years and as had been the previous pattern, they were told of yet another promising place. "Here also, they heard stories of a magical place called *Gran Quivira* from a native yarn spinner named El Turco." (loc.cit.) Although the natives used many different names, it did not matter to the Spanish for its description sounded like Aztlán and/or Chicomoztoc.

Again, expeditions were sent responding to Indian stories, which is called disinformation by today's military standards. "Finally in 1542, the disappointed expedition returns to Mexico City," writes Mr. Trimble.

Chavez theorizes, "Since the Spanish had conquered and brutally occupied pueblo villages, the Indians most likely fabricated the urban wealth of Quivira in order to lure Coronado into a wilderness from which they hoped he would never return."[31] Keep in mind the cycle explained earlier: stories become documents, documents become maps, and maps become fact. These fantasy maps through intergenerational transference become "factual maps" and become the Xicano cornerstone of *proof* in the twenty-first century, or over 450 years after the pursuit of Aztlán officially began.

It was another 40 years before the Spanish government made any serious attempts to find Aztlán, Chicomoztoc, Cibola or Gran Quivira or whatever of the names was being presently used. The expeditions had been numerous, costly and fruitless.

Robert Julyan in *The Place-Names of New Mexico,* writes:

> "Both as a name and a place bearing the name, Gran Quivira is as elusive today as it was for the Spanish Explorers who sought its fabled wealth more than four centuries ago. They associated Quivira with a fabulous realm <u>always</u> just beyond the horizon, and it was in search of Quivira that Coronado in 1541 journeyed from today's NM onto the great plains.
>
> …at one time the name, Quivira referred to all the unknown land in what is now the western U.S. Michael Lok's 1582 map shows Quivira at the western tip of the continent…(p. 152)

Gran Quivira as pointed out kept moving beyond and northerly just as Aztlán and Cibola kept doing when expeditions met failures. Still cartographers however portrayed Aztlán, Cibola and Gran Quivira as if they had direct knowledge of its existence and approximate location.

"Now Coronado sent out his captains to explore... they had heard of numerous kingdoms, especially of golden Quivira – reputed to have much gold that the ordinary dishes were made of "wrought plate," the pitchers and bowls of solid gold, and the chief of the kingdom slept under a tree with little golden bells that lulled him to rest during his siesta. What a dream – golden Quivira! This kingdom was sought for so long, as was so well publicized that it became an established point on the maps of European mapmakers."[32]

"However, while at Pecos, Coronado became keenly interested in two captives held by the Indians as slaves. One of them was a Pawnee, whom the Spaniards called "El Turco" because of his headdress... They led Alvarado and his men into the high plains at the head of the Canadian River... (loc. cit.)

"...Alvarado rejoined Coronado at Tiguex, he found that winter quarters had been set-up... With the coming of spring, Coronado marched eastward to find Quivira with El Turco and Isopete as guides. The army of 1500 marched past many camps of nomadic Indians... Eventually, they found themselves among Indians who spoke to them about *Tejas* (in the language of the Indians, "friends, allies"), and told them that the land toward which they were heading was barren and forbidden. At this point, the two guides broke down and confessed that they had been leading the Spaniards not to Quivira, but to *Tejas* (Texas). The people of the Tiguex Pueblos had promised El Turco and Isopete their freedom if they would guide the Spaniards to certain death on the arid plains. The two guides were slapped into irons. This army changed directions, now moving northward. After some days they actually came to Quivira which turned out to be a collection of poor villages located near present day Lyons, Kansas" (p. 27).

Gran Quivira like Cibola was also used at times to represent the southwest in general. We begin to see the instabilities of names and locations, also their multiple and conflicting names but not their golden promises and descriptions. So, it was with place-names like *Cibola* or

Gran Quivira. When were they talking about a specific place-name village or a very large generic area involving millions of square miles?

As you can see this was a massive and well-organized effort by the Spanish government to find and conquer the seven cities of Cibola. Using the map and writings of Fray Marcos de Niza, the Spaniards in general and Coronado in particular were gravely disappointed and extremely angry with Fray Marcos. Coronado had actually been face to face with Fray Marcos immediately after he returned to New Spain. "This done, he hurried southward back to Culiacan, then on to Compostela where he met Governor Cornonado. Here he wrote the report to be used by Coronado when in the following year he would lead his famed expedition of conquest and exploration. Little did Coronado know that the report would prove to be inaccurate and filled with fiction. No one knows why Fray Marcos wrote this false account. He had shown he was an able mapmaker and that he understood what he observed. But the report had been called by some historians the worst geographical document ever written."[33] Ironically, the 1847 Disturnell map would earn the same disrespect later.

As I researched through the many pages of documents, I could not help but begin to conclude the Spaniards were fools out of their minds to believe in such undetermined nonsense as the seven cities of Cibola and Calafia, for example. But then I came across this paragraph: "Because they believed these, Spaniards might seem usually gullible to twentieth-century readers. We must however, take seriously Dr. Hammond's reminder that the atmosphere of the sixteenth century was "super charged with dreams." Spain's explorers had not only absorbed popular legends of chivalry in which *fact and fiction melded indistinguishably,* but those same explorers knew that in the new world dreams beyond imagining had come true. For the discoveries of fabulous Aztec cities in the valley of Mexico, it required little stretch of imagination to suppose than an even more fabulous New Mexico might lie somewhere else" (p. -18). Add to that the gold discovered and robbed by Spaniards in the Inca empire further south.

1556
MONKEY SEE, MONKEY DO:
CARTOGRAPHERS GO LOOKING 4 AZTLÁN

"So far as we know, that earliest western wanderer made no map, nor did any of the names used by him for his stopping points find their way onto contemporary European maps. But though the next-comer also made no map himself, the names he gave in 1539 to the "seven cities of Cibola" and to the other fabulous places he claimed he saw on his northern pilgrimage were avidly seized upon by the European cartographers. The appearance upon their maps of these names from Fray Marcos de Niza's *narrative* was an event of prime importance. For the first time the "northern mystery" had been cartographically pierced – though ever so slightly – and the seven cities of Cibola and Niza's other place names were soon the common talk of Europe."[34]

Again, stories came from the natives of great villages of wealth further north or northwest (told to rid themselves of the brutal Spaniards) became documents such as Niza's narrative in this case. These documents became maps and once mapped (written in stone) as place-names, therefore in the minds of people it becomes unquestionable fact or truth.

"It was not until 1556 that the third volume, dealing with discoveries in America, appeared in Venice. In this book is a significant woodcut* map (at pp 455-456) entitled "Univesale de la Parte de Mundo Nuovamente Ritrovata" probably drawn by Eastaldi, on which Quivira, Cicuich, Axa, Cucho, Tiguas and Cibola – all but the last being Coronado place-names. This was the first published map to carry such legends, and though Quivira was placed far to the northwest, rather than northeast of Coronado's Tiguex, this earliest cartographic reflection of the explorer's efforts was an advance of first importance, so far as the mapping of the American West is concerned." (loc. cit.)

This would be called a codex because it is a slice of the trunk of a tree.

This again illustrates how world-renowned cartographers of Europe would read any documents, which "leaked" from the Spanish empire and without first-hand knowledge or observation, create maps and distribute them as accurate facts. This pattern of *monkey see, monkey do, was repeated* for centuries to come. What is frightening is that in the year 2002, some people indiscriminately view some of these maps as factually accurate and original. My caution to these individuals or groups is this, *if monkey see, and monkey do, and it ain't true, then the white man, before the world will make a fool out of you.*

1565
COPALA: ANOTHER NAME 4 AZTLÁN

"These tales of elusive wonders in the west that have charmed man for many years require some reference to Copala and to Teguayo. The kingdom of Copala, marvelous to relate, was first heard of in the time of Diego de Ibarra, he who became one of the original millionaires on the discovery of mines at Zacatecas about 1545. Like Coronado's Quivira, Copala was just over the horizon. Francisco de Ibarra, nephew of the millionaire, was commissioned to find it, and in 1565 he did make tremendous exploration of the country north and west of Zacatecas. He probably reached the Casas Grandes area of northern Chihuahua, may even have seen a part of southern Arizona, but found no kingdom of Copala, no rich Indian communities to conquer, only a wild country inhabited by nomadic tribes."[35]

The lure of Copala persisted. However, "What a wonderful story! Now we have Copala pictured as the mythical place of origin of the Mexican people, who of course migrated from somewhere in the north. And we have the story of Lake Copala intertwined with other stories of the unknown. With each advance of the frontier, these kingdoms tended to disappear over the horizon. In this instance Copala did not find a fixed resting place till the Dominguez-Escalante expedition of 1776 into Utah, when it found lodgement in the valley of the Great Salt Lake" (p. 30). And still another name is used to identify Aztlán and or Chicomoztoc. And is this Lake Copala the same mysterious Lake of gold we had heard of long before the place name Teguayo or Copala were born? Why is it that native Mexicans also use the name Copala or only Copala instead of the name Aztlán?

1570

In 1570, Abraham Ortelius produces a map of the world, which with few exceptions is a *plagiarism* of a world map earlier made by Mercator. "In fact, Ortelius' map of the world… is a reduced-size copy of the 1569 Mercator with its great westward bulge of North America and its use of Niza and Coronado place-names in the white space thus produced."[36]

Plagiarism is a nice and intellectual way of saying *monkey see, monkey do.*

1577
THE FIRST MAP SHOWING THE NAME, AZTLÁN

"In 1577 Abraham Ortelius, the famous Dutch Cartographer published his hemispheric map of the Americas based upon his interpretation of the New World exploration and discovery. Although filled with errors regarding his placement of the area that would soon be called New Mexico, his maps nonetheless had publicized its approximate location. Indeed, Ortelius had misplaced the Rio Grande and showed it flowing into the Pacific Ocean... Also significant was his misplacement of Gran Quivira in the northwest corner of his map."[37]

In *Explorers, Trader, and Slavers, Forging the Old Spanish Trail, 1678-1850,* author Joseph P. Sanchez includes copies of the 10 earlier and most influential maps of the Spanish presence in the colony of New Spain. On the 1577 Ortelius map in addition to notating Gran Quivira it notates *Astatlan* which is considered the same as *Aztlán*. Neither Aztlán or Gran Quivira had been discovered yet, but a map of great influence was being circulated throughout New Spain and the world showing their existence and even approximate location.

Because of the poor quality of the copied map (I used), it was difficult to determine if Aztlán (Astatlan) was in the now southwest United States or in now Mexico. I would guess that because it is south of Culiacan on the map it would most likely be in Mexico.

First of all, for all map worshippers who think that maps are as magical as a flying magic carpet (carrying you magically to your destination)here's your proof to the white man that Aztlán once existed. However, the downside is that Aztlán on the map is notated south of the southwest and in today's Mexico. This would be or will be very disappointing to Xicanos who claim and are convinced Aztlán was in the southwest. In fact, Xicanos have restricted their research for *Aztlán* in the southwest. If that is the case then try to be patient, another map will appear later and you will find what you are looking for; Aztlán designated indirectly on a map in the southwestern United States.

1578
THE CIBOLA FANTASY CONTINUES

"Most interesting… is a manuscript map in the British museum thought to have been drawn in 1578… Many place-names appear along the northwest coast, but only one is shown inland. There in the largest letters on the entire map, is the single word Civola, with seven separate vignettes of seven lordly cities, each with its banner, its gilded domes and its lofty towers. Here, the ultimate glorification of Fray Marco's meanderings."[38]

The author adds "so much for the 'Northern Mystery' in the sixteenth century. To the close of that earliest period no map still extant can be said to have been made directly from actual exploration and observation" (p. 45).

Here, on this map we see many things of interest. The name Cibola used instead of Aztlán; Cibola is designated as an extremely vast area and not an island as Aztlán was originally described to the Spaniards by central Mexico' Mexica Indians. The name-place Cibola includes "seven lordly cities." Even at this late date, Cibola and the seven cities of gold are depicted on maps.

1581, 1582, 1583, 1587
THE MYSTERIOUS LARGE LAKE OF GOLD

"In 1581, three Franciscan friars... with a small escort did reach the area that Coronado called Tiguex... the Friars were soon murdered... Unaware of this Espejo set out in 1582 to rescue them... On his return he reported his peaceful reception and also told of a large lake somewhere in that far country. "Espejo returned with ore specimens and a wild tale about a lake somewhere in Arizona."[39]

The earliest map seen by the writer on which the lake appears is the map of the New World, which Richard Hakluyt published in his Peter Martyr of 1587, some years after Espejos returned. The lake had certainly become known in Europe *before* that map was drawn, and it is of interest that Hakluyt 1587 map is also of interest because of its legend of "Nuevo Mexico" ...thus was born a place-name that had come down to our day."[40]

This mysterious large lake will grow in importance and serve as a benchmark in the search for Aztlán (Chicomoztoc, Cibola, etc.). Lakes in the southwest are rare and are therefore good landmarks for other places.

1598
OÑATE RETURNS TO FIND THE MYSTERIOUS LAKE OF GOLD

In 1598, Juan de Oñate the first to colonize New Mexico went across Arizona looking for that "Lake of Gold" (the natives talked about) but failed to find it. One of his officers did find silver ore in the vicinity of Prescott, Arizona. The story of the lake of gold and the finding of silver ore was at least encouragement enough to make Oñate want to return later. This momentum will give birth to the colony of Santa Fe a few years later.

Remember, I earlier mentioned a 1597 map by Cornelius Van Wyfliet, which shows seven cities surrounding a lake. One has to believe that this map and that lake were being put together in the mind of Oñate.

1604-05
SANTA FE: BASE CAMP IN LOOKING 4 AZTLÁN

Oñate again returned to the southwest and again was unsuccessful. And again was told by natives of great riches in other places such as "... a great lake where the natives decorated their bodies with gold jewelry."[41] Part of if not the major reason a Spanish colony was established in new Mexico north and south along the Rio Grande was to have it serve as a permanent base camp for more exploration. Exploration was no longer a luxury for the Spanish Conquistadores and day-to-day physical survival became paramount. All concentration and efforts were focused toward the colony's stability. Aztlán was put on hold, officially. "New Mexico was first conquered and settled because there was some truth to the myth of the seven cities... In new Mexico there were sedentary Indians who, while not rich in precious metals, could provide an agricultural base for a colony."[42] John R. Chavez goes on to say, "once the Spaniards became established in New Mexico, it settled into a frontier life based on subsistence farming, and the north gradually lost its glossy image" p. 64). Because the Spanish colony was under constant attack and threat of attack from surrounding Indian nations, the stability of the colony was always insecure.

To further support my claim that Santa Fe was at least originally intended to be a base camp, I quote the book, *New Spain's Far Northern Frontier*. "Now came Oñate's exploration of New Mexico, the land that was supposed to rival Mexico in its riches. Everywhere the picture was much the same – a large Indian population living in houses of adobe, often built to a height of more than one story. But these Indians possessed neither silver nor gold, nor abundant or fertile farms, nor good mining prospects. Still, Oñate considered New Mexico's prospects great, as shown in a letter of his to the king dated April 7, 1599... "I trust in God that I shall give your majesty a new world greater than Spain, to judge from reports I have received and from what I have seen and explored, and I shall preserve in his effort to the end of my life."[43]

Further supporting this belief is this description of the Spanish government's participation initially. "Fresh rumors of mineral wealth and Indians to convert brought a wave of explorers north from Mexico to the Rio Grande Valley in the 1580's. Their initial probing led to a government-sponsored party, headed by wealthy Juan de Oñate, which began the permanent European occupation of New Mexico in 1598. Yet, the province had no strategic value at this time and was costly to maintain. In 1608, when the crown learned that precious minerals had not been found, it ordered New Mexico to be abandoned. Rather than see them revert to their "pagan" native religion, the crown permitted the Franciscans and colonists to stay" (p. ix).

It would be over a hundred years before the gold epidemic would reappear and Spain would officially again seek such places as Aztlán, Chicomoztoc, Gran Quivira, etc. Independently and unofficially there were always individuals and small groups seeking Aztlán in the name of Aztlán or at least in its earliest documented description.

It is important to note that this pattern of being told "stories" which inspired great enthusiasm and activism followed by failures and frustration, then eventually long periods of abandonment and then once again some time later the cycle would restart with the tenacity of a forest fire only to burn itself out. This pattern continues today and will probably end the same to restart at some later period by a different group or groups. The only change today for Xicanos (of these groups) is that gold is not sought by Xicanos, but the supposed prestige, power, and magic that the southwest location discovery of Aztlán would bring to Xicanos.

History, as taught today, asserts that the primary reason for the southwest invasion was to Christianize and save native souls. But it was not the soul being sought; the Spanish were seeking the gold. They came to Santa Fe and other parts of the southwest not to Christianize but to capitalize. The colony of Santa Fe's primary function was to serve as a base camp initially in the search for Aztlán, which would take them to Chicomoztoc.

1650

1650 Map by Nicolas Sanson "Amerique Septentrionnale."[44]

"A predominant map for remainder of seventeenth century... California is still a large island." (loc. cit.)

It makes this notation "Cibola" representing the large northern empty space of the map. It seems also to notate on a southwest lake as "Lago de Oro".

We see here, that as late as 1650, some cartographers still mistakenly map California as an island. Cibola continues to be a region and even though this golden lake has not been observed it continues to be included on maps on the basis of "stories" or "hearsay."

1652
QUIEN SABE?

"In 1652 after the Pueblo areas of New Mexico had been colonized by Spain, another chronicler took up the issue of Aztlán. In his *Cronica Miscellanea*, Fray Antonio Tello placed the original Aztec homeland "between the north and the west", but he meant the territory beyond what we now call the southwest, for the frontiers of the unknown had moved farther north by the mid-seventeenth century. Tello stated that the Aztecs on their journey to central Mexico had "passed the strait of Anian, and the province of Aztatlan (Aztlán) lies on the other side of the straits."[45] One has to wonder if the Spaniards in general and this chronicler specifically confused the east to west part of the Colorado River with that of the mythical strait of Anian.

As the Spaniards methodically searched and settled north and northwest of Mexico City their constant failure of locating Aztlán resulted in them pushing the mysterious Aztlán further and further north in theories and on maps. By now, Aztlán began to migrate north and west of the southwest.

1678
TEGUAYO, ANOTHER NAME 4 AZTLÁN

"Nearly a century later, a new word appeared that would add perspective to Ortelius's cartographical error and place Gran Quivira on the great plains to the east where it belonged and where every Spanish frontiersmen in New Mexico knew it to be. That word was Teguayo, a large area near a Great Salt Lake associated with mythical origins of the Aztecs and other indigenous legendary place-names such as *Copala, Sierra Azul,* and *Siete Cuevas.* In their writings about the origins of the people of Mexico and central America, early Spanish writers recorded their belief that American Indians came from seven caves near the Lake of Copala which was later associated with *Gran Teguayo,* northwest of New Mexico."[46]

This description in general no doubt describes Aztlán and Chicomoztoc, however, yet another name referring to Aztlán is used. Keep in mind, Aztlán was vacated at least in part by the Azteca. What's the likelihood the name would be kept and used so many centuries later, even if the descendants of original Aztlán continued to reside there?

Life was so simple when we were looking for a place called Aztlán but then over the centuries, the word Aztlán experiences the biological process of mitosis (figuratively).

"In a 1686 report, Franciscan Custodian of the New Mexico Missions Fray Alonso de Posada writes: " By the same ancient traditions, it is said that from Teguayo comes not only the Mexican Indians, which were the last, but all the other nations which in different times were inhabiting these lands and kingdoms of New Spain. They say that Guatemala and all the other kingdoms and provinces of Peru and those close by have their beginning there" (p. 9).

However, it is this same document in later paragraphs Fray Alonso writes, "Beyond this some seventy leagues in the same northwest directory one enters afterwards between some hills at a distance of fifty leagues or less, the land which the Indian of the north call *Teguayo,* and the Mexican Indians by old tradition call *Copala.*" (loc. cit.) First he now speaks of Teguayo in the present tense and claims at one time Mexicans called this nation *Copala* yet maybe another name for Aztlán? Non Aztlán residents themselves could have identified Aztlán by different names as shown here. What does not change are the "location" stories of Uto-Aztecan speakers origin and migration recognized and told by many southwestern nations of Arizona and New Mexico. Eventually, this area of Gran Teguayo will be mapped without first hand cartographic observation and study. Strangely, it will incorporate a very large lake.

Also, from the first paragraph, we have seen Teguayo and Gran Quivira cartographically coexisting on the same map. Yet, I had pointed out how some believe Teguayo and Gran Quivira to be one and the same, while for others Gran Quivira generically meant the southwest. Lastly, Gran Quivira was relocated from the northwest corner of the southwest to the great plains (east). Remember, "History makes maps and maps make history."

If the original Azteca as a nation-state people left Aztlán completely or emigrated then whoever replaced them of course replaced the name of Aztlán as well. If the Azteca nation-state (or tribe) remained intact while a portion of them left to found Mexico-Tenochtitlan several generations and a century later then the natural dynamics of nationhood would itself change the name or word to identify the former Aztlán. That is emigration, immigration, and or successful invasion by other groups.

The Azteca likely left around 1126 and began their empire building about 1225 with the founding of Mexico-Tenochtitlan. In 1521 they were finally defeated in the germ of their empire. Then in about 1677 the word or name Teguayo officially appears and seems by description to be similar to if not in fact the same as Aztlán. That is a 551 years minimum of existence of this mythical or real homeland once called Aztlán. Nations and communities throughout their history seldom reach this period of identity (name-place) stability and it would be unreal to believe that at this time any nation-state or its neighbors would still refer to it as Aztlán.

In other words, Aztlán may come to us eventually or have already come to us as another name or word such as Teguayo. Aztlán may have been or is right before our eyes. However, our accumulated stereotype of what Aztlán is in name may prevent us from recognizing if we should or had already made eye contact with it.

Fray Alonso wrote, "... the land which the Indians of the north call Teguayo and the Mexican Indians by old tradition call *Copala*." (loc. cit.) Was Copala the name <u>also</u> used to identify Aztlán before, during or after the name Aztlán was used by the original Azteca? Nation-states can and do go by several names, i.e. United States and/or America to describe this country.

LAKE COPALA

Explorers in earlier times had spoken and written of a *mysterious lake* or *mysterious lake of gold*. Their information was not personal observation, but by word of mouth from the natives of the Nuevo Mexico province. Though lakes are rare in the southwest, I still was confused as to where this lake may have been until I came across a book while doing research in Salt Lake City. Its title, *Great Salt Lake, a Scientific, Historical, and Economic Overview,* was produced by the Utah Geological and Mineral Survey, which is a division of the Utah Department of Natural Resources Bulletin 116. In the chapter titled, *Great Salt Lake: a historical sketch,* the author Professor David E. Miller clarifies in my mind not only what lake was being referred to but where it was actually located. He writes, "Reports and rumors of the existence of a huge salty lake somewhere in western America circulated quite freely for more than a century before any white man actually obtained authentic information about it or visited its shores. Numerous maps purporting to show such a lake appeared in print from time to time beginning as early as 1710 with the La Hontan map. One of the strongest and most prevalent traditions, based on information gained from Native Americans, centered on Lake Copala. Since it seemed quite easy for cartographers to draw maps of a lake no white man had ever seen, it is not surprising to find these various maps showing lakes quite different from each other in size, shape and location" (pp. 1, 54). Lake Copala seems to be the Great Salt Lake of Utah.

Though Mr. Miller is extremely vague in saying, "One of the strongest and most prevalent traditions, based on information gained from Native Americans, centered around Lake Copala." (loc. cit.) He must be referring to the stories, histories, myths, theories or earliest maps indicating the Salt Lake area as the original homeland of the Aztecs called Copala, Teguayo, Aztlán or by whatever other name. It is strange that and makes you wonder why he and other modern historians would not highlight at least the vague possibility that the Aztecs may have originated there. The grammar he used I believe purposefully camouflaged* this possibility. Mr. Miller actually quotes in his writings Chavez and Warner, *The Dominguez-Escalante Journal,* which elaborates often on the subject of Teguayo as possibly being the original homeland of the Azteca. Why?

The original Mormons and the Mormons of today who dominate the Mormon state of Utah do not have an impressive historical profile in its dealings with the indigenous peoples of Utah. In fact, the name Utah was forced upon their territory by the American union as they entered statehood. They despised the name and the people it represented, who like the Aztecs were and are Uto-Aztecan speakers. Is racism their motive? Today, Salt Lake City has a large population of Mexicanos, both legal and illegal. Would they feel uncomfortable letting these Mexicanos know that very possibly the Indian ancestors they glorify and identify with most (the Azteca) possibly originated in and around Salt Lake City hundreds of years before the foreign Mormon invasion. In Carey McWilliams classic, *North from Mexico,* he states very clearly and strongly: "Migration from Mexico is deeply rooted in the past. It follows trails that are among the most ancient on the North American continent. Psychologically and culturally, Mexicans have never immigrated to the southwest: they have returned."[47] Maybe, this is why!

SIERRA AZUL

"Though New Mexico was remote and cut-off from its sister provinces in Mexico, its occupants continued to dream, and some of its governors played with the magic of finding new and rich kingdoms, long after the early rumors of Quivira had been so completely scuttled. One of these dreams was a certain Sierra Azul, or Blue Mountain, apparently

---

**David Miller in fact in 1976 led a team of 10 scholars to retrace the route of the Dominguez-Escalante expedition. It was a monumental achievement.*

a mountain of silver. In the time of Governor Diego de Vargas, who reconquered New Mexico after the disastrous Pueblo Revolt of 1680, the Viceroy of Mexico wrote him in 1691, urging the discovery of certain quicksilver deposits thought to exist in the form of small lakes and pools in the province of Moqui, according to information he had received. Vargas in turn did not fail to emphasize the possibilities of finding riches in Sierra Azul, using this as a fulcrum to keep the royal officials interested in the reconquest of New Mexico. In fact, one can hardly escape the conclusion that the bait of the Sierra Azul was tailored to fit the desires of the crown, eager to re-establish Spanish control over the Pueblos in New Mexico that had rebelled. The psychology of the times nourished such thinking. The Sierra Azul continued to dance about, like a distant mirage, every time an expedition went out to explore. It did not vanish till a better knowledge of geography dispelled its attractive power in the nineteenth century maps also!"[48]

Sierra Azul was believed to have existed initially. When it was apparent that it may not or that it would likely not be discovered the Spanish crown found use in still promoting the idea to promote exploration, settlement, and expansion of its colonial territories. Find Aztlán, Chicomoztoc, Cibola, Teguayo or Copala and you will find Sierra Azul.

This same tactic would be used by white Americans in the inspiring of more Anglo settlers to move to the territory of New Mexico in the 1880's. That will be discussed in a later section.

1686
TEGUAYO VS GRAN QUIVIRA, A CARTOGRAPHIC DIVORCE

Teguayo now officially comes into existence cartographically and Gran Quivira is distinguished from Teguayo and relocated.

"Mysterious and mythical, *Teguayo* marked the way to the Yuta country. To the northwest in the same way, Quivira drew Spanish explorers to the Great Plains. Once knowledge was gained, cartographers would correct Ortelius's map in regard to his placement of Gran Quivira and add Teguayo to the toponyms on their maps. In 1686, Alonso de Posada offered a first view of *Teguayo* to Spanish officials when he wrote: "Many cosmographers and astrologers confuse this kingdom of *Teguayo* with that of *Gran Quivira,* but the facts are that *Gran Quivira* is to the east and borders on the north sea (Atlantic Ocean) while *Teguayo* is north and borders on the sea of the west (Pacific Ocean)."[49]

FRANCE
WANTS TO GO LOOKING FOR AZTLÁN

"...The kingdom of Teguayo was reported about the middle of the sixteenth century in New Mexico. It became an object of speculation and official concern, especially after Governor don Diego de Peñalosa, who had gotten into trouble with the church and had been humiliated by the inquisition, <u>fled to France and sought to interest that government in establishing a base on the Gulf of Mexico from which France might conquer the interior of North America,</u> and in particular acquire the wonderful kingdoms of Quivira and Teguayo."[50]

"This threat from an old enemy, France, called for action. The Viceroy of Mexico was instructed to investigate and report. Fortunately, he had a well informed, Fray Alonso de Posada, who had been a missionary in New Mexico for many years before retirement from the mission field. Posada gave a famous report of the northern country, about 1686. By this time, Quivira had become firmly rooted northeast of New Mexico, and he placed the mythical kingdoms of new Teguayo far to the northwest, beyond the lands of the Utahs. It was he said, the same place as Copala, according to the Mexican Indians. He had obtained his information while a missionary among the Jemez Indians, one of his tribe having visited Teguayo and having been imprisoned there. Father Posada urged that exploration be made, but he did not repeat the usual stories of great riches" (p. 31). Again, we see the motive for the Spanish crown being so secretive in its documents protecting the possible location of Aztlán (aka Teguayo).

1694
KINO DISCOVERS AND NAMES CASA GRANDE

"As much as the blackrobe had traveled in Northern New Spain, no other archaeological ruin captured his imagination as much as the imposing walls of the great house, Casa Grande. Although, he had never seen the impressive ancient city of Casas Grandes in Chihuahua, this soaring, thick walled citadel fit the descriptions he had heard so often from soldiers and missionaries stationed near these ruins. From the heights of Casa Grande, <u>leading him to believe that his sector must have been of the seven cities of Cibola</u> for which Coronado and Marcos de Niza had searched in vain. *Moreover, this location fit into the contemporary notion about the migration of the Aztecs from the north to Mexico City. Why not?* From here on the Gila to Casas Grandes, to Mexico! At least it was sufficient justification to label an adjacent reservoir, Montezuma's tank. Kino's record of the ruins of Casa Grande became the *first report by a European* of such puzzling, crumbled cities in the desert."[51](italics and emphasis added)

It is interesting to extract and comment on these points from this paragraph.

1) These ruins, which were discovered by Father Kino, were named Casa Grande, as a spin-off of the larger Chihuahua Casas Grandes.
2) It was believed that this ancient city was one of the mythical seven cities of Cibola, which is contrary to the original belief that the seven cities were grouped closely together.
3) It was also believed that the original Aztecas in their migration from north to south stopped here. Because it was believed, Casas Grandes was an Aztec place of residence on their way to the valley of central Mexico then the smaller but similar ruins at Casa Grande in Arizona must have also been a place of residence prior to Casas Grandes. Because of the Aztec stereotype

of pyramids, monuments, palaces and stone houses, the Spaniards automatically assumed and theorized any ruins made of stone they encountered must have been Aztec built. When the original Aztecs left Aztlán, however, it seems they were hunter-gatherers with no stone building skills. The Aztecs once entering Central Mexico learned these crafts from the surrounding civilized nations such as the remnants of the Tolteca. From the earlier quoted paragraph it is clear that the claim and belief that either Casa Grande or Casas Grandes is from the *"contemporary notion"* and not evidence. However, cartographers of the future who read documents such as that of Kino's observations and conclusions believed this to be fact; therefore, making it a fact for map users and map-making copycats.

4) Montezumas' name is used to label an adjacent tank. The emperor(s) Montezuma were in power in 1440-1469 (Motecuhzoma I) and 1502-1520 (Motecuhzoma II) in Central Mexico playing no part in the original migration, so why would the name Montezuma be used to identify the possible original Aztec inhabitants?

Author Charles Polzer writes: "It was Monday, November 18, 1697. the Sobaipuris talked about an ancient chief named Ciba (the bitter one) who had ruled these vanished peoples until they abandoned the cities and their huge aqueducts to go southeast. Perhaps, the Spaniards thought, these were the precursors of Moztezuma, after all, the legends said the Aztecs came from the north to Mexico" (p. 61)!

It also could have been the stories Father Kino had heard from soldiers in Mexico and or his extensive readings on the myths of Teguayo as indicated here that influenced his thinking concerning this area and these ruins. "Interest in *Teguayo* was not exclusive to New Mexican frontiersmen. Far to the southwest of New Mexico, Sonoran frontiersmen also marveled at what lay beyond the Grand Canyon and the Hopi Indians. They were also attracted to the mystery of *Teguayo*, of which they had learned by word of mouth from New Mexicans and by reading reports that had mentioned it. In the 1690's the Jesuit Eusebio Francisco Kino and his soldier escort, Captain Juan Mateo Mange took a keen interest in *Teguayo*. From a geographical viewpoint in their writings, they indicated a scholarly curiosity about the seven caves, linked with the genesis story of the Aztecs, which were associated with *Copala and Teguayo*. Indeed, they expressed the hope that *Teguayo* was not far from the *Sierra Azul,* another geographical legend that was thought to exist beyond the tribal lands of the Sobaipuris in Sonora's Primería Alta. Kino and Mange believed that cartographers were correct in placing *Teguayo in* a region adjoining the Sierra Azul."[52]

On maps of Father Kino's time at least up until 1848 a river tributary which ran north and south of the Rio Gila located just west of Casa Grande was named *Rio Azul*. Why was this river named Rio Azul and was it believed it would take someone north to the mythical mountain *Sierra Azul?*

Though Spanish explorers credit the Azteca with building Casa Grande it is scientifically estimated construction for the house was began between 1300 and 1350, according to Edwin Corle in *The Gila: River of the Southwest* (p. 26). If the 100-year Azteca journey from north to south started in 1126 approximately and or ended approximately 1225 in the central valley of Mexico then it would have been impossible for the Azteca to construct this ruin. Still early explorers and cartographers consider it as the second stop of their journey in spite of the fact that Casa Grande was constructed at least 75 years after the Azteca founded and settled Mexico-Tenochtitlan.

At the beginning of this book, I had mentioned that the Spanish sailor *Ulloa* (1539) had been given credit for proving that California was not an island and Queen Califa was not its ruler. With few exceptions, however, cartographers continued to show California as an island. "The earliest printed maps of America all show a continuous western coastline from the far south to the far north. Mercator 1531, Ortelius 1570 and Wyfliet 1597 all show California correctly as a peninsula."[53]

The idea of California as an island is supposed to have originated with a Caremelite Friar, Father Antonio Ascension, possibly on a misconception of the reports of the Spanish navigators Juan de la Fuca, 1592 and Martin d' Aguilar, 1602, one of whom reported a great opening in the west coast and the other a vast inland sea north of Cape Medocin. Father Ascencion about 1620 drew up a map of his idea of California as an island and dispatched it to Spain. The ship was captured by the Dutch and the chart taken to Amsterdam." (loc. cit.)

It was in England that California as an island picked up approval, popularity, and momentum. And as the monkey see, monkey do attitude among cartographers of the time it was all they needed as proof. "California was almost invariably depicted as an island till well into the 18th century" (p. 111).

Father Kino is also given credit like *Ulloa* (1539) for discovering and claiming California was not an island. "A Jesuit, Father Eusebio Kino, was the first European to cross from the mainland to the peninsula of California, and to point out the fallacy of the island theory. His map compiled in 1698, was printed in 1705. this map, however, was not generally accepted: in fact it provoked a fairly strong reaction." (loc. cit.)

Approximately fifty years later the matter was settled. "Finally in 1746 Father Consag sailed completely round the Gulf of California and at last settled the vexed question. Ferdinand VII in 1747 in a royal decree, stated: "California is not an island." (p. 111).

1724-26
THE LEGEND OF TEGUAYO CONTINUES TO GROW ON PAPER

"In his inspection of presidios in 1724-26, Pedro de Rivera took a scant note of the land northwest from New Mexico. As he passed from Chihuahua to El Paso, however, he came across some ruins northwest of the mission San Antonio de Casas Grandes. Of the ruins, he noted with an air of authority, albeit in error, that he had seen "the ruins of a palace which the Emperor Moctezuma constructed when, from the area northwest of Mexico, about 300 leagues from a place called *El Teguayo,* he and 6,000 people left there to inhabit the city of Mexico." His use of the word *Teguayo* indicates that even at that late date in Spanish colonial history the legendary and geographical dimensions of that place name persisted as far south as Chihuahua and, as lore would have it, Teguayo was still *associated with the origin of the Aztecs.* Rivera's cartographer, Francisco Alvarez Barreiro, moreover, indicated the location of the "Rio Azul" and the "Laguna de Teguaio" on the top left hand side of his map, indicating the far northwest and *annotating on it the origins of the Mexican people (Map 6).* Although, Rivera was not the least bit interested in Teguayo, he did contribute to its cartographical longevity."[54] (italics and emphasis added).

Here the author speaks authoritatively naming now only the leader of the emigrating Mexica but the emperor's name, the number of people who followed him, where they stopped, and what they built. Pedro de Rivera even gives the exact distance and location of Aztlán; which in this time period is being called Teguayo.

Cartographers such as Francisco Alvarez Barreiro here who also read the same and or similar documents without personal observation incorporate these "stories" as fact on their maps.

1727
THE
MOTHER MAP
FIRST MAP TO SHOW 3 AZTEC STOPS

1727

BARREIRO CREATES THE MOTHER MAP OR CARTOGRAPHIC DNA

"It is now possible to consider a group of maps which we can now sink our cartographic teeth, they represent the work of a trained engineer, Francisco Alvarez y Barreiro (or Barreyro), who accompanied Brigadier Don Pedro de Rivera on his tour of inspection of the *Provincias Internas* during the years 1724-1728… Rivera's task was to inspect the Presidios along the northern frontier of New Spain…"[55]

"He joined the Rivera expedition an engineer, cartographer and statistician and prepared six maps, which together may be said to form the first reasonably scientific cartographic description of the areas covered. The sixth map is a general map of the entire area including the province of Texas. This overall map was by far the most accurate yet made of much of the area we now know as the American southwest, though it must be supplemented for many details by reference to the individual maps… It is a cartographic landmark of first importance" (p. 81).

I call the 1727 Barreiro Map the *Mother Map* because of the domino effect it has upon cartographers after him and even Xicanos today who continue to look for Aztlán using archaic maps.

"…Although he was apparently confused in respect of the far northwest, for he shows the coastline of the Gulf of California extending north from the mouth of the Gila to the northerly limit of the map. At the head of the River Azul (A Gila tributary), is the interesting legend "Laguna del Teguario o' estero de donde salieron los Indios Mexicanos con su principe a poblar a Mexico." (Possibly this was the first cartographic appearance of the long current legend concerning the origin of the Aztecs in this northwestern land of mystery.)" (p. 82). On this map, its author has *Rio Azul* running in a northerly direction until it reaches *Lake Teguayo* (Lake Copala) and Teguayo (Aztlán).

1727 BARREIRO MAP

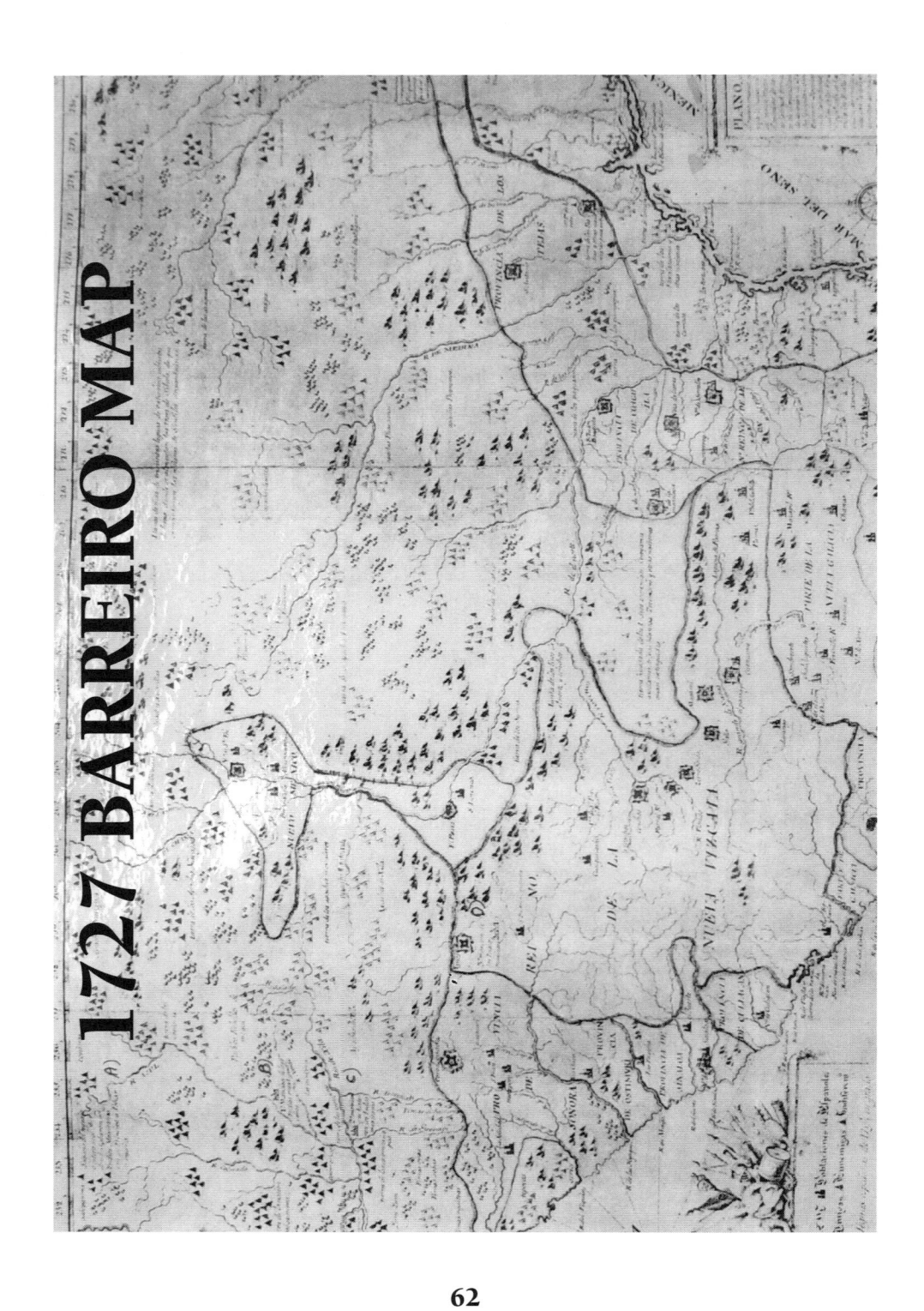

Barreiro does not stop here, for he maps even the three major stops of traditional residences of the Mexica on their 100-year journey into what is now central Mexico and Mexico City. Fact or fiction, accurate or inaccurate, this cartographic inscription of the Aztecs three stops will have the future impact of petroglyphs even for the world's most renowned cartographers for over a hundred years.

On his general map, Barreiro shows the R. Colorado as merely a westerly northern affluent of the Gila. On the Azul, above where it reaches the Gila is the "Ia Mancion de los Indíos Mexicanos," and just south of the Gila, near the tierra de los Cocomaricopas, is the "2a. Mancion que hizieron los Indios Mexicanos," while still farther southeast, at Janos in Nueva Viscaya, is the "3a. Mansion de los Indios Mexicanos. (Almost a century later, Baron von Humboldt was to introduce somewhat similar legends on his famous map of New Spain)." (loc. cit.)

Barrerio was apparently ignorant of Kino's maps and reports… (p. 83).

It is regrettable that these maps were not published when they were drawn, but the Spaniards preferred to retain such information for use by their official's only. (loc. cit.)

By keeping these types of maps secret, Spain was able to expand its empire. This permitted the uncontested and continued search for Aztlán under its many names.

On Barreiro's map of 1727 "1a.Mancion de los Indios Mexicanos," is nicely tucked in between the confluence of two rivers; their names are the Colorado and the Gila rivers as named by this particular map. In fact, both rivers are misnamed as will be shown by the map drawn in 1777 by the Dominguez-Escalante expedition cartographers. However, the spatial location within the southwest and the way this area is located at the confluence of two rivers will not change.

These locations were made and given concerning the Mexica origin and exodus without the benefit of personal observation also, up to this point there was no official observation in the name of the Spanish crown. So how did and why did Barreiro conclude this was the authentic origin and route of the Mexica centuries earlier? The concept of rescates and bondos may provide a possibility as to his source.

RESCATES AND BONDOS

"In the beginning, contact between Utes and Spaniards, unless officially sanctioned, went unrecorded. Later, when Spanish officials prohibited trade with Utes in their country, Hispanic frontiersmen wisely chose not to leave a paper trail, which could implicate them in disobeying Spanish law. Only when some were caught and the legal process generated a historical record was knowledge about the Yuta country recorded."[56] [It is known and acknowledged by historians that individuals and small groups did go off on their own at their own risk.

For a number of reasons trade and exploration into Yuta country or amongst other warlike nations had to be carefully controlled and observed to prevent another uprising as in the 1680 Pope uprising. Also, there was the purpose of preventing non-Spanish Europeans (like France) to gain knowledge or advantage from the discoveries of others. These laws preventing such operations were called *Bondos*. "To strengthen the conviction that regulation and control of trade was a sound policy preferable to military intervention, Governor Francisco Cuervo y Valdes issued a *Bando* (proclamation) on August 1705 providing that no one could trade without a license from the governor under penalty of forfeiture of goods to be traded or received in trade and a fine, and half of which would be paid to the local war fund..." (p. 18). Later proclamations would be created that would add jail time to violations of these types of bondos.

Still they were violated and many stories must have returned from their journeys along with them stories of golden lakes, golden cities, lost shipwrecked Spaniards, bearded Indians, and Aztec Ruins. It was when violators of the bondos were caught that there became a public record. Violation and capture meant the violators having to go to court, which is where documentation was initiated. Here if officials serving their governor, viceroy and royal family come across "information of interest" it would surely find its way to the top as well as other levels of society along the way.

"In the eighteenth century, *Rescates* were held throughout New Mexico in such places as Taos, Picuris, Pecos, San Juan, Santa Clara, Abiquiu, Tierra Amarilla, and Santa Cruz de la Canada" (p. 9). Rescates were trade fairs where traders Indian and non-Indians would meet to bring and trade their wares, which even included captives. Actual proof of this common practice is in this statement of how it is believed Teguayo was learned of: "Apparently, Posada's knowledge about *Teguayo* was learned just prior to the Pueblo Revolt of 1680, when contact with Utes most likely occurred uneventfully at the yearly trade fairs in Taos, Picuris, or even Pecos."(loc. cit.) This would also contribute to the Spanish initiative of reconquest of New Mexico twelve years after their defeat.

It is probable or most likely that story after story was told about new discoveries and more stories of distant riches. And, no story was too good for a Spanish official to over hear, document and eventually if possible to investigate. In fact, it was one of these Rescates that a Ute Indian was trading with a piece of silver. Sanchez writes "the first Rivera expedition stemmed from news that had spread throughout New Mexico of a Yuta warrior who had traded a piece of silver ore to a blacksmith in Abiqiu." The government kept this expedition and its route as secret as possible. So, we know that words or stories from wherever they came were taken seriously, no matter how fantastic they may have sounded.

"Apparently, Posada's knowledge about *Teguayo* was learned just prior to the Pueblo Revolt of 1680, when contact was made between Ute traders who, crossing the Rio San Juan, had ventured southward. To New Mexico and Spanish frontiersmen who dared to meet them at certain northern rendezvous points for trade. Early Spanish contact with the Utes most likely occurred uneventfully at the yearly trade fairs..." (loc. cit.)

Contact with the Yuta are believed to have been as early as 1601 and *knowledge of Teguayo* as well. This would be over a century before in 1727 when Barreiro placed on his map, Teguayo, Lake Teguayo, and the three stops the Mexica are to have made. "The earliest known cartographic reference to *Teguayo or Tatago,* appear in Diego de Peñalosás proposal to explore the area in 1678. In his report of 1686, Fray de Posada, who had served as the Franciscan custodian of the New Mexico missions during the period 1664-65, acknowledged a relationship between *Teguayo* and the Utes... Knowledge of the Utas, however, may have been acquired much earlier. In 1601, after his expedition to the Great Plains, Juan de Oñate met with a delegation from Quivira... One Quiviran leader told Oñate that if he sought gold he had gone the wrong way" (p. 7). The leader not only gave directions but also offered to take Oñate, which he considered but declined.

In that same report of 1686, "Fray Alonso de Posada stated that on his expedition to the Colorado River from New Mexico in 1605, Juan de Oñate met with Indians from many nations," among them two men "who said they were from the kingdoms of *Teguayo* and seeing him eat from a silver vessel, they told him that in their land there was much of the same metal." (loc. cit.)

Sanchez writes of an account that Posada made that clearly shows cartographers were not eyewitnesses to Teguayo could have used documents such as this one to place Teguayo on a map. Sanchez writes:

> When he was minister in New Mexico, an Indian called Don Juanillo from the Pueblo of Jemez told him of the many people and different nations in the kingdom of *Teguayo*. Don Juanillo had been a captive for two years in the provinces of *Teguayo*, as he described the area. Posada wrote... they have in them a very large number of people of different languages some of which were spoken in New Mexico and also a large lake with its circumference populated. On different occasions he told the governors of New Mexico they should make a journey to these provinces and that he would go as a guide for the Spaniards. Although Captain Francisco Luján petitioned once and again a second time for this journey, he was unable to secure permission. This is the most that can be said and is known at present of the river and provinces of *Teguayo*.
>
> In the seventeenth century some New Mexicans sought official permission for expeditions of the Yuta country. Interest among Spanish frontiersmen in Santa Fe ran high, but officials continued to deny licenses for expeditions to the northwest. (p. 10)

It is important to establish how and why Barreiro notated the Mexica homeland and the three notated Mexica *stops* on his map. His map took on a domino effect with other cartographers following him and eventually on the 1848 Treaty of Guadalupe, Disturnell map that Xicanos today are waving in the face of gringos as evidence that Xicanos and other supposed descendants of the Aztecs are indigenous to the United States. Did Barreiro use the Mexica codices to establish these notated locations? Or, did he use documents he had read about in the Spanish archives? Or, was he responding to "stories" as told to him by others, whose sources may have come from rescates? He never eye witnessed Teguayo or maybe even the Mexica *stops*. The 1727 Barreiro mother map is the womb or source of what seems to be many mistaken claims made that the Aztecs made at least three exactly identified major stops as annotated cartographically. Today in year 2002, his volcanically explosive map of yesteryear continues to ripple Xicanos with aftershocks.

What is interesting however, whether intentional or accidental is that there are what I call echoes of Aztlán in the area of Teguayo, things that point to the possibility of this area once housing Aztlán or Chicomoztoc or both.

Finally, Barreiro's map, which was created under the auspices of Rivera, succeeded in doing something else. "Although, Rivera was not the least bit interested in *Teguayo*, he did contribute to its cartographical longevity" (p. 11).

1736-1743
CODICE BOTURINI

"One of the most indispensable documents in the reconstruction of the mythic narrative surrounding Aztlán is known as the Codice Boturini. This document is considered to reflect in style, content, and format the traditional pictorial manuscripts of pre-conquest times. Composed during the sixteenth century outside bounds of Spanish patronage, it is fortunate that it did not fall prey to the zealous frames of colonial proselytization. It became part of a collection of Mexican Indian documents gathered by Lorenzo Buturini Bernaduci during the years 1736-1743. this codex portrays... their exit from Aztlán until their arrival at the hill of Chapultepec and subjugation by the Culhuacanos. A series of glyphs, ideographs, and phonetic symbols codices such as this one assisted the story talkers' memories. Although produced after the conquest, this text evidences the retention of a strong sense of historical consciousness and identity among the indigenous population."[57]

Earlier we were informed that "it seems shortly after 1433, they burned their books and rewrote their history." Pina, therefore, encourages caution when sifting through historical documents.

Secondly, it was gathered and completed over 200 years after the conquest. It is likely a Spaniard or other European as in this case an Italian recorded their conversations on Aztec history from the informants' traditional oral education and as stated the primitive code of writing (comparatively speaking). No doubt, there is much room for mistakes, and inaccurate interpretations by everyone involved.

When one hears or reads the term "codex" immediately it radiates an aura of authority and specialness. The use of the word codex was the word used by the several Europeans who documented Aztec history, thought and culture. However, there is much conflict and confusion between the different codices themselves when speaking of the same subject matter.

In the dictionary, for example, it describes a codex: "1. *a manuscript volume, especially one of the scripture or of a classical author.*" That sounds pretty powerful and serious but it is a mistake to without question view any codex as authoritative and exact. This may have been the strategy at the time of their compositions by their author to give their documents an image of authority or the final exact say on the subjects covered.

The word "codex" came from its ancestor word "caudex," a Latin word. Codex as defined in Cassell's New Latin Dictionary means: "the trunk of a tree. (3) a book made up of wooden tablets, covered with wax; a book." So, it's a sophisticated way of saying a book or document. The codex is often named after its author and other times the people it is written about. By demystifying the connotation Codex, you challenge its infallibility.

Can the codices today lead us to Aztlán? Better, did the codices lead the Spaniards to Aztlán? Whatever these particular documents actually revealed to the Spaniards they were unable to accurately and immediately decipher them to the point of discovering Aztlán. Or did the Spaniards discover Aztlán? And how would we know? Even more important, who would be the final authority on whether Aztlán has been discovered? Would we seek or need our oppressors' approval? Its actual identity may be more elusive than its location in the end.

1765
RIVERA
SECRETLY GOES LOOKING 4 AZTLÁN

"In 1765 Juan Maria Antonio Rivera led the first two recorded expeditions to Yuta country."[58] And why would these expeditions continue into the land of the "Northern Mystery?" The author Sanchez gives the traditional motive, the possibility of discovering precious metals. "The first Rivera expedition stemmed from news that had spread throughout New Mexico of a Yuta warrior who had traded a piece of silver ore. To a black smith in Abiqui. The expedition undertaken in June 1765 left Abiqui shortly thereafter" (p. 29). To the Spaniards this was vivid evidence that they were on the verge of a great discovery and maybe even greater than that of the Mexica and the Inca gold empires. Always under the watchful eyes of the curious Europeans Rivera was told of the importance of secrecy, Sanchez continued. "One peculiar detail adds historical interest to the expedition: it appears Rivera was ordered not to describe portions of his march over well-known territory" (p. 21).

Though Rivera's short first expedition which was followed by a second short expedition of about 15 days both were failures in terms of not finding gold or silver or the supposed mother lode (Aztlán?) It did provide the Spaniards with meaningful information. "...Above all, Rivera's expedition served as an impetus for the next major expedition to the Yuta country. That led by the Friars Dominguez and Escalante" (p. 38). Between the two major expeditions of Rivera and Escalante or about 11 years the recently colonized California had grown in importance.

Governor Velez instructed Rivera additionally, "to determine the location of the large river they had heard about and to see if silver could be found within the environs" (p. 29). Also, "… Rivera was to learn whether there were large towns in the area, what nations lived along its banks, and the truth of the twice-told tale that flitted throughout Abiquiu that white bearded men "dressed in a European manner" lived there." (loc. cit.)

Curiously, Velez wanted to know whether the Río de Tizon discussed here is in fact the Colorado River. From preliminary explorations of the Colorado, the Spaniards were not able to determine accurately its length or course. Therefore, many times, this same elongated Colorado River was believed to be different rivers and given as a result different names causing greater confusion. The Colorado River, "called the Tizón because the Indians on the lower river carried tizones, or firebrands, with them in winter to keep them warm."[59]

"In 1769... shortly after arrival, Portola led the first Spanish overland march along the coast following closely the present coastal highway, from San Diego to Monterrey, discovering San Francisco Bay. In the next decade, Monterey, the capital of Spanish Alta California grew in prominence - so much that by 1775 Spanish officials began to consider an over land connection between New Mexico and California."[60]

Even in the 1776 Dominguez-Escalante expedition the route taken arouses suspicion that they too were actually looking 4 Aztlán. Though we are told, it was an exploratory expedition to discover an overland route connecting Santa Fe with Monterrey.

1768
DON COPYCAT

On the map captioned: Nuevo Mapa Geographico de la America Septentrional, Perteneciente al Virreynato de Mexico dedicado a los sabios miembros de la academia real de las ciencias de Paris, por su muy rendido servidor y capelan, - don Joseph Antonio de Alzate y Ramirez, año 1768, are the following notations. [Warning: because of the very poor quality of the map I located and used, it is quite possible I have made errors in the spelling of certain words].

On the northwestern part of the map are the notations: "*Laguna de Teguayo,*" "*Sierra Azul*" and "*De Los Centerros Deserta Laguna Dizen haver salido Los Indios Mericanos* (or Americano or Mexicanos?) *a fundae* (fundar?) *su impero.*"

Just north of Teguayo (Aztlán) is strangely "*Quivira Fabulon.*" Remember the kingdom of Quivira? (Often earlier cartographers confused Teguayo with Quivira or as here, put it near Teguayo and eventually placing it separately and further east.

Just south of Teguayo (Aztlán) is notated "*Primera Mansion que hazieron Los Yndios Mexicanos.*"

Further south is notated: "2a Mansion de Los Mexicanos."

It is interesting to note that a short distance directly east of this notation is the notation *Casa Grande*. I thought from my readings and the Francisco Alvarez Y Barreiro's general map of 1727 that Casa Grande was the second stop of the Aztecs. This map however seems to indicate they are not and are two separate notations and locations. In any event, this 1768 map was no doubt greatly affected by the 1727 general map.

Because of the poor legibility of the map, I was not able to locate the third stop of the Aztecs, which is considered Casas Grandes in Northern Mexico. This map and other maps following the 1727 would indicate how Teguayo (a.k.a. Aztlán) and the three notated stops of the Aztecs took hold cartographically and would continue to be placed on maps even though worded slightly different for over a century as late as 1848.

Don Antonio Alzate was known as a famous astronomer and naturalist. I am not sure of his recognition as a cartographer. However, one author in a footnote gave a harsh criticism of this particular map. He writes: "Although Alzate was at this time one of the most learned men in Mexico, his map is certainly one of the poorest of the northwest coast ever published, whatever may be said of its value in other parts."[61] To be evaluated as having made a poor map during a time of poor map-making in general is pretty bad.

1774
MISSIONARIES
CONTINUE LOOKING 4 AZTLÁN

"A few years after Barreiro's visit to the *Provincias Internas,* Father Jacobo Secelmayr, a veteran of Pimería Alta, urged missionaries be sent to the Gila-Colorado River area, remarking that if this were done the king's representatives could learn what sort of people lived beyond the river Colorado, "a part of America as yet unknown."[62] This was in 1744, and Father Sedelmayr also referred to the legend (mentioned by Barreiro and later perpetuated by Humboldt) that the Aztecs originated some where in the northern country. If missionaries could only be sent there, he believed that they should be able to find the original "cities or caves whence issued the Mexican nation and where they learned that organization and method of government which enable them to found an empire so far removed from the cradle of their race" (pp. 83, 84). And the learned Friar suggested that such missionaries, if sent to these far countries, could "find out whether the *Gran Quivira* or *Gran Teguayo* are kingdoms which the French have succeeded in discovering." (Loc. cit.)

This quotation reveals many important principles. 1) Barreiro's general map of 1727 had strongly secured for over a century the belief that the Aztecs originated near Teguayo and this map and belief had a domino effect upon cartographers, explorers, settlers, and other Spanish citizens. 2) The Spanish were intensely driven to locate the Aztec (Mexica) origin because they believed it would take them to the seven *cities* or *caves*. Why would Spaniards who conquered, despised and oppressed the Mexica, their descendants, and all central Mexican and Indians in general, be interested in the Mexica place of origin? As stated earlier, Aztlán was synonymous with Chicomoztoc and both with the Aztecs (Mexica) and all with *Gold*. After all the Mexica were saturated with gold when Cortez arrived in 1519 it made sense *cities of gold* could have still been found if the Aztecs had anything to do with a *place*. 3) It is shown here that Spain was concerned that France was on the verge of discovering these cities of gold in advance of Spaniards.

The missionaries were not primarily interested in saving souls but finding gold as is shown again and again by their writings and suggestions that precious metals lay further north to be discovered. Still, history has a sacred place for these "conquistadores par excellance."

1774
MYTHICAL RIO TIMPANOGOS

"In promoting his discoveries in 1774, Fages wrote a *Historical, Political and Natural Description of California* pointing out the importance of the resources in the interior. After the establishment in the interior. After the establishment of missions, presidios and farmlands, California's importance grew rapidly in the eyes of Spanish officials. Similarly, New Mexico's Governors took notice of California as a possible trading partner."[63]

"Although Fages and his men at the time were ignorant of Teguayo and the Yuta country, they had contributed information which would extend the myth of Gran Teguayo to the San Franciso Bay area. Indeed a latter *Mexican-period map* showed a Rio Timpananogos flowing from the Great Salt Lake to San Francisco Bay, where Fages's Rio San Joaquin and Rio Sacrament were located. Perhaps hope sprang eternal that an easy route from Timpanagos to the Monterey –San Francisco Bay Area existed" (pp. 44, 45). That Mexican period map would place it at least as late as 1821. So, if RioTimpanagos is believed to be connected to the Great Salt Lake land of Teguayo (another name 4 Aztlán), then as late as this period, Mexicans are continuing to claim Aztlán is in the vicinity of the Salt Lake City area under a different name or names instead of Aztlán as we call it today.

1776
DOMINGUEZ-ESCALANTE EXPEDITION GO LOOKING 4 AZTLÁN

For two centuries, this expedition was called the *Escalante Expedition*. Recently, however white American historians have renamed it the *Dominguez-Escalante Expedition*. It was actually Friar Dominguez who organized and led it. But, it was Friar Escalante who kept the monumental daily journal of this amazing expedition. It was therefore, known originally as the Escalante Expedition.

In 1776, "Two Catholic Fathers, Francisco Antanasio Dominguez and Silvestre Velez de Escalante- set out from Santa Fe, New Mexico, at the head of a ten-man mission exploring party bound for California. Before completing its work, that expedition had accomplished one of the most remarkable explorations in the history of the United States. It had penetrated deeply into the vast, as yet unknown interior region of the great American west."[64]

According to most historians, there were two major objectives, (1) to open a line of communication and transportation between Santa Fe, New Mexico and Monterrey, California. Monterrey because it was the newly established capital of the California Mission Colonies. Because of the encroachment of other European nations into North America, it was important to cartograph, document, settle, claim, and defend the northern mystery. A route from Monterrey to Santa Fe would be the start of such an objective. (2) To take Christianity to the natives. Actually, missionization was one of the very first steps often before military conquest in the domination and oppression of indigenous peoples and their regions. It was not as "*Holy*" as it may have sounded.

I would myself add a third motive, which may in fact have been the very first. The use of the mythical name-place Aztlán had slowly faded in use and by now at least in this instance had been replaced by the name Teguayo. Teguayo was the latest in a list of names that represented Aztlán. Unofficially, but I expect even officially but covertly the Spanish government wanted Dominguez-Escalante to attempt to discover Teguayo. In fact, the earliest Indian scout during Rivera's earlier expedition was a Ute and from the very beginning of Dominguez-Escalante, their scouts were also Utes. They were called Laguna Indians by the Spaniards because they lived in an area with a large lake the Spaniards were calling Teguayo.

Cartographically, Teguayo had been on a map at least since 1727 with Barrieros general map of the southwest. Did the Spaniards believe this to be the large mysterious lake of gold they were not successful in finding? Also, an ancient Mexican codice had shown Aztlán to be on an island in the middle of a lake. It seemed also that many if not most of the Indians of the southwest in their oral tradition pointed to this area as the genesis of most Indians and especially the Mexica. Remember, as stated earlier, find Aztlán and you will find Chicomoztoc, which was in Spanish eyes and hearts the seven cities of gold.

In my own opinion, I believe the Dominguez-Escalante expedition had purposely deviated from their publicly stated intention to create a route north and westerly directly across to Monterrey, California. As shown by this particular author, Escalante was well versed in the knowledge of Teguayo.

Fray Alonzo de Posada's written report in 1686, was regarded for many years subsequent to that date as the most authentic source of information relating to the regions outside the settled portions of New Mexico, and particularly with respect to Quivira, Teguayo, and other provinces. Escalante had made careful studies of and familiarized himself with many of the explorations, which had been made into the territory, which interested him so deeply. He had access to many documents relating to these explorations and discoveries, which, unfortunately, were destroyed during the Indian revolts in New Mexico, or have during the years, disappeared for one reason or another."[65]

Another document of interest and access to Escalante may have been this one. "Although Teguayo appeared to be a mythical place in official Spanish thinking, Franciscans dreamed of creating a mission field there before Spanish settlers, miners, traders, or soldiers could get there. One such Franciscan was Fray Carlos Delgado, the missionary at Isleta Pueblo in New Mexico.[66] In 1744, sixty-seven-year old Fray Carlos proposed to work among the Hopi, Navajo, and the people of Gran Teguayo... his proposal was based on information he had learned from the Navajos, who were ever so eager to conjure up stories to satisfy the Spanish quest for new discoveries. To that end, he gave the following account of Teguayo:

"... It is a distance of about two hundred leagues more or less from this custodia. On this entry that I made to Nabajoa, I heard some of the natives tell how this Teguayo, so renowned, is made up of various nations, for in it are found people from all of them, both civilized from among those who we are governing as well as others who are heathen." (loc. cit.)

And of course as always precious metals just happen to be there as well. Fray Carlos continues to write "... and I am sure they desire to be acquainted with the holy habit, for they say that in former times a religious went there and contracted a fatal illness. After his death they kept him in a box, which they give one to understand is of silver. The said religious merited this honor because of his having catechized the king. All his successors regard as relics a shrine of gold, and the articles used in saying mass, as well as other things that he used." (loc. cit.)

As you can see, at least on paper Teguayo (Aztlán) was rockin' with diversity, large populations of civilized and uncivilized Indians, and the promise of precious metals. It is no wonder why the Dominguez-Escalante kept their probable number one objective a public secret. Adding to my suspicions is this fact I discovered in reading the Dominguez-Escalante journal. The author using the journal determines; "Near the present city of Provo, Utah, Silvestre left the group, but Joaquin agreed to stay on as they moved back to the south. Miera had been taking astrolabe navigational sightings, and about two-hundred miles south of modern Provo, he determined that moving straight west would bring them to Monterrey, in California"[67] This calculation and determination pointed specifically at Monterrey was made *after* they decided to return to Santa Fe, New Mexico.

One of the explanations for the expeditions for going so far north before they went west was because of the inhospitable mountains, terrain, and hostile Indians. However, as the Spanish Trail and its many variations would later show, it was not necessary to go so far north in Utah before heading west *unless* you were going to Teguayo.

Most convincing is this passage in Escalante's journal on August 30. "On the 30th in the morning the interpreter Andrés and the guide Atanasio arrived with five sabuaganas and one laguna. After we had regaled them with plenty of food and tobacco, we informed them of our purpose, which was to pass on to the Pueblo or Pueblos of the Lagunas (the Yutas had told us that the Lagunas dwelt in pueblos like those of New Mexico) telling them that, since they were our friends, they should give us a good guide who would conduct us as far as these peoples and that we would pay him to his satisfaction. They replied that to go to the place we were trying to reach there was no other trail than the one passing through the midst of the Comanches and that these would impede our passage and even deprive us of our lives and finally that none of them knew the country between here and the Lagunas. This they repeated many times, insisting that we had to turn back from here. We tried to convince them by arguing and then by cajoling, so as not to displease them. Then we showed the Laguna a woolen blanket, a big all-purpose knife, and white glass beads, telling him that this is what we were giving him so that he would accompany us and serve as a guide all the way to his country. He agreed, and the things mentioned were turned over to him."[68] So in spite of initial refusal on the part of Indian guides and warnings of great danger, the expedition party was insistent until it got its way and they went on to Teguayo.

The greatest achievement of the expedition was the map composed by their cartographer Don Bernado Miera y Pacheco. It was his assignment to map the route. "In many ways the Dominguez-Escalante expedition defined the Yuta country, for Miera y Pacheco had depicted it graphically, thus influencing colonial cartographers of the period. The subsequent cartography of eighteenth century added little new information regarding the Yuta country; In fact, it appears to have relied on Miera y Pacheco's work."[69] It also secured the European principle of conquest and discovery, as mentioned earlier by discovering and documenting their discoveries as proof of their new possessions. As we will see later, another famous and very key cartographer will be influenced by Miera y Pacheco's work, his name; Alexander Von Humboldt. Von Humboldt's map in turn will serve indirectly as the basis for the 1847 Disturnell map, which is also called the 1848 Treaty of Peace map.

THE 1778 MIERA MAP

Though at the time the Miera map was completed it was considered monumental in importance and accuracy, however, it was not without many shortcomings. Miera in the vast wilderness was limited in the technology of the time period for mapmakers; the Quadrant. In *The Dominguez-Escalante Journal their Expedition through Colorado, Utah, Arizona and New Mexico in 1776*, the author comments on the instrument used and its inaccuracies. The only time the Quadrant was mentioned in the journal was September 14. (loc. cit.) "A Quadrant measures angular attitudes. This instrument generally consists of a graduated arc of 90° or more, an index arm, and a sighting arrangement with a plumb or spirit level.

"The Quadrant was superceded by the sextant, which determines geographic position by measuring the altitude of the sun and the stars. They made their astronomical observations some fifteen times during the course of the expedition. Seven times, they fixed their positions by the sun and eight times by the North Star. It appears that most of their calculations were somewhat too high in latitude. Just why is not known. They were concerned about the accuracy of their calculations and made several readings at the same place in order to check it more accurately."[70] This is important to remember because mapmakers who map similar regions use earlier maps and as we have seen will often do so indiscriminately and uncritically.

There are several parts of the map that I believe are important to resurrect and discuss.

RUINS

It is interesting to note that of the 3 proposed stopping points of the Mexica (Aztecs) on their way from Aztlán to Mexico-Tenochtitlan – that these places all have extensive architectural ruins. Stereotypically, today we identify the Aztecs with great architectural achievements in their pyramids, palaces, and monuments. Did the earliest cartographers, historians, and explorers stereotype the Aztecs as well? We must keep in mind two important points: 1) The original Aztecs (Mexica) who existed from Aztlán were *hunter-gatherers* – the science of building pyramids and monuments would be learned later from the Tolteca in central Mexico;

2) There are no great ruins in the cartographic areas designated as Teguayo, or any other name representing Aztlán.

On the Miera map these words are notated: "*Aqui se manifiestan las ruinas de grandes poblaciones de Indios antiguas.*" (Here are the ruins of large ancient Indian settlements). The question has to be asked, is this notation in the 1777 Miera map the reason for the 1847 Disturnell map notation of "*Antigua Residencia de los Aztecas?*" Or is it a Barreiros general map of 1727 or the Von Humboldt map of 1811 or any combination of the three? And why was the name Azteca used instead of Mexica, which had been used for centuries before?

Also, does this correspond with the 1727 Barreiros general map, which notes the 1st Mexica stop? The approximate locations seem similar in that this area is sitting in the proximity of the confluence of two rivers.

In a letter written to the King of Spain after the expedition, Miera as a retired soldier, engineer, and cartographer advises the king to create 3 Spanish frontier settlements. This description helps in modernizing the area's actual location. His letter can be found in its entirety in, *Pageant in the Wilderness, the Story of the Escalante Expedition to the Interior Basin, 1776,* by Herbert E. Bolton on pages 243-250.[71]

Miera writes, "With three Presidios, together with three settlements of Spaniards, the door will be open to a new empire which may be explored and colonized. The chief one, and the one that should be the first objective, should be on the shores of the lake of the Timpanogos,…" (loc. cit.)

It is the next one that is relative to the Miera map. "The second Presidio and the settlement of families attached to it also are very desirable, and should be founded at the junction of the River Nabajoo with that of Las Animas, along the beautiful and extensive meadows which its margins provide for raising crops, together with the convenience of the timber, firewood, and pastures which they offer. There skill remain in those meadows vestiges of irrigation ditches, *ruins of many large and ancient settlements of Indians, and furnaces where they apparently smelted metals.*"[72] (italics added)

Even though Miera does not call this particular notation a Mexica stop or homeland, specifically, he was aware of the Mexica migration as indicated here. "In the British Museum is a large manuscript map… which bears at least some evidence of being the original map which accompanied Escalante. *Diario Derreoteo* when in May of 1777 it was sent from Santa Fe to the viceroy of New Spain… " (p. 101). The title of the map gives the name of the maker of the map, the key individuals of the expedition and to whom the map is dedicated. "Below this title appear two extended legends, one terming the alleged "sea of the west a myth, 12 -… " (loc. cit.) (footnote omitted) The footnote to this myth in the English translation reads: "The sea of the west, shown on the new maps extending in this direction more than 500 leagues from east to west and the same from north to south, communicating with the Lakes of the Bueyes, and from them to the Bay of Utsom, is indicated as beginning at 41 degrees of latitude on the south side, which apparently and without doubt is in error. I believe that all they show as the said sea is dry land, populated by various peoples who are able to live in organized societies, which is why our ancient Spaniards, from the time of Don Fernando Cortes down to the present, have longed to discover and settle the coast of California, because of may reports they had of the people who lived in those places, *and the fact that the Mexican nation emerged from them.*" (loc. cit.) (italics added) Adding to and convincing me he was aware of the "hypothetical" Mexica stops are these quotes. "…Francisco y Barreiro (or Barreyo), who accompanied Brigadier Don Pedro de Rivera on his tour of inspection of the *Provincias Internas* during the years 1724-1728… He joined the Rivera expedition as an engineer, cartographer and statistician, and prepared six maps, which together may be said to form the first reasonably scientific cartographic description of the area covered.

The sixth map is a general map of the entire area including Texas. It is a cartographic land mark of first importance" (p. 81). It is here; we for the first time see the original homeland and exodus of the Mexica and the three *stops* on their 100-year journey south. Miera had to have also been aware of Barreiro's 1727 general map. Remember, *cartographers are copycats*. Miera must have felt this was an ancient Aztec (Mexica) stop but regardless; he did not use the term Mexica as a notation.

On the Miera map the location of these ancient ruins are described as being "… at the junction of the River Navajo with that of Las Animas…" The Nabajoo or Navajo River today is called the San Juan River and El Rio de Las Animas is called the Animas River. Today this area houses the town of Aztec. "Aztec (population 5,500)… is on of New Mexico's true jewels. Over a mile high in elevation and straddling the Animas river in the fecund San Juan River basin, Aztec is green and vibrant and in the heart of some of the prettiest country in the southwest." (loc. cit.)

AZTEC RUINS

"This is among the most well-preserved and best reconstructed of all the Anasazi villages and is part of three-pueblo cultural chain that also includes Chaco Canyon to the south and Colorado's Mesa Verde to the North."[73]

Metzger continues:

>   First recorded by the Dominguez-Escalante expedition in 1776, which passed by the ruins on its way to the Pacific, Aztec was thought by earlier settlers to have been part of the great Aztec empire. In truth, the pueblo was built in the 11th or 12th century by Chacoan Anazasi Indians, who had lived in pit houses and smaller pueblos in the area for hundreds of years.
>   Like Chaco, Aztec was abandoned by the end of the 12th century, lay deserted for several decades, and was repopulated and added onto in the mid-to late 13th century by less advances people migrating south from Mesa Verde. By 1275 or so, though, the Mesa Verdeans had left Aztec as well, and the pueblo probably lay virtually untouched until the mid-19th century, when Anglos began to settle the area and scientists started taking an interest in early southwestern cultures" (pp. 68, 69).

In *The Place Names of New Mexico,* Miera is mentioned together with the ruins.

Europeans first saw the ruins in 1776 when Dominguez and Escalante passed through the area, and their cartographer, Bernado Miera y Pacheco, put them on his map.

English-speaking settlers arrived in the area in the 1870's and they, mistakenly assuming a northern branch of the Aztecs of New Mexico had built the ruins, called them Aztec Ruins. The name stuck" (Julyan, p. 26).

THE GREAT SALT LAKE

If you look at the expedition map composed by Miera and dated 1778 you will see in the northwest corner two lakes connected by a river to each other and named as one lake or "Laguna de los Timpanagos." Author Carl J. Wheat writes, "It was Miera who affixed the word Timpanagos to the lake beside which the party camped, and on some types of his map Timpanogos is also applied to the larger, saltier Lake to the north, of which they did not see."[74]

The September 23 entry of Escalante's journal reads, "On the 23rd, knowing that we were approaching the lake..."[75] The lake he was referring to is today's *Utah Lake,* which I will discuss later. It is the *other lake* as referred to by Escalante that is of interest here. This lake was not seen on this expedition, not even by its mapmaker who applied it to his map. Escalante enters; "The other lake (Great Salt Lake, which is connected to Utah by the forty mile-long Jordan River) with which this one comes in contact covers many leagues, so we are informed, and its waters are harmful and extremely salty, for the Timpanois assured us that anyone who wet some part of his body with them immediately felt a lot of itching in the part moistened" (p. 72).

Miera realizing they meant a salt-water body figured it was water from the Pacific Ocean. That is why he added a river running east to west believing it would lead to the Ocean and most likely the San Francisco Bay area. But Miera had to be preconditioned when assigning the Great *Salt* Lake to a river running westerly to the Pacific.

Garcés, a contemporary missionary and cartographer earlier wrote: "I have been very sorry that advantage has not been taken of this occasion, so opportune for discovering the course of the San Francisco river, which

I believe is connected with the Colorado, and both with some very large lakes, or a water which is still and is very large, as the Gileños have told me."[76] The author Sanchez writes of Garcés written comments. "The San Francisco River was the San Joaquin, which had been discovered in 1772 by Fages and Crespi. It is possible that Garcés comment may have been the origin of the notion that the Great Salt Lake was connected to San Francisco through the mythical Rio de Teguayo." (loc. cit.)

Sanchez further explains why Garcés is regretful. "Upon arriving at San Gabriel, Garcés was disappointed at having missed the opportunity to join Anza on his expedition to Monterrey, for he had been specially charged "by high authority to investigate the feasibility of opening communication between Monterrey and New Mexico." (loc. cit.)

In promoting his discoveries in 1774, Fages wrote *A Historical, Political, and Natural Description of California* pointing out the importance of the resources in the interior. It is written:

> Although, Fages and his men at the time were ignorant of Teguayo and the Yuta country, they had contributed information, which would extend the myth of Gran Teguayo to the San Francisco Bay area. Indeed, a later Mexican-period showed a Rio Timpanogos flowing from the Great Salt Lake to San Francisco Bay, where Fages' Rio San Joaquin and Rio Sacramento were located. Perhaps, hope sprang eternal that an easy route from Timpanagos to the Monterrey-San Francisco Bay area existed (Sanchez, p. 45).

If you examine the far northwest corner of Miera's map, he clearly points out his belief though wrong of why he believes *Rio Timpanogos* runs to the Pacific Ocean. It reads: "*ade ser este rio el de el Tizon, descubierto antiguamente por el adelantado D. Juan de Onate el que no pudo pasa por su mucha anchura y hordor, puede, ser nabegable; se dice haber de la otza banda, muchas poblaciónes grande de Indios que viven en politica.*"

It is important to restate that Miera went on the basis of hearsay and not first-hand observation in mapping the Great Salt Lake and the river, which would eventually be called *Rio Timpanogos*. As cautioned much earlier by Mr. Greenwood, one has to be careful and critical when using maps for they surely can be dangerous especially as we have learned in their infancy during the Spanish period.

GREEN RIVER

"The Green River was known to the Spaniards by the name Rio San Buenaventura... Escalante knew a little about the Rio San Buenaventura, for he had studied previous Spanish reports of the area... Posada had said that the river was the boundary between the Comanche and the Utes."[77]

The Dominguez-Escalante expedition first discovered the Green River in Jensen Utah, which is located at the northeast part of the state today. They after a short while would leave it and mistakenly believe at a much later time on their way back to Santa Fe further west and south that they had reconnected with Rio San Buenvenura (Green River). On Miera maps this caused him to not connect the Green River with the Colorado as its tributary (which it is in reality) and secondly had it running almost in an east to west direction across today's Utah.

This footnote explains in detail why Miera would map the Green River as he did:

"Although in later years a great apocryphal Buenaventura River was to loom large on maps, and although that invention was at times ascribed to Father Garcés, the name Buenaventura for a westward or south-westward – flowing river in the eastern Great Basin was initially proposed by Escalante when he crossed what is now known as Green river near the present day town of Jensen, Utah. Later, after leaving its northern most camp near the Shore of Utah Lake, his party came to the stream now known as the Sevier River, where, though Escalante seems to have known better, Miera apparently believed he was again on the Buenaventura."[78]

This map like the earlier maps was closely guarded. "For more than a century this map remained unpublished, though few cartographers – notably Baron Von Humboldt – seem to have had access to it in some form and to have made use of the information it records" (p. 96).

TIMPANOGOS:
STILL ANOTHER NAME FOR AZTLÁN

And so, some understanding of mythical Teguayo had been reached for the small Spanish expedition, myth, and reality met on the edge of a place the Yutas called Timpanogos.[79]

"The San Buenaventura River could represent what Spanish officials and explorers knew about the Yuta country. Since 1686 when Father Posada had written about it, albeit vicariously through the eyes of colonial informants, until 1776 when the men of the Dominguez Escalante expedition saw it and described it, knowledge about the river was only hearsay evidence. New Mexican Frontiers-men who had been there kept what they knew about the area to themselves, for they had been there without license. Their illegal entry into the area would not have been without penalty. BUT NOW, the Dominguez-Escalante expedition stood on the threshold of a new land. Beyond the Rio San Buenaventura lay *Teguayo,* a place few if any, Spanish New Mexicans had seen" (p. 67).

Can you imagine the difficulty of the expedition members trying to keep their excitement under control. After centuries of stories, documents, maps and theories of whether or not and where this place was, and of the many names to label this special place starting with Aztlán, Chicomoztoc, Cibola, Quivira, Copala, Teguayo and Timpanagos. They were just a few days travel away. What would they find?

Beautiful fantasy ran smack into ugly reality at the doorstep of Teguayo, however. "Of *Teguayo* Escalante wrote: It is nothing but the land by which the Tihuas, Tehuas and other Indians transmigrated to this kingdom; which is clearly shown by the ruins of the Pueblos which I have seen in it, whose form was the same that they afterwards gave to theirs in New Mexico; and fragments of clay and pottery which I also saw in said country are much like that which the said Tehuas make today. To which is added the prevailing tradition with them, which proves the same; and that I have gone on foot more than 300 leagues in the said direction up to 41 degrees and 19 minutes latitude and have found no information whatever among the Indians who today are occupying that country of others who live in pueblos" (p.13).

Why were the Spaniards so disgusted? Because they were expecting to find, I believe, the seven cities of gold. In Friar Posada's 1686 report he actually tries to explain the exact location of Teguayo by starting at 37 degrees latitude with Santa Fe and giving directions north.

> "It remains only for us to tell of the location and direction of the kingdom and provinces which they call *Teguayo*. To provide some understanding of this land, let us recall again the location of the villa of *Santa Fe*, the capital of New Mexico which is stated as thirty-seven degrees – taking from the villa a straight line to the northwest between north and south and crossing the *Sierras* called *Casafuerte* or *Nabajo*, one reaches the large river which runs directly west for a distance of sixty leagues which are possessed by the *Apacha* Nation. Crossing this river, one enters the nation called *Yuta*, a warlike people.
>
> Beyond this nation some seventy leagues in the same northwest direction one enters afterwards some hills at a distance of fifty leagues more or less, the land which the Indians of the north call *Teguayo*, and the Mexican Indians by old tradition call *Copala*" (p.8).

World renowned scientist "Alexander von Humboldt after researching Mexican historical documents guessed that Aztlán had to be located no further south than forty-two degrees of latitude somewhere in the present-day states of Oregon, Idaho, and Wyoming." [*Aztlán, essays of the Chicano Homeland*, p. 33] By Escalante saying, "... I have gone on foot more than 300 leagues in the said direction up to 41 degrees and 19 minutes latitude and have found no information whatever..." It seems he was also of the same general opinion as von Humboldt would be in the next century. The "information" seems to be information as to where the precious metals were located. I gathered from his written statement.

He did believe that this was the original birthplace of the Indians of the Americas. In other words, this was thought to be Aztlán, Chicomoztoc, or both. Because of the centuries of "blending" Aztlán into Chicomoztoc, it became confusing, which was which, or which was meant to be which? But no big deal was made of the birthplace of the Indians because again they were hunting for gold and they couldn't care less where the Indians of North America originated unless that location was accompanied by precious metals. It was the expectation but actual absence of a Mexico-Tenochtitlan gold saturated city or cities that caused disgust in their findings.

First of all the expedition did view the area of mythical Teguayo (Aztlán) as a beautiful area as is documented in Miera's written report to the King of Spain. Miera recommended the establishment of three settlements with this area being the first to be established. "The chief one, and the one that should be the first objective, should be the shores of the Lake of the Timpanagos, on one of the rivers that flow into it, for this is the most pleasing, beautiful, and fertile site in all New Spain."[80]

The Spaniards renamed the lake and the surrounding valley, its rivers and mountains. The peoples who resided in the valley were Lluta Indians. Also called Utes or Yutas, this was the generic term for most of the Indians of today's Utah. Within the Utah named nations they were further subdivided by outsiders and the Utah themselves. It is not always clear when you hear or see a *Yuta* subdivided nation, whether it is an outsider or insider name. "The names of each comes from the area it inhabits, whereby they are distinguished according to several provinces or territories – not according to nations, all the Yutas known heretofore compose a single nation, or let us call it kingdom, divided into five provinces which are the ones known by the common name of Yutas."[81]

WHERE DID THE HISPANIZED NAME TIMPANOGOS COME FROM?

The lake being referred to here is today's Utah Lake. "Timpanogotzis are named after the lake where they reside, which they call Timpanogo, and this name is the proper one for this lake since the name or word by which they designate any lake is *Pagarri*". [Dominguez-Escalante

Journal, p.73] The Lluta Indians who resided in what the Spaniards called Valle de Timpanogos were called *Timpanogos*. In a July 8, 1998 edition of the Ute Bulletin newspaper from Fort Duchesne, Utah, they describe their ancestoral name. The Utah Lake area Indians were called "*Toompah Nah-wach*." You can see that the Hispanized Timpanogos and the Ute version are obviously cognates.

The Spaniards also referred to these lake residents as *Laguna* Indians obviously because of the lake. Some outsiders called these residents fish eaters in their native tongue which the Spaniards called in Spanish come pescado or fish eaters instead of Timpanogos. "The Sabuaganas call these Indians *come-pescado* (fish eaters), and it is true that they have good fish."[82] The Sabuaganas were another nation within the Yuta collection of nations. Today, the direct descendants of the Laguna Indians are the Utes* who were forcibly relocated to other parts of the state. It is interesting today how Xicanos are intensely interested in discovering Aztlán and point to this area or state but not to the Indians of Utah. Why shouldn't we be since they would be more directly descendants of Aztlán (if Aztlán is in Utah) than Xicanos and Mexicanos who come from beyond the boundaries of the state Utah?

"*Timpanogotzis* appears to be an Aztecan rendition of a Ute name. According to George Steward, it would seem to be derived from an old Ute name for the mountain now called Timpanogos. Not having gender, the name seems to mean, "the stone person" or "stone one" and refers to the image of a reclining human being formed by the rides of the Mountain Timpanogos."[83]

The lake was named Lagos de los Timpanogos and the valley, Valle de Timpanogos. Miera in his report to the king wrote: "It alone is capable of maintaining a settlement with as many people as Mexico City, and of affording its inhabitants many conveniences, for it has everything necessary for the support of human life." The next sentence immediately caught my attention when reading it, he writes: " This lake and the rivers that flow into it abound in many varieties of savory fish, <u>very large white geese</u>, many kinds of ducks, and other exquisite birds never seen elsewhere..."[84]

---

*Noochew (the people); Nooah Paggot (Ute language); Nooduveep (Ute lands); [Special information handout by the Ute Bulletin, July 8, 1998]

Aztlán, the probable contraction of Aztatlan is said to mean place of the *white crane* or *place of whiteness*. Adding to this is a footnote by the author of the Dominguez-Escalante Journal and he writes: "Mount Timpanogos (11,750 feet high). In late September it was probably covered with snow and this gave rise to its name to the Spaniards of the "white mountain of the Timpanogos Indians."[85] Or in Spanish, la Sierra Blanca de los Timpanogos. Just north of this valley which today is called Paradise Valley and Utah Lake is the Great Salt Lake. The large area surrounding the salted lake because of the residue of salt crystals in the soil give off a bright lighting effect or "whiteness" which is unusually brighter in my experiences from other areas. This area and flat lands are called the "salt flats." Are any of these or all of them the "whiteness" referred to in the Aztlán definition?

Is this area earlier Aztlán or Chicomoztoc of the Mexica?

"Escalante's description of the valley and lake of Timpanogos (present Utah Lake), and of the people he observed living along it, called the *Timpanogotzis* or *Timpani Cuitzis*, was the first *reliable** eye-witness account of it. Because the people there ate a great amount of fish, he said they were called fish eaters (*come pescado*) by a neighboring tribe the Sabaguana Utes."[86] Author Sanchez further writes, "Four medium-sized rivers flowed into the lake from the Sierras that surrounded it." I find this interesting because there is a professor whose name is Cecilio Orozco of California State University at Fresno who has said the word *Nahautl* means "*People of the four rivers.*"** As you know, the Mexica (Azteca) spoke Nahautl (Ute-Aztecan). But, Professor Orozco claims the word Nahautl was also used to designate a migration nation associated historically with the Aztecs (Mexica).

The name the Timpanogos used to refer to themselves *Timpanagotzis* or *Toompahnahwach* as stated earlier is of the Ute-Aztecan language family, another interesting coincidence.

**Italics added because it implies stories may have circulated prior to Escalante from earlier eyewitnesses.*

***...Several hundred years earlier, one of the migrating tribes had been called Aztecs, and the original name of their migrating descendents were the Náhuatl (people of the four rivers)..." "El Seminario," 1 de Octubre de 1998, Denver, Colorado.*

These modern four rivers connected to Utah Lake would be: Spanish Fork river, Provo river, American River and Hobble River.

I had pointed out earlier how in establishing the 3 major stops or temporary residences of the Mexica (Aztecs) in their 100 year journey south to central Mexico each of the 3 stops had obvious advanced architectural *ruins*. Spanish cartographers and explorers I felt had stereotyped the original Mexica (Aztecs) with the recently conquered but impressive builders of Mexico-Tenochtitlan. And, simultaneously it was believed by these same explorers and cartographers that Teguayo was the point of origin and departure of the Mexica (Azteca). Well let us see what Escalante's journal has to say about the *Lagunas* (lake dwellers) or Timpanogos of Teguayo (now Timpanogos).

"Their dwellings appeared as "little wattle huts of osier out of which they have interesting crafted baskets and other utensils for ordinary use." They dressed poorly, thought Escalante; some wore deerskin jackets and long leggings, or in cold weather, they wore robes from rabbit pelts. He noted the people possessed good features and most of them were fully bearded, an uncommon trait among indigenous peoples they had met throughout the Americas."[87]

How can you intelligently credit the 3 major stopping points of the migrating Mexica (Aztecs) as proof because of the *ruins* that existed in these places? At the same time, they came from a place that did not have any similar *ruins*. My understanding in my readings was that the Mexica (Aztecs) learned the art of architecture and building from the remaining Tolteca in central Mexico after the downfall of their own empire.

However, on the other hand this does not disqualify Timpanogos (Teguayo) as not being the area of Aztlán or Chicomoztoc or both. In the codices depictions of the Mexica's (Aztec) emigration, migration and immigration into central Mexico shows them as primarily hunter-gatherers with bows and arrows nearly naked dressed in clothing made of rabbit and deer furs. Also, the Mexica are said (in Mexican codices) to have originated from an island surrounded by water. Just north of Utah Lake is the Great Salt Lake populated by at least six islands, which were inhabited by Indians until the arrival of and conquest by the Native Americans (white American people).

Much earlier in the book, we looked at the name Cibola as one of the many and earlier names 4 Aztlán. In Escalante's journal he states: "Besides this, they gather the seeds of wild plants on the bottoms and make a gruel from them, which the supplement with the game of jack rabbits, cottontail rabbits, and fowl, of which there is abundance here. They also have bison handy not too far away to the north – northwest..."[88] The word Cibola is believed to have derived from the Nahautl word *Sibulada* meaning buffalo. Indians were telling Spaniards for centuries that Aztlán was associated with the land of the buffalo and therefore, Spaniards either copied the Indians place-name or independently created that place-name.

1803
ALEXANDER THE GREAT
GOES LOOKING 4 AZTLÁN

I first came across the name Alexander von Humboldt when I was researching for my monograph: Xicano, an Autobiography. This man is given credit for either inventing or reintroducing the name Aztec. One of his greatest admirers, the Arizona historian William Prescott learned of this name (Aztec) through his readings of von Humboldt's' works. It was through his own writing of Mexican history that Prescott made the word Aztec enjoy worldwide popularity and especially in the United States. As a result Mexicanos and Xicanos have been confused about our Indigenous identities and ancestries ever since, for *Aztec* is a phonic misnomer. I will return to this point later in this section.

Still von Humboldt was no dummy and during his period on this earth, he was hailed as a genius among scientific geniuses. He was in demand throughout the world and when Spain found he was interested in visiting and researching the American hemispheric colonies of Spain he was given the *royal* treatment.

In March of 1779, von Humboldt appeared before the King of Spain and gave his presentation on the mutual advantages of his proposed multi year visits to the New Spanish colonies.

"The specifications for Humboldt's and Bonplano's passports mentioned as destinations Cuba, Mexico, New Granada (Venezuela), Peru, Chile, Buenos Aires, and the Philippines… The passport would have to mention a permission to carry out all the manner of exploration, collect plants, minerals, and animals, measure mountain heights, make astronomical observations. The same document would serve as instructions to governors and magistrates to aid in every way possible, as Humboldt had been asked to collect scientific objects for the museum and gardens of his Catholic majesty. Finally, it would give specific permission to travel in all his majesty's vessels."[89] This was all granted in spite of the fact that Spain as mentioned earlier was very secretive, strict, distrustful and suspicious of all non-Spanish citizens. Von Humboldt was a German (Prussian) but considered a cosmopolitan scientist.

"Never," Humboldt acknowledged, in the same travel book, "had a traveler been granted greater concessions and never before has a Spanish government placed greater confidence in a foreigner." He received two passports, one from the secretary of state and another from the *Council of the Indies*. In return for such courtesies he promised to deliver copies of his reports to the governor and to present several geological collections to the museum in Madrid" (p. 84) (Italics added).

Alexander von Humboldt started his journey through the Spanish colonies in South America and in March of 1803, he arrived in Mexico (Colony of New Spain). One of the strongest requests made to von Humboldt by its government was that von Humboldt make a map of the colony of New Spain. In addition to all the other scientific skills mastered by von Humboldt he was also a cartographer. In fact, von Humboldt was personally in possession of the world's most updated equipment for mapmaking. He was in constant use of these instruments because, "At that time there was real need for travelers like Humboldt to improve upon sailing charts and maps, the method for measuring geographic longitude at sea having been perfected only in 1756… <u>As for geographic maps of the Americas, no explorer as conscientious as Humboldt could have relied on any of them.</u> Hence the need for constant astronomic observation including the determination of fixed stars in relation to the traveler's actual position" (pp.87, 88).

Humboldt is given credit as the first European to research and review to the world the great pre-Columbian civilizations of the Andes and Mexico without prejudice. "In his time, Europe was unaware of the great civilizing achievements of pre-Columbian traditions. By calling attention to their importance, Humboldt contributed to a new orientation toward America, whose natives had been pictured as barbarians devoid of any higher aspirations. Humboldt's writings on the subject inspired men like John Lloyd Stephens to explore the splendors of ancient Maya temples in Yucatan and prompted William Prescott to write his *Conquest of Mexico*" (p. 136).

Humboldt was given unlimited access to Mexico's (Colony of New Spain) secret documents and unlimited assistance. "Time in Mexico City passed more quickly than was good for Humboldt's' crowded schedule. Copyists were kept busy for him, extracting from government archives statistics on commerce, mine-production, population censuses, and farm commodities. The large map of Mexico had been started, and a smaller one dealing with the valley of Mexico was almost ready. Every day Humboldt was seen working in the school of mines, directing the draftsmen, studying reports and attending classes" (p. 167) Mexico would not only express immediate gratification but historically generation after generation of Mexicans would show their admiration for his contributions. "It is as if circumstances had favored Humboldt's scientific genius. Geographic variety of scenery, mineral wealth, volcanism, and the impressive records of pre-Columbian traditions. From each of his subjects his mind had struck new sparks, all of which would interest another generation, helping it to inspire the leaders of Mexican Independence and the founders of the United States. The great Mexican patriot and statesman Benito Juárez was to confer on Humboldt the title, 'Benefactor of the Nation.' (*Benemerito de la Patria*)" (p. 217).

In fact at the Biblioteca Nacional, there… "stands a marble monument to Humboldt" (p. 156). So appreciative and impressed was the Mexican colony that Humboldt was offered among many other things a prestigious job. "Humboldt's unique knowledge of South American conditions and his research into the economic and geography of Mexico had resulted in an offer from the Mexican government."[90]

Even in the United States as a scientist, he is recognized and rewarded for in the west there is for example the naming of the Humboldt River and Humboldt Mountains.

THE DAUGHTER MAP

"However, one final and truly magnificent cartographic achievement demands attention here. It is the map of New Spain by the celebrated savant, Baron Alexander von Humboldt. Although dated 1811 and presumably published in that year, it was drawn in Mexico City in 1803 while the geographer was visiting New Spain…"[91]

1811 VON HUMBOLDT MAP

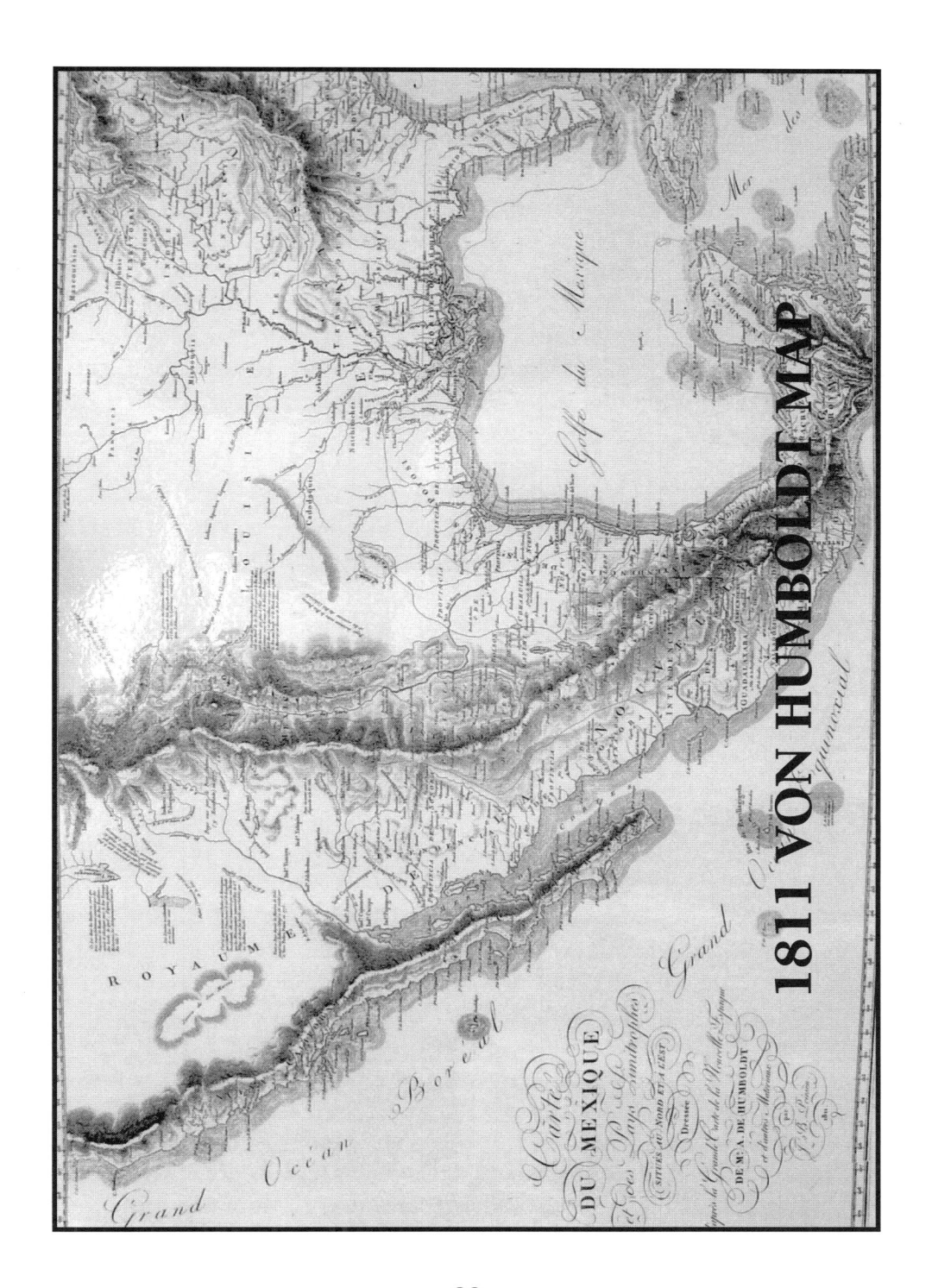

Author Carl I. Wheat continues: "When the celebrated German savant arrived in New Spain under royal auspices, he proceeded at once to assemble all possible materials for a new and accurate map of the "kingdom," and he drew his basic map at the Real Seminaria de Mineria (the Royal School of Mines) with every then available facility, report, map and document at his command. He found these materials meager and their information quite inadequate, but he went to work with vigor. Soon he decided that it would require too large a sheet to include on his map both California or the west and Texas on the east, so he left those areas for an overall map to be engraved for him by J. B. Poirson in Paris, while he concentrated on Mexico and the frontier provinces directly to the north, first gathering together and attempting to reconcile all the astronomical observations he could discover" (pp. 132, 133).

Von Humboldt was very critical of the most recent map of New Spain (1803) by the famous English cartographer Arrowsmith. "From Mexico to Vera Cruz the names appear to be scattered at random." (loc. cit.)

The information from Lewis and Clark and the United States government in to the northwest did not appear until 3 years after his 1811 map was published. This is why he stated, "It must be allowed that all that part of the west of North America is still but very imperfectly known," (loc. cit.)

Wheat writes: "He marveled that the once intrepid Spaniards had not yet been able to discover a practical land route from this to Monterrey." This would clearly indicate his knowledge of, and possible use of the Miera Map of 1778. The author Wheat continues this paragraph by saying; "However, he swallowed entire the myth of the Aztec Journey the fabled Quivira, or the Lake of Teguayo, to the Valley of Mexico, <u>and showed on his map of New Spain no less than three of their "resting places" en route</u>" (p.134) (emphasis added). Like so many cartographers before him, he did not observe the *Northern Mystery* but relied on earlier maps, documents and *chisme*. "In any event, he had before him a remarkable group of earlier maps, including, selected ones of Costansó, Mascarò, Alzate, de Fer, Urrútia, Pichardo, Lopez, Garcés, Font, Venegas, Lafora, and perhaps Miera (though possibly only indirectly), and he declared that his map had two main advantages over all previous ones of New Spain, (1) "I chose rather to leave vacant space in my map than to draw from suspicious sources," and (2) "I have traced on my map of New Spain the direction of the Cordilleras, not from vague suppositions or hypothetical combinations, but from a great variety of data from people who had been there" (pp. lxv, 134) (footnote omitted).

It is interesting to note that at the approximate point on the Miera map of 1778 at the confluence where it is written by Miera "*Aqui se las ruinas de grandes poblaciones de Indios Antiguas,*" von Humboldt on his 1811 map notates here in French "*Pays vus Par le Pere Antonio (Y Escalante) en 1777.*" This to me says he had a direct interest in the Miera map. Further: "Humboldt, like Miera, has a Buenaventura River flowing westerly into the lake to which Miera affixed his own name (Sevier Lake)" (p. 135). Unlike Miera though he does not have a river flowing from Lake Timpanogos to the Pacific. For Humboldt said it was "a bold supposition," which would give that river "an enormous length" (p. 133).

In a footnote Wheat seems to clear up why he uses the word *indirectly* to describe von Humboldt's use of the Miera map. He writes, "Humboldt's Escalante (Miera) material seems to have derived from the maps of Costansó and Mascarò – as already remarked – included much of it on their maps drawn between 1779 and 1782" (p. 135).

Author Carl I. Wheat writes of the Mexica map legends:

"Far to the northwest, west of Lac Timpanogos, is the legend:
"Ce Lac dont les limites ne sont que trés imparfaitment connues par les Journaux de route de Père Esclante, seroit-il identique avec le Lac de Teguayo des bords duquel, d'après quelques historiens, les Azteques passèrent au Rio Gila?" (p.135).

<u>This is the very first time in cartography that the word Azteques or Aztec is used replacing the word Mexica.</u> At the close of this section, I will explain possibly, why von Humboldt does this.

Of the Aztecs, aside from the already-quoted legend near Lake Timpanogos, Humboldt remarks – at about the spot where in reality Navajo Mountain rises in its solitary majesty – that here was the:

Première demeure des Aztèques sortis d'Aztlán en 1160: Tradition uncertaine." Or, the first stop of the migrating Azteca. This is a critically inaccurate interpretation of Miera's 1778 map, whether directly or indirectly through other cartographers. This puts the notation too close to Navajo Mountain and at the wrong confluence of rivers. This is important because this mistaken location will be replicated by future cartographers all the way up to Disturnell's map of 1847. (p. 136)

Farther south, near the Gila, he states:

"Casas grandes Seconde demeure des Aztèques d'ou ils passerent de la Tarahumara à Haeicolhuacan (Culiacan)." (loc. cit.) Or, the second stop of the Azteca.

And, finally, southwest of the Pres[idio] del Paso del Norte, and east of Arispe, is the legend:

"Casas grandes Troisieme demeure des Azteques." (loc. cit) Or, the third stop of the Azteca.

This is why I have referred to this important map as the *Daughter* Map. No doubt whether directly or indirectly von Humboldt was affected by the 1727 *Mother* map of Barreiro. And like the mother map, the daughter map will continue to be the source of future maps. This map still managed to become (and deservedly) the most accurate of the southwest up to this time. However, if he drew it for the Spanish and the Colony of New Spain, why did he do it in French?

"Both editions bear the imprint date 1811, but it appears on the map itself that it was drawn in Mexico in 1803, and that it was corrected by Humboldt and three associates in 1809." (loc. cit.)

Though author Carl I. Wheat makes no mention of an 1822 map of Mexico authored by von Humboldt, I luckily discovered its existence. This time it is in Spanish. It is titled, "Mapa de Megico y de los Paises Confinantes situados al norte y al este. Redacido de la grand Mapa de la Nueva-España de Mr. A. de Humboldt y otros materiales. 1822."

In this map, he continues the "Aztec" legend of emigration and migration. Near Lago de Timpanogos he notates: *"Este lago cuyos limites son muy imperfectamente conocidos por los diarios de ruta de P. Escalante. Seria acaso identico con el Lago Teguayo, desde cuyas orillas segun algunos historiadores pasaron los Aztecas al Rio Gila."* Notated across three rivers (which run north to south), east to west and above the, then, Rio

1822 VON HUMBOLDT MAP

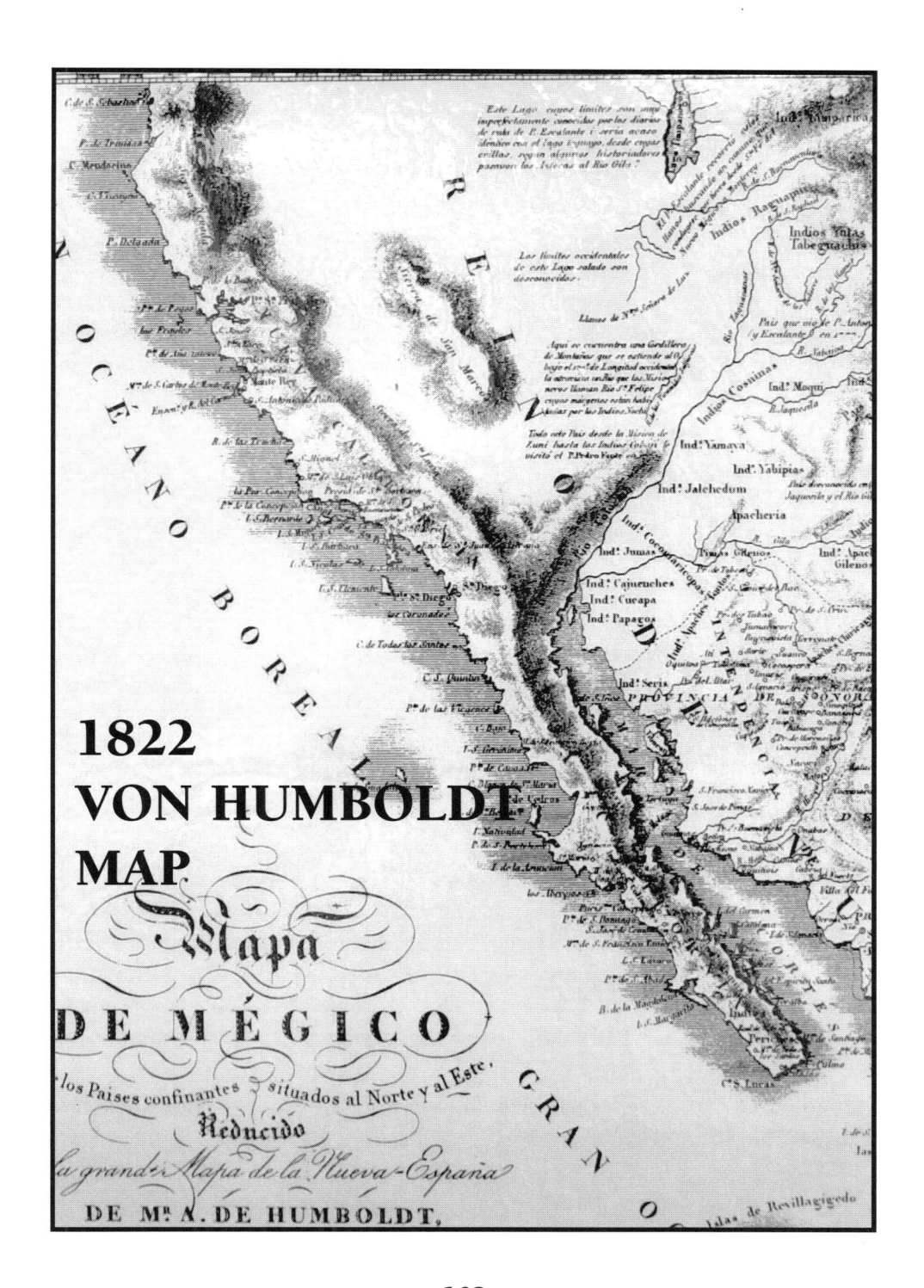

Nabajoa, Humboldt notates: *Pais que vio le P. Antonio Velez (y Escalante) en 1777.* Strangely, on this particular map there is no specific mention made of the first, second, or third stopping places for the Aztecs. The Dominguez-Escalante expedition is notated in such a vague manner and it covers a vast area consuming hundreds of miles allowing it to be possibly misinterpreted by future copycat cartographers.

Surprisingly, 1822 is the same year that the 1848 Treaty of Guadalupe map can be traced to its origin. In *The Treaty of Guadalupe-Hidalgo* its author, Richard Griswold del Castillo gives a general evolution date wise of this map. "Disturnell's map of Mexico published in 1847. This map was appended to the Treaty of Guadalupe-Hidalgo. This map was a reprint of an 1828 plagiarism of an 1826 reproduction of an 1822 publication entitled *Mapa de Los Estados Unidos de Mejico,* published by H.S. Taner of Philadelphia."

As we finally near the Treaty of Guadalupe-Hidalgo map of 1848, it is important to note that directly or indirectly von Humboldt's map of New Spain 1804, 1811, and 1822 was used. In addition to being copycats, some cartographers are outright thieves who steal from others without giving credit to their original sources. A word, name, or phrase changed here and there is made to give the cartographer a look of originality.

Von Humboldt very likely had fallen victim to such thievery as this footnote explains. "There has been some question as to how Captain Pike and Aaron Arrowsmith were able, separately, to include Humboldt material on maps published by them in 1810, a year before the *Essay on New Spain* appeared. Respecting Piker, however, Humboldt later wrote, "The maps of Mexico, which are annexed to the narrative of his journey, are reduced from my great [large?] map of New Spain, of which I left a copy, in 1804, at the secretary of state's office in Washington" (Alexander de Humboldt and Aimé Bonpland, *Narrative of Travels to the Equinoctal Regions of the New Continent during the years 1799-1804,* Philadelphia, December 23, 1815, p. xxii). Humboldt also stated (ibid., p. xxi) that Arrowsmith's map of Mexico (presumably that of 1810) was also based on the 1804 materials used to develop the map of New Spain."[92]

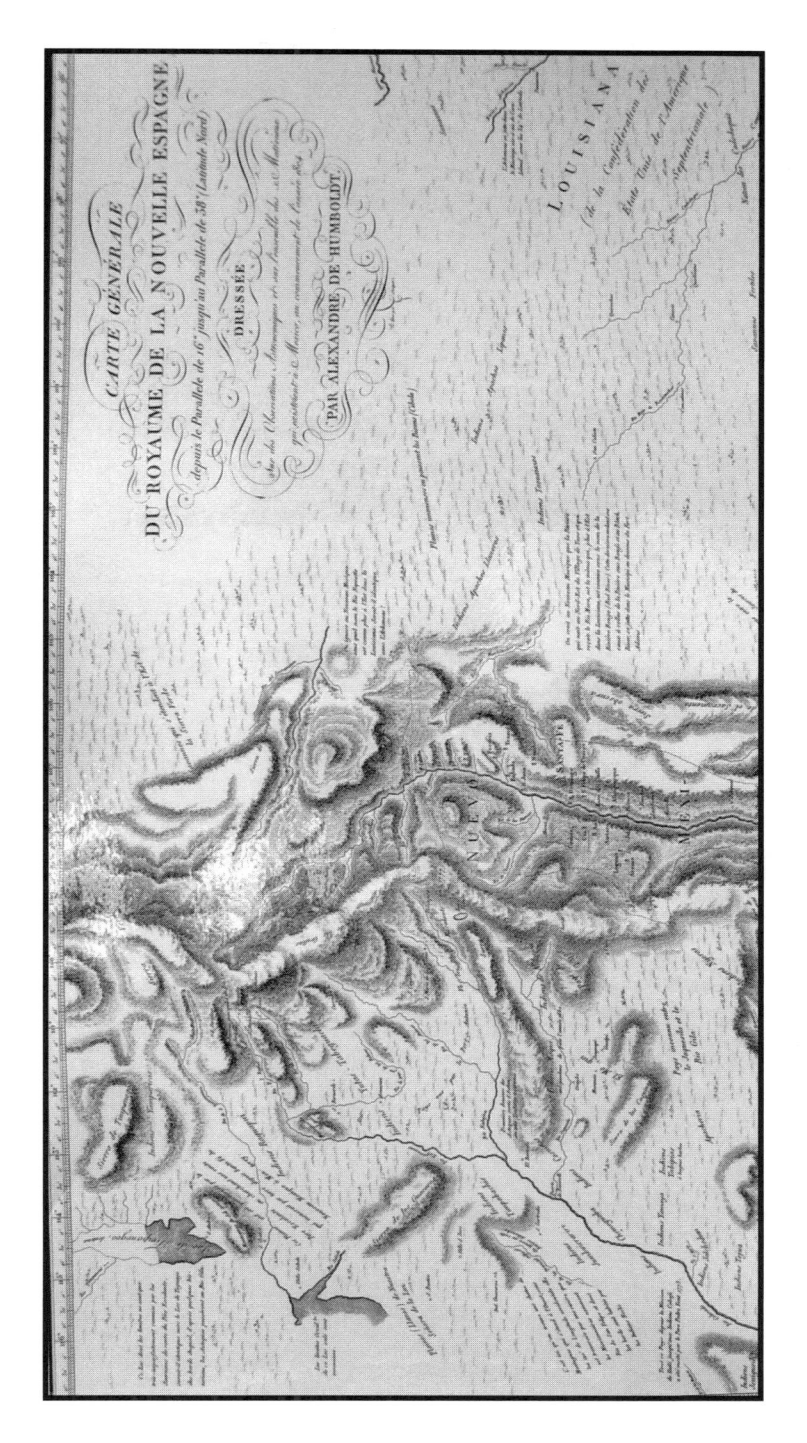

1804 VON HUMBOLDT MAP

It is ironic how von Humboldt criticized the accurateness of Arrowsmith's map of 1803 and then in 1810 the same Arrowsmith produced a map using von Humboldt's map as a guide. "In 1810 Arron Arrownsmith published his *"New Map of Mexico and Adjacent Provinces"* (p. 138) largely copied from Humboldt as the latter stated.

Finally, Humboldt left Mexico but his work for and commitment for the Spanish colony did not stop as writes Friedrich Wilhelm: "From 1804 until 1827, Humboldt lived in the main in Paris...In Paris he found the scientific collaborators and the libraries he needed to collate the results of his expedition and to carry out the experimental research demanded by the data he has collected. There he also found the engravers to draw his maps and illustrations and the publishers willing and able to undertake the publications of his great work."[93]

Humboldt was given the same *carte blanche* freedom in researching, copying and even transporting information on the ancient Mexica of Mexico. His studies and writings were not restricted to France for Italy was a treasure of ancient Mexican history as well as Mexico City.

"...But it was the library and museum of the Vatican that Humboldt benefited in his American research from a wealth of ancient Mexican manuscripts."[94] This resulted in Humboldt pioneering the elevation of the Mexica (or Aztecs) to the most highly recognized Indians in the world and the most documented because of the initial excitement he stirred world-wide by writing about them.

Humboldt no doubt knew a lot about the Mexica and was particularly fascinated by the north to south ancient Mexica migration. On his 1804 map, he notates the original homeland of the *"Azteques"* which means he viewed this area as originally Aztlán. He then goes on to *"copy"* very likely step for step Barreiro's map of 1727 with the three exact *resting stops* on the Aztecs original 100 year migration south. However, years later and of course after much more familiarity with Mexica history in general and migration in particular von Humboldt strangely does not notate these same three *resting spots* on his 1811 and 1822 map of Mexico. After extensive research, did he by now realize the lack of credibility of or the mistake of notating the three resting stops or did he feel unsure himself?

He does notate *"Teguayo"* however, and as stated earlier he believed Aztlán was no further north than the 41degree latitude. His notation states, "Este lago cuyos limites son my impertamente conocidos por los diarios de ruta de P. Escalante i seria acaso identico con el Lago Teguayo, desde cuyos orillas. Segun algunos historiadores pasaron los Aztecas al Rio Gila." <u>This would imply also that the Dominguez-Escalante expedition though they didn't find gold or other precious metals did believe they had arrived in original Aztlán.</u> Though under the name of Teguayo or Timpanagos once they discovered the present indigenous name for it.

I earlier in the beginning of this section had credited von Humboldt and William Prescott as being the cause for so much of our confusion about our identity because of their injection of the term *Aztec*.

Richard F. Townsend in his book: *The Aztecs* writes of the word Aztec. "Probably during the early 12th century a tribe departed from its ancestral homeland, described as an island within a lagoon somewhere to the north. The name of this place was *Aztlán,* meaning "place of the cranes," from which the archaic name Aztec was taken. It was not until later during the migration that these peoples assumed the name *Mexica* by which they were known by the Spaniards."[95]

In all Spanish documents and especially Barreiros Mother Map of 1727 the word Mexica is used and not Aztec. A century later when von Humboldt enters Mexico (Colony of New Spain), researches, evaluates, concludes, and documents his conclusions and then the word *Azteque* or *Aztec* or *Azteca* appears. Townsend continues, "the original term "Aztec" reappeared again in scholarly studies of the 18th and 19th centuries, and is now accepted as a generic name for the peoples of the valley of Mexico at the time of the Spanish Conquest." (loc. cit.) (italics added).

Townsend writes the original Aztecs and Mexica were two different Indian nations who merged to become the Mexica discarding the name Aztec on their way south to discover and develop Mexico-Tenochtitlan. "The original Aztecs may have had some knowledge of agriculture, for it was not until after leaving their homeland that they were joined by a second group of nomad hunter-gatherers who called themselves "Mexica" (p. 56).

In my monograph *Xicano, an autobiography* I wrote of this critical confusion caused by the phonetically disruptive word Aztec.

"Why was there a transition of names from Aztec to Mexica? One historical explanation offered was, "…Before that, the Aztecs were said to have come from a legendry place, Chicomoztoc, or the seven caves. They had been desert rats, used to long migrations. Their present leader was Mexi. A new found god, Huitzilopochtli, had given signs to the Aztec priests to change the tribal name from Aztec (people of Aztlán) to Mexica in honor of Mexi." (footnote omitted)

Several authors refer to the Aztecs and the Mexica, as being the same people. "The word Aztec means "People of Aztlán," although they rarely called themselves by such a term. They were usually known among themselves and their neighbors as the Mexica, or sometimes the Culhua-Mexica to emphasize their connection to the old lineages established at Culhuacan. However, William Prescott's *Conquest of Mexico,* published in 1843, popularized the term Aztec (introduced by Alex von Humboldt earlier in the 19th C.) as a catch-all reference to all Náhuatl speakers in central Mexico at the time of the conquest." (footnote omitted)

C.A. Burland in Montezuma wrote, "It was in the thirteenth century that the Aztecs appear, although they were not called Aztecs until after the conquest by the Spaniards. At first they claimed that they came from a place called Aztlán, which seems in fact to have been called Aztatlan (Beside the White Heron.)."[96] (Footnote omitted)

What is most significant is that the Mexica did not call themselves Aztecs. The label, 'Aztec' was a word that was reintroduced, popularized, or possibly even *invented* by white Europeans. More than 300 years after the Spaniard conquest the Mexica are suddenly identified as Aztec. The label of Aztec has remained since its introduction and has created more problems in tracing our roots as Xicanos and Mexicanos, than any other obstacle. The word, 'Aztec' has camouflaged the evolution of the cognate words Mexicano and Chicano. Specifically, it deviates from the smooth and sensible phonetic transition, which takes place for the root word, Mexi, to the final word, Xicano. In my introduction to *Xicano: an autobiography,* I stated, "Once you abort the German imposed label Aztec and decode the mystery of the letter X the word 'Chicano' takes the reader through the course of phonetic evolution."

When historians adopted the "catch-all" phrase of Aztec, they never questioned its accuracy, examined the impact, or recognized the importance of properly labeling a people. Their purpose was to simplify for themselves the diverse identities of indigenous peoples of Mexico. "The famous German naturalist, Baron Alexander von Humboldt, was one European with enough influence to win entry to Mexico, and his account of his journey there, published in French in 1813, further fanned excitement over Aztec lore. He reported that Aztecs, hitherto classified a primitive and non-literate culture, had actually been highly advanced. When the gates were opened after Mexico gained its independence in 1821, an era of feverish interest in the Aztecs commenced. Tourists, scientists and adventurers descended on Mexico then returned to Europe with tales to tell (many of them fanciful) illustrations to publish (a few quire accurate), and, in some cases, trunkfuls of purchased or purloined artifacts." (Footnote omitted) This description of the foreigner's onslaught of Mexico's history and its treasures reflects their lack of sincerity and accuracy in defining Mexico's multiple indigenous identities.

1829
ANAHUAC
IN THE NORTHWEST U.S.A.

"On his large map, "United States," H.S. Tanner published an insert "Oregon and Mandan Districts," a name to be found on many maps subsequently, but its first appearance was this of 1829, with a sub-insert "outlet of the Oregon River" (The mouth of the Columbia)." Just west of the "Mountains of Anahuac," the "Boundary of 1819, is the legend "sources of the S. Buenaventura River of the Pacific."[97]

It is very interesting that not only early Spanish cartographers but also American cartographers early to the northwest seemed to believe this was the homeland of the Mexica and Aztlán. This is just another piece of their (cartographers) thinking during this time period. Anahuac as we know is the name given to central Mexico while under Mexica Dominance.

1847

"ANTIGUA RESIDENCIA DE LOS AZTECAS"
OR STOP NUMBER ONE

The absolute most critical question here is who, when, why and how was this cartographic notation originated?

Finally, we have arrived at the *eye of the storm*. It is the credibility of the 1847 map attached to the 1848 Treaty of Guadalupe Hidalgo. It is the notation on this map "Antigua Residencia de los Aztecas"* that is being used by contemporary Xicanos as *"proof"* that the original Aztecs are indigenous to Aztlán (southwest area). Therefore, their descendants, Xicanos and Mexicanos are indigenous as well. In addition to this notation, another notation further south states: "Ruinas de los Aztecas,"** which I will also discuss here.

Let us look at what the experts say about this map and its inventor. I found no historians who had respect for either John Disturnell or his 1847 Disturnell map. None were more direct and hard-hitting than the author Jack D. Rittenhouse in his booklet, *Disturnell's Treaty Map: The map that was part of the Guadalupe Hidalgo Treaty on southwestern boundaries, 1848.*

The author begins by saying; "few maps in United States history have had a role as interesting as that of the Disturnell map – the map that was attached to the Treaty of Guadalupe Hidalgo at the end of the Mexican War in 1848."[98] And, I would add that now that Xicanos have resurrected this map it would continue to have ripple effects if not a tsunami effect eventually whether used by and *for* Xicanos or *against* Xicanos.

The Mexican-American War officially began on May 11, 1846 with President Polk's war message. "The major fighting ended when U.S. troops captured Mexico City on September 14, 1847." (Disturnell's Treaty Map, Rittenhouse, p. 6) President Polk in early 1847 appointed

---

*By the way, there is no island at this location.
**By the way, there is no island at this location.

Nicholas Philip Trist as a peace commissioner to negotiate a treaty in Mexico City. Because the treaty was signed on February 2, 1848 at the town of Guadalupe Hidalgo it had been named the Peace Treaty of Guadalupe Hidalgo.

"As part of his baggage, Trist took with him the most recent 1847 edition of a map of the Mexican States. It was not a government map, but one published and sold commercially by John Disturnell, a map firm in New York City" (p. 6).

<u>The map had been filled with so many errors and was of such poor quality that the United States Senate did not approve the Treaty until April 25, 1854.</u> Though you cannot fault the map entirely for this, it no doubt in its poor quality contributed in fact. "But because there were errors on the map, <u>it took eight years of discussions, surveys and Gadsden Purchase to straighten out the major disputes that arose</u>. Part of the disputed territory – the Chamizal area of El Paso – was not determined finally until 1963, a hundred and fifteen years after the original treaty was signed" (p. 5).

While the Mexican and American governments were struggling to correct the Disturnell map and its inadequacies before and after the signing of the Treaty, the man himself John Disturnell continued his profitable venture of selling indiscriminately and carelessly this Disturnell Map of 1847. Rittenhouse writes, "During all these years of debate and confusion, John Disturnell continued to sell maps. He was no skilled cartographer, no eminent geographer, and no topographic engineer who surveyed the west. Instead he was a business man – a publisher of guide books and maps; an energetic salesman who promoted his wares so well that Disturnell maps were readily available where ever maps were sold" (p. 12). Adding to the confusion and suspicion of the maps used was the fact that the U.S. and Mexican government had two slightly different 1847 Disturnell maps. "It was Martin's so-called "seventh-edition" of this map, printed early in 1847 that was attached to the American copy of the Treaty of Guadalupe (signed February 2, 1848) but – oddly enough it was a copy of martin's so-called "twelfth edition" that was attached to the Mexican government's copy."[99]

"When Texas was admitted to the United States in 1845, there was a surge of public interest in this new region. Disturnell saw a good opportunity to sell a map of that area, so he acquired a set of copper plates that had been used by another publisher eighteen years before and, after a few revisions, started re-issuing it as the Disturnell Map of the United States of Mexico."[100] John Disturnell it becomes obvious cared nothing of the accuracy of his product and only the monetary benefits.

To help identify the original source and evolution of "Antigua Residencia de los Aztecas" it is necessary to examine the source of John Disturnell's map. Rittenhouses' booklet traces the history of John Disturnell's 1847 map.

The Disturnell map was based on a series of earlier maps issued by other cartographers. "In 1822 an American map publisher named H.S. Tanner issued "A Map of North America, Constructed According to the Latest Information." In 1823, he stated that the Mexican map was based upon several regional maps. "A Map of New California" drawn in 1805 by Don Juan Pedro Walker; "A General Map of the Kingdom of New Spain" drawn about 1809 by Alexander von Humboldt; "Map of the Internal Provinces of New Spain" drawn in 1810 by Zebulon M. Pike, and which Carl Wheat says, "was probably copied from a Spanish original not yet identified;" "Chart of the Internal Parts of Louisiana," also by Pike; "Map of the Southern Part of the Province of Texas" by William Darby; "Plan of the Port of Vera Cruz" by Bernado de Orta; and "Chart of the Gulf of Mexico" by Juan de Longara."

"At any rate, Tanner's map of 1822 was an advanced compilation, not copied from a single source. It showed all of North America. In 1825 Tanner made a map of Mexico by using the southwestern part of his 1822 map."[101] We see how many of the earlier maps we examined were used in combination with each other. The same maps in fact that based some of their cartographic notations on 'stories', 'hearsay', and wishful thinking.

It is the <u>Tanner map of 1822</u> that I draw to your attention here. <u>It is this map that is the ancestor of Antigua Residencia de Los Aztecas of the 1847 Disturnell map.</u> At the exact location, but in English, on this map is the notation *Former Residence of the Aztecs*, which is also known as the first stop. At the second Aztec stop, or where the 1847 map reads

113

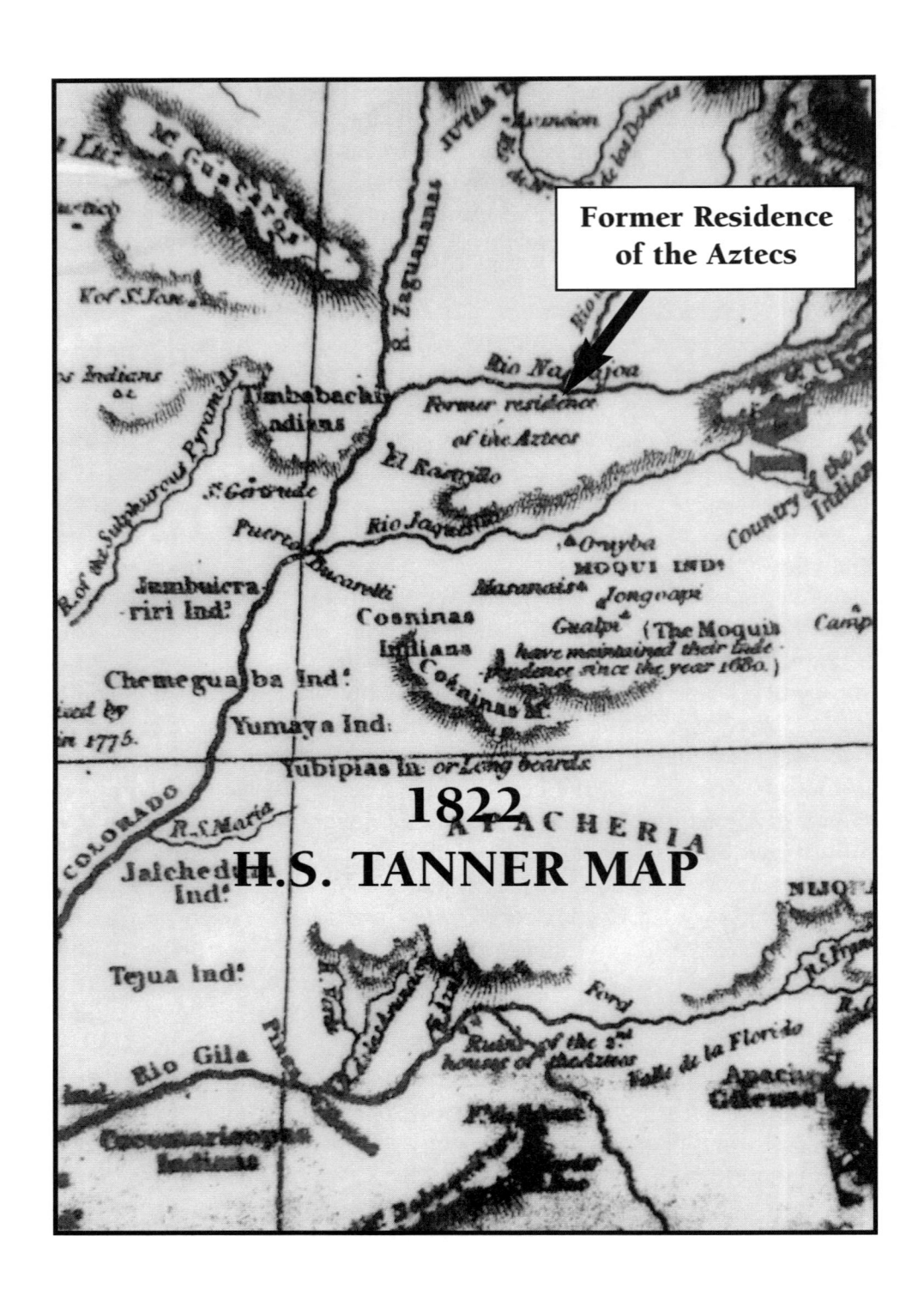

Former Residence of the Aztecs

**1822
H.S. TANNER MAP**

"Ruinas de Las Casas de Los Aztecas" on this 1822 map it reads *Ruins of the House of Aztecas*. The third Aztec stop in Chihuahua, Mexico reads *Houses of the Aztecs*.

Just as Von Humboldt swallowed Barreiro's 1727 map of the three Aztec stops, Tanner swallowed Alexander von Humboldt's map of 1804, hook, line and sinker. But, why? Tanner expresses his confidence in and admiration for the world-renowned scientist von Humboldt.

Tanner writes in his 1823 publication, A New American Atlas: "*A general map of the kingdom of New Spain, from 16° to 38° north latitude,* founded upon astronomical observations and materials which had been collected at Mexico previous to the year 1804, by Alexander de Humbolt. The high reputation for scientific knowledge, and the celebrity which the works of this distinguished traveler have acquired, offers a sufficient guarantee for the accuracy of the present map." Tanner continues his humble appreciation. "The map he has given to the world, so far as he has become responsible for its correctness, bears the stamp of accuracy, which the test of twenty years has not impaired. It will no doubt, continue to be, what it has been since its first publication, the basis of all similar maps, until the country shall have been submitted to the operation of an actual survey." The final sentence of this quote clearly points out how *personal observation* at this time was not a prerequisite to reliable mapmaking, unfortunately.

Contrary to the many who have chosen to plagiarize Humboldt, Tanner clearly points to his sources. Tanner expresses how his initiative will give his map a slightly different look than von Humboldt. "I have accordingly sought for, and obtained, many valuable items of information never before published, which give to some minor districts an appearance essentially different from the view hitherto presented of them."

The next map of importance is the *granddaughter* Tanner map of 1825. This map was the same as the 1822 map except that it was in Spanish. It is here (I believe without the benefit of having seen the map), that *former residence of the Aztecs* becomes *Antigua Residencia de Los Aztecas*; the same hook, line and sinker, except in Spanish.

?
H.S. TANNER MAP OF 1825
— THE MISSING LINK —

    The name Tanner arises again and again as the original (and most credible) source of maps of the (American) southwest or more accurately of Mexico's northwest (pre-American). And as stated, here above his sources are from much earlier and many Spanish map makers. Therefore, it is easy to believe and understand how he would continue recognizing and possibly notating if not Teguayo at least the three resting stops for the former Mexica (now Aztecs). Carl Wheat writes of Disturnell's map; "The map issued by Disturnell was his first printing of the "Mapa de Los Estados Unidos de Mejico" (termed by Lawrence Martin the second edition). It displayed certain significant items not present on the White, Gallaher and White map of 1828 from which it was taken."[102] In a footnote to this statement, Carl Wheat explains each maps relationship to each other chronologically and why the original Disturnell map is sarcastically called a "second edition."

    "The progenitors of this famous map have been discussed in volume two in connection with Henry S. Tanner's 1825 map of Mexico (which was itself a portion, somewhat enlarged in scale, of his 1822 map of North America), and in connection with the 1828 White, Gallaher and White PLAGIARISM of Tanner's 1825 production. This latter map* was

---

Also, this may explain why the map uses both English and Spanish names as well as Spanish names with English spelling principles.

in Spanish, and Disturnell merely *changed the date* and *substituted his own name as publisher.* He even used the old plate, for the earlier copyright notice was imperfectly eradicated and appears faintly on many of Disturnell's issues. Martin, in his *Disturnell Map* (Washington. 1937), calls the Disturnell's earliest edition the "second edition" because it is so nearly identical with the earlier map of White, Gallaher and White, (White, Gallaher and White, by the way, got out a new printing of their old map in 1844)."[103] (italics added) In other words, Tanner's map of 1822 is the *mother lode* of this group of maps.

Martin distinguishes four more "editions" of Disturnell's maps in 1846, seven in 1847, four in 1848, four in 1849, two in 1850 and one in 1858. Most of these differ in minor elements relatively few exhibiting significant alterations" (p. 5).

Carl Wheat explained how Tanner responded to his plagiarized maps of 1822. "With Disturnell coming out with a map of Mexico, largely copied from one of Tanner's early productions, Henry S. Tanner could ill afford to sit by in silence. In 1846, therefore, he brought out a "second edition" of the 1832 issue of his "map of the United States of Mexico" (even retaining the original copyright date). So far as areas now in the United States are concerned, this is a throw back map, with the Timpanagos, Buenaventura and the St. Felipe Rivers (and even the Los Mongos River!) flowing from the Intermountain area to the Pacific Coast."[104] It is interesting that Tanner would continue with the term Timpanagos to identify the river and having it flow entirely to the Pacific coast. It is obvious here of the *influence over him by earlier Spanish cartographers*. It was supposed this map was done in a hurry and because of its inaccuracies; this great cartographer's reputation suffered a blow.

As for White, Gallaher and White this can and is being said historically: "One of the Tanner maps, that of 1826, was copied and published in 1828 by the firm of White, Gallaher and White, of New York City. This map whose plates were brought by Disturnell and used for printing the Disturnell maps of 1846-1858.

It has often been said that White, Gallaher, & White (and Disturnell) *plagiarized* or "pirated" this map. It was obviously *copied* from Tanner's map, but there is no proof that it was done with intent to defraud. It might have been the result of an agreement. The White, Gallaher &

White map was issued in 1828... there was a market demand in Latin America for a map with all legends and place names in Spanish." The Tanner map was in English; White, Gallaher & White made a map with all legends in Spanish..."[105]

A few years later, there was another plagiarism of the Tanner map, this time in France. "Rosa's Mapa de los Estados Unidos was published in Paris in 1837. It was a literal copy of Tanner's 1834 edition, on the original scale and translated into Spanish. Rosa produced another edition in 1851.

When the boundary disputes arose after the Treaty of Guadalupe Hidalgo, all three publisher's maps were brought into the argument – the Tanner map, the Disturnell (or White, Gallaher & White) map, and the "Rosa Map" (p. 14). It is strangely ironic how these authors directly or indirectly plagiarized Alexander von Humboldt who finalized and published his maps of Mexico (Colony of New Spain) while in France.

Von Humboldt as described in his own section heavily used earlier Spanish exploration maps along with his personal scientific calculations. He did however gather the materials hurriedly since he was running short of time on his visit to Mexico. He also finalized his map of 1809 across the ocean in France, which had to have had some disadvantages. Rittenhouse claims Tanner used Von Humboldt's 1809 map to cartograph Mexico, but I have not been able to locate an 1809 map. It is very possible it is the same map dated 1811 titled in French *Catre du Mexique*. On this map contrary to his earlier map of 1804 of which he notates: *premiere demeure des Azteques sortis d'Aztlán en 1160 tradition incertaine*. In his 1811, map he does not make mention specifically of the Aztecs (the name he introduced or reintroduced) but makes a very general notation, which sounds very similar to the 1777 Miera map. Von Humboldt writes and even makes reference to Escalante: "*Pays ous par le pere Antonio Velex (y Escalante) en 1777.*" As written earlier, Miera did believe this was an Aztec resting place but cartographers and explorers before him may have influenced him. The point here is he did not refer specifically to the Aztecs in his notation. The question is did Tanner originate the phrase "Antigua Residencia de Los Aztecas?" I have been unable up to this time to see a copy of the Tanner 1825 map. However, there is little doubt in my mind that I will retrieve a map and little doubt

<u>it will prove that H.S. Tanner and his 1825 map is the exact source of Antigua Residencia de Los Aztecas.</u>

Another mapmaker mentioned earlier as part of "a series of earlier maps by other cartographers" was Zebulon Pike. The name place Pikes Peak in Colorado was named after Zebulon Pike. These other cartographers plagiarized the same Daughter mapmaker as Tanner. "*A map of the internal provinces of New Spain*... In its larger aspects this map is a *direct plagiarism* of the northern two-thirds of Alexander von Humboldt's celebrated map of New Spain, Though there are many slight differences and numerous misreadings and misspellings of Spanish words. Since Humboldt's map was not given to the public until 1811, it has not always been understood how Pike (or those who may actually have prepared his maps for publication) obtained access to it for use in Pike's account in 1810... Humboldt himself resolved the problem in his *travels to the Equinoctal regions of the new continent during the years 1799-1804...*" Mr. Pike displayed admirable courage in an important undertaking for the investigation of western Louisiana; but unprovided with instruments, and strictly watched on the road from Santa Fe to Natchitoches, he could do nothing towards the progress of geography of the provinces internas. The maps of Mexico, which are annexed to the narrative of his journey, are reduced from my great [large?] map of New Spain, of which I left a copy, in 1804 at the secretary of states office in Washington."[106](italics added) As you see again all roads lead back to von Humboldt who himself was a plagiarist of earlier Spanish cartographers. *Monkey see, monkey do.*

It is interesting what Carl Wheat in his footnote has to say about Pikes map, his translation of French and his misreading of the Mexica legends. "The fact is that, if the translation's misreading of some of Humboldt's legends be disregarded, we see here precisely what the Baron doubtless placed on the early draft of his magnificent map, so laboriously constructed with such high scholarship, at the Royal School of Mines in Mexico City, between 1799 and 1804. <u>Some of his legends are here shortened, the various resting places of the Aztecs on their way south are missing,</u> except that just west of the Lac de Timpanagos, where "Azteques" is seen or Humboldt's map, it here appears as "ARETEQUI". A good many other words are unconsciously misspelled... Certain words are omitted (as the last name of the exploring Friar, Pedro Fort, who appears as Father Pedro), and other terms are altered (as when Humboldt speaks of "les Bisons (Cibola)", the Pike map reads "the Cibolas")…"[107]

Returning to and closing on John Disturnell here are some pertinent quotes explaining his finished product. "Obviously an engraving for a large map would be costly, so when Disturnell wanted to publish a map it was better to buy an old plate or set of plates. The Disturnell map was actually printed from two plates – a right plate and a left plate, printed on separate sheets that were carefully overlapped and pasted. Colors were added by painting them on by hand, using watercolors.

The original White, Gallaher & White was *Grabado* (engraved) by Balch & Stiles of New York. Their name, together with Disturnell, but the copy right notice was imperfectly removed and appears faintly on all Disturnell maps printed from these plates from 1846 through 1858." (Disturnell's Treaty Map, p. 15] Reading and understanding the map was extremely difficult and impossible at times for me. Further damaging the accuracy and credibility of Disturnell's 1847 map, Carl Wheat writes: "Most commercial maps were found objectionable in some degree by those familiar with the still imperfectly known west, and Randolph B. Marcy in 1849 entered a bill of particulars against Disturnell map, terming it "<u>one of the most inaccurate of all those I have seen</u>, so far as relates to the country over which I have passed. He makes a greater error than most other in laying down the Pecos and has the Colorado, Brazos and Red River all inaccurately placed."[108] Keep in mind this is the map we are presenting to Xicanos and gringos as "proof" and as having "credibility." In reality, gringos have historically, cartographically, and scientifically destroyed its "credibility." This can become not only embarrassing to Xicanos but also revealing of the superficial commitment and efforts we apply to problem solving. It reminds me of the lyrics that go "if feels good do it, do it if it feels good!" National public embarrassment does not feel good.

Ruinas de las Casas Aztecas
Or Stop Number Two

If this notation "Ruins de Las Casas de los Aztecas" is also on the same map, why isn't a big fuss also made about this? Is it because it is too close to the Mexican border and Xicanos would like Aztlán to be further north of the border to show we are descendants of "Native Americans," in the eyes of white people.

We learned earlier that Father Kino documented these ruins as "Casa Grande" because he had heard of the ruins in northern Mexico called Casas Grandes. He believed they were connected because *he had heard* that this *Casas Grandes* ruins were *theorized* as being stopping or resting places for the Mexica (Aztec) migration south into central Mexico. Cartographers, however, treated the theories as if they were fact and therefore created the domino effect in mapmaking.

Another example showing the inaccuracy and distortion of the map can be shown with the notation *Concepcion*. It is located directly to the west and next to (at the rivers confluence) the notation "Antigua Residencia de los Aztecas." For several years, I thought this notation *Concepcion* to be a town or village and I looked for its history in documents. Finally, I did find mention of it in Escalante's journal and historical notes supplementing his journal. The upper Colorado River has vicious and dangerous currents and the canyon walls help to make most of it uncrossable by foot or horse. *Concepcion* was notated on the map because it was one of the few safe places to ford the upper Colorado.

On November 7, 1776 Escalante makes this entry into his journal. "We got down to the canyon, and after going a mile we reached the river and went along it downstream for about as far as two musket shots, now through the water, now along the edge, until we came to the widest part of its currents where the ford appear to be, one man waded in and found it all right, not having to swim at any place. We followed him on horseback, entering a little further down, and in its middle two mounts which went ahead missed bottom and swam through a channel. We held back, although with some peril, until the first one who crossed on foot came back from the other side to lead us, and we successfully passed over without the horse on which we were crossing ever having to swim."[109]

In a footnote, the author describes in detail the crossing. "This is located where a permanent sandbar was found at the base of the west canyon wall. Diagonally across that sandbar was a similar one on the opposite side of the River. A ripple in the water surface indicated the shallowest point leading directly to that sandbar. It was evidently from this point that the camp gear was lowered over the cliff to the sandbar. The journal statement that the ford was little more than a mile wide would have to mean from Padre Creek to the sandbar at the east side of the river. The water at the ripple was not more than three feet deep. The actual fording place probably changed slightly from time to time, depending on the shifting sandbar." (loc.cit.) It now made sense to me to permanently notate the ford *Concepcion* on the map.

The name *Concepcion* is explained in Escalante's Journal notes as well: "On the eastern side at the ford itself, which we named La Purísima Concepcíon de la Virgin Santísima…" (pp. 119, 120) or in English "The Immaculate Conception of the most Holy Virgin" (p.121).

Today this crossing is known but inaccessible. "This marks the famous *"Crossing of the Fathers"*. Most of the area traversed by the 1776 Spanish party now lies beneath the water of Lake Powell. At the point where the Padres crossed, the lake is now about 550 deep. Several research teams explored this region in 1938, 1950 and 1958, prior to the construction of the Glen Canyon Dam." (Dominguez-Escalante Journal, p. 120) This Crossing of the Fathers used to be one of Utah's most famous historical sites. The exact location by today's standards would be about three miles north of the present south central Utah and north central Arizona boundary.

If the *Aztec Ruins* in Aztec, New Mexico is the actual location of "*Antigua Residencia de los Aztecas* and *Concepcion* is just 3 miles north of the north-central Arizona-Utah border that means these two places and locations are separated by about 300 to 350 miles! However, if you look at the 1847 Disturnell map it looks as if the two notations and places are right next to each other! For Xicanos to put so much weight on and trust into the 1847 Disturnell map would open us up to ridicule and a loss of any credibility. By Alexander von Humboldt inaccurately copying the correct rivers confluence of Miera's 1778 map it cartographically becomes written in stone to be incorrectly copied again and again. Once again as Alexander, (the Great), von Humboldt has confused us with his misuse of the identity and word Aztec; he has also confused us with the actual location of *Antigua Residencia de Los Aztecas*. And because of our misuse of the identity Aztec we have yet to recover and may not recover unless we start researching and thinking for ourselves.

The Confluence of Confusion

The first theorized Mexica stop* is consistently located at or near the confluence of two rivers. These two rivers, however, are inconsistently named and located. This is especially true of the 1847 Disturnell map. This confluence of rivers is so misnamed and mislocated that it places the location of "Antigua Residence de Los Aztecas" in the wrong state. Here is the chronology of the changes starting in 1727 to present times.

I. On the 1727 Barreiro map at the notation of the first "Mexica" stop, the rivers of confluence are "*R. Azul*" and "*R. Venie.*" The "*R. Colorado*" also runs north and south like *R. Azul*, but to the west of it.

II. On the 1778 Miera map at the notation "*Aqui se manifiestan las ruinas de grande poblaciones de Indios Antiguas,*" the rivers of confluence are *Rio de Nabajoo* and *Rio de Las Animas*. The modern Colorado River on this map was divided into one north and south rivers name wise. The south was called *Rio Colorado* and the north *Rio de los Zaguaganas*. It is crucial to visualize that the *Rio Nabajoo* forks east from the *Rio de los Zaguaganas* (today's upper Colorado River). *Rio Nabajoo* then confluences (forks) with *Rio de las Animas*. This is where we find the above-mentioned notation.

Miera was completely off when he referred to the *Rio Nabajoo* as the river to confluence with the *Animas*. The scholarly historian David Miller led a team that retraced the route of the expedition in 1976. This excerpt will help us understand why he

---

*Referred to depending on the author, as resting place, homeland, Residencia, or stop, as is here.

placed the Nabajoo as the source of confluence instead of the *San Juan*. Fortunately, members of his research team detailed how the Dominguez-Escalante team got lost. They wrote, "...they finally come to a high point from which they could see the distant channel of the San Juan River, which they mistakenly thought to be the Navajo." As a result, to begin with the confluence of rivers was incorrect.

III. On the 1804 Humboldt map at the notation of the first "Azteques" stop, the rivers of confluence are *Rio Zaguananas** and *Rio Nabajoa*. By modern standards, this would be the Colorado River (Upper, north to south) and the San Juan (west to east). This is critically wrong. Critical, first because Humboldt must have misinterpreted Miera's 1878 map or some other map that also copied Miera. And, or was confused because of Miera's misnaming of the San Juan River calling it the *Nabajoo*. On his 1911 map, he reduplicated this mistake except that he placed the notation above (north) of the Rio Nabajoa instead of below (south). It is also critical because this man and these maps were held in such high esteem that cartographers did not question their accuracy. This map, however, creates the chain reaction of cartographic descendants like Tanner who used Humboldt's approximate terminology in English (*former residence of the Aztecs*) and location.

IV. On the 1847 Disturnell map we have the results of von Humboldt's mistake since his maps were used indirectly and primarily to construct the 1847 map before Disturnell simply changed names plates.

The 1847 Disturnell map at the notation, "*Antigua Residencia de los Aztecas*," the rivers that confluence are *Rio Zaguananas* and *Rio Nabajoa*. This confluence is wrong and further wrongfully interpreted by Xicanos. It has been interpreted as the Colorado River and the Green River, which puts the location in the state of Utah.

---

*Spelled Zaguaganas on Miera's 1778 map.

V. Modern and accurate cartography at the notation *Aztec Ruins National Monument,* places the rivers that confluence as the *Animas* and the *San Juan*. It is in the northwestern corner of New Mexico (Aztec, New Mexico). It is over 300 miles east of the confluence interpreted by Xicanos as being the Colorado and Green River.

In the 1847 Disturnell map the reason the Colorado River crossing "Concepcion" (Crossing of the Fathers) is mistakenly right next to, it is because the cartographer von Humboldt and his subscribers thought the confluence of rivers to be today's upper Colorado River and San Juan River. The crossing Concepcion is also over 300 miles east of the actual confluence of rivers.

This also explains why many Xicanos initially thought the notation Antigua Residencia de los Aztecas was located in Arizona on the map. If you look at modern maps the San Juan/Colorado confluence though in Deep South central Utah, it is only a few miles north of the north central Arizona border.

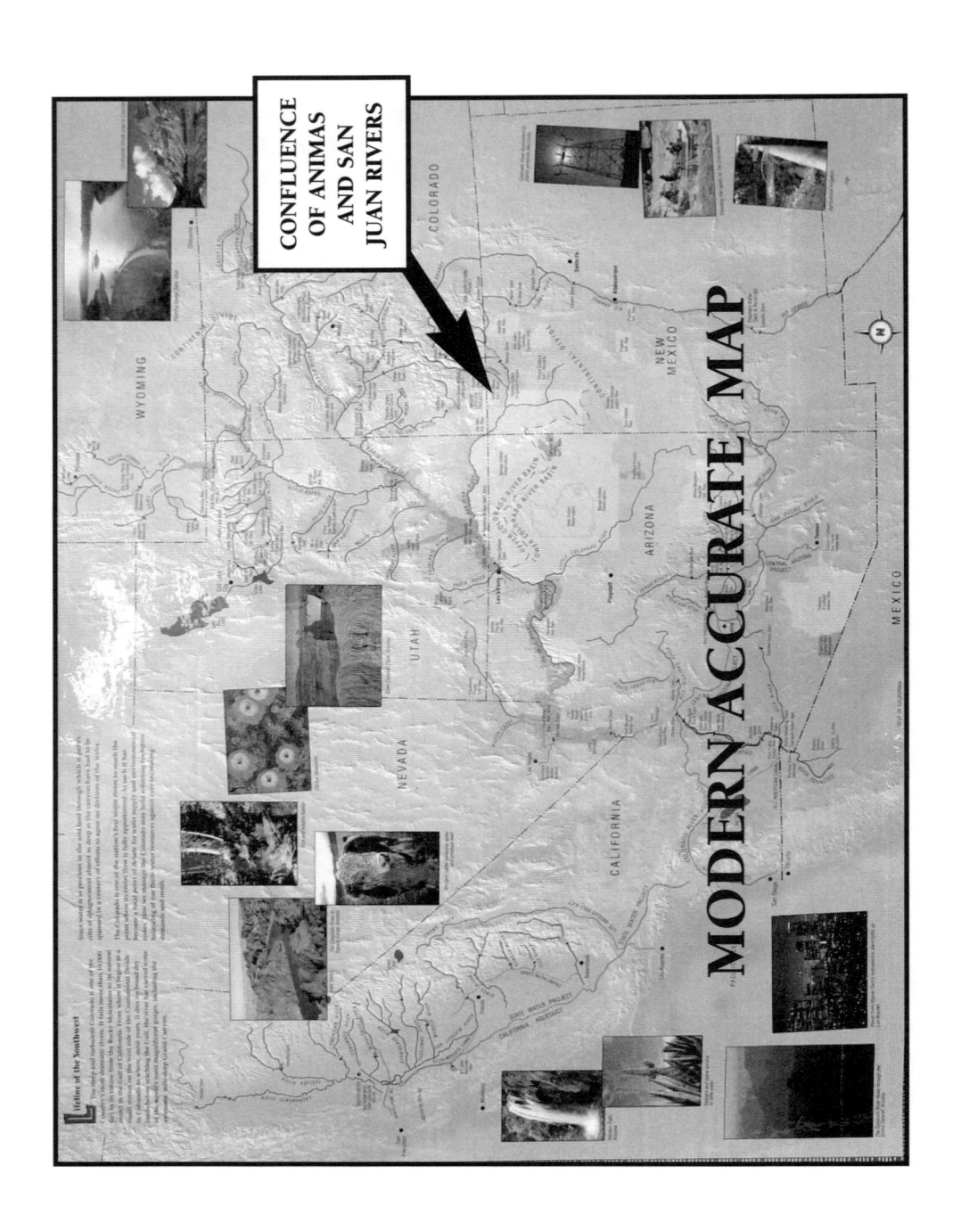

CONFLUENCE OF ANIMAS AND SAN JUAN RIVERS

MODERN ACCURATE MAP

1850
THE NAME TEGUAYO FADES AWAY

"Unfortunately Spanish and Mexican maps did not depict all the variations of the Old Spanish trail; but historical documentation described its varied routes prior to 1850. By then, the word Teguayo, which had inspired Hispanic Frontiersmen from New Mexico to go the Yuta country, had long been forgotten."[110]

Starting with the name Aztlán and ending with Teguayo and Timpanagos all these names representing Aztlán died a slow death only to be selectively resurrected even up and beyond the year 2000.

1870
GRINGO SCHOLARS
GO LOOKING 4 AZTLÁN:
THE RESURRECTION OF AZTLÁN

As a footnote in the back of his book, author Sanchez writes of Teguayo and its resurrection in the late nineteenth century. "Facination with Teguayo continued beyond the Spanish Colonial Period. In the late nineteenth century scholars such as Cesaro Fernandez Duro, John Gilmay, Adolph F. Bandelier, and Oscar W. Collect *renewed the search for* mythical Teguayo by sifting through historical documents, maps, and archaeological reports... regarding the relationship of Teguayo to the great Salt Lake, Burns writes: "Teguayo, just as unstable cartographically as Quivira, had been variously identified with Salt Lake, Utah, and regions from which the Pueblo Indians originally came" (p.159)(italics added).

To find truth these scholars sifted through documents and maps that as we have seen were not always based upon fact but myths, stories, documents and maps that were riddled with suspicion and in many instances unproven over the centuries.

Adolph Bandolier and his sidekick Lewis Henry Morgan are of particular interest to us here and will serve as the preface to the next section.

"Adolph Bandolier has been called anthropologist, archaeologist, archivist, ethnographer, explorer, geographer, historian, and scientist. He was a leading figure in the anthropological and historical study of American Indians that was nascent in the nineteenth and early twentieth centuries. Although he had almost no formal education, Bandelier succeeded in blending the data and methods of disparate academic disciplines to paint a rich portrayal of pre-historic American Indian life."[111] That picture he painted was (in my opinion) very racist against *Indios* both past and present (during his lifetime). Also the science of archaeology and anthropology in this hemisphere was very raw and under developed as write Lange and Riley: "His interests were well ahead of his time; even if he had sought professional instruction in his field of interest he would have been hard pressed to find it." (loc. cit.)

"Adolph was a true pioneer and explorer academically as well as in the field. He had no manuals or handbooks to tell him how to proceed. Many times he was naive or aggressive or willing to settle for less than the whole story." (loc. cit.) Here is a researcher, scientifically embryonic, as is his field, sifting through documents, which have faulty foundations. The "scientific" outcome has to be received with great concern for accuracy.

There were two major influences in Bandeliers thinking. One started while he was very young and the other was later in his career and life. Both were heroes to him and both were completely opposite. One was a champion of oppressed people of color and the other a champion of the oppressor.

"A major influence on Bandolier's career was Lewis Henry Morgan, the "Father of Anthropology." Morgan brought Bandolier to the attention of prominent scientists in the 1870's as well as fashioning Bandiliers (sic) thoughts from the time of their first meeting in 1873, in Rochester, New York, until Morgan's death there in1881. An equally valid claim could be made for Baron Alexander von Humboldt the world-renowned German anthropologist, geographer and historian whose writings were known to Bandolier even before he even met Morgan. As long as he lived, Bandolier paid homage to Humboldt and his thoughts." (loc. cit.) Bandelier is reported to have said he began reading Humboldt as early as eleven years old. It seemed to me however, that Lewis began a stronger influence over Bandelier in his view of Indigenous peoples as inferior savages.

Around the time, he first met Bandelier; Morgan was working on a more general theory of cultural evolution in which the various social groups in the modern world represented way stations – "social fossils," as it were – of a unilinear evolution involving all mankind. Morgan's idea rested on three developmental stages – savagery, barbarism, and civilization. Each stage was more advanced that its predecessor, and more advance in *every field of human endeavor* – language, religion, political and social organization, technology, art, and so forth. Given the right conditions and enough time, every group of humans would presumably work its way through savagery and barbarism to reach civilization. By the nineteenth century, however, only Europeans and, to a lesser degree, certain Asians had reached this civilized stage. This social Darwinism made good sense to the colonizing European powers of time, because it gave an intellectual underpinning to colonialism with its assumption that Europeans were culturally and racially superior to the rest of the world. It made Morgan internationally famous as the champion of the unilinear evolutionary school. (p. 24)

Bandelier was an extremely focused and hard working researcher but he did not seem to have the desire and or ability to express himself freely and independently. "By degrees, Adolph became a strong champion of Morgan's views before the world, though it seemed unlikely that he fully understood these views. Bandelier had a fact oriented mind; theory was beyond his ken" (p. 25).

I thought it was important to introduce these two individuals because of their collaboration of the book *Ancient Society,* which is used politically and economically to stimulate migration to and domination of the primarily Mexican-Americans of New Mexico. "It is clear that in these final days of 1879, Adolph Bandilier's mind was fixed on Aztec Society, and the ramifications of Morgan's new work, Ancient Society, as it applied to Native American high culture" (p. 27).

Bandelier is himself to have reported that he began his study of Mexican high culture in 1869. Bandelier wrote to and eventually became friends with, "…the great Mexican historian and bibliographer don Joaquin García / Cazba / Ceta (1825-94)…and largely concerned the Tezozomoc work. This was the beginning of an extended contact. The two men eventually met in 1881, and they became intimately connected, corresponding until 1891" (p.25). In spite of Bandelier's intensive interest and study of Mexican high culture and or the Aztecs he will conspire to make a complete illogical and unprofessional contradiction along with Lewis as discussed in the next section.

And like his hero Alexander von Humboldt, Bandelier became intensely interested in all documents related to ancient Mexican history and also the Mexica exodus was of special interest to him. He like von Humboldt consumed himself in reading documents by the Spanish explorers. He eventually went to study the archives in Seville, Spain at "The Archives of the Indies." Spain was the repository of much of the documentary data on Spanish America, and most of this vast treasure of documents was contained in the archives of the Indies in Seville. In the early centuries of Spain's overseas empire, the Council of the Indies, a body that directed American affairs under the authority of the Spanish Crown, had its headquarters in Seville, and accordingly built its archives there. Thanks to the bureaucratic nature of Spanish rule, documents were usually duplicate or triplicate, with one copy going to these Seville Archives.* Even today this great archive has been only incompletely examined."[112]

Gradually in his later years, he gravitated toward the southwest and away from central Mexico becoming a pioneer. "Bandilier was right about the "unknown south," if by that phrase he meant the area of northern Mexico between the American southwest and the high cultures of central and western Mexico. It was not until after World War II that this region (Sonora, Chihuahua, and portions of Coahuila, Sinaloa, Durango, and Zacatecas) received the archaeological attention it deserved. And Bandilier can be given considerable credit for blazing a trail, especially for alerting future generations of archaeologists to such great sites as Casa Grande in Chihuahua" (p. 72).

Bandelier took great interests in two very famous ruin sites in the southwest United States and northern Mexico. This area is archaeologically called the *southwest.* "Bandilier next rode eastward to investigate the great ruin of Casa Grande in the Gila Valley between modern Phoenix and Tucson. This ruin (now a National Monument) is still famous for its four-story high rectangular building of Puddle Caliche – it was constructed about 1300 A.D. but had been abandoned before the earliest Spaniards came into this region" (p. 90). If this Ruin was originally constructed about, A.D. 1300 as modern scientists have established then these structures were built far *after* the theorized Mexica exodus from Teguayo (Aztlán). This would then disqualify these

---

*"For two centuries Seville was the port through which gold, silver, and other riches had moved back to Spain; ...King Carlos III had ordered that there be gathered in this building from throughout the country, all decrees, government and court records, correspondence, maps and architectural drawings having to do with the Spanish conquest of the Americas. Collected under one roof, these eight-six million handwritten pages have made the general archive of the Indies one of the great repositories of the world," Adam Hochshield <u>King Leopold's Ghost</u>, p. 37.

ruins as being built by or even used by as a *resting* place by the Mexica (Aztec). Depending on its author, the proposed departure date from Aztlán is about 1126 A.D. and within a hundred years or about 1225, the Mexica had settled Mexico – Tenochtitlan.

Whenever at Casa Grande, Bandilier would stay with a gringo friend who was also a judge. His name, Judge John d. Walker. "Walker had settled among the Pimas in the 1860's. He spoke Pima and was able to give Bandelier a considerable amount of information on these Indians. (loc. cit.)

While doing research and residing at the New Mexican Nambe Pueblo Bandilier came upon an important discovery. He "…became intrigued by a newly found "campaign document" that related to the Montezuma legend. It had been concocted in Mexico in 1846 in an effort to win support among the Pueblos in the fight against the United States. Bandelier borrowed the manuscript from a friend at the Historical Society and made a copy of it" (p. 124).

I want people to be cautious in accepting the author's quotation stated above. Was the idea of making Montezuma (as a man or man-god: Messiah) indigenous to the southwest strategy by Mexico against the U.S? In oral tradition and in documents we can see that Pueblo Nations believe themselves to share common origin, history, and culture with the Mexica of Mexico and its great diversity of Indian Nations. My advise to you is to research and think for yourself rather than taking this at face value.

As scholars, why would they be interested in Aztlán? For many there is fame, glory, and financial compensation as its reward. Bandelier had many shortcomings as a researcher, writer and as a *"scholarly"* person. On the other hand, he unlike many scholars of today literally lived in poverty to pursue reconstruction of the past. He was *driven* by a demon that drives many individuals who have made their mark in our world. His pursuit for Aztlán may have originally been personal, professional, and innocent but as we will see in the next section by 1885, the unscientific virus of prejudice had contaminated him.

As thorough as Bandelier was I've yet to come across any materials indicating his actual belief that "Ruinas de as Casas Aztecas" (Casa Grande) was an actual resting stop or structure built by the Azteca. Nor has he ever mentioned the use of the 1847 Disturnell map in his writings that I've read.

1880
QUIEN SABE II

"In contrast to Claviejero, the historian Manuel Orozco y Berra, found the question concerning the location of Aztlán as "inextricable." In his *Historia Antigua y de la Conquista de Mexico,* published in 1880, he cites the difficulties in untangling the mass of conflicting evidence of the experts in the field as support for his non-position."[113]

Evidently, Claviejero did not see the 1847 Disturnell map, or did he? And, if he did, why didn't he recognize it?

1885
GRINGO POLITICOS
GO LOOKING 4 AZTLÁN

In the very beginning, I mentioned how over the centuries different people for different reasons have been looking for Aztlán. Author Ramon A. Gutierrez gives a sound example of what he calls political uses. He writes: "In 1885, William G. Ritch, then secretary of the territory of New Mexico and the recently elected president of the New Mexico Bureau of Immigration, issued a promotional book on the resources of New Mexico entitled *Aztlán: The History, Resources and Attractions of New Mexico*, which was meant to attract immigrants to the territory."[114]

But what is Aztlán without Aztecs and what are Aztecs without Montezuma? And most importantly what would any of these components be without gold or at least the promise of gold. These elements were all woven into this book with the fibers of powers of suggestion, myth, uncertainty and outright lies.

"Aztlán was a handsomely produced case – bound book. Its brown cloth cover was intricately embossed with a gold foil engraving of Montezuma, the Aztec emperor, holding a scepter in one hand and a ceremonial staff in the other, seated on an eagle with outstretched wings. Below Montezuma was the North American continent with two cities prominently marked – Mexico and Santa Fe. Ritch began the very first line of the text in his book by asking: "From whence came the tribes who founded and settled the city of Mexico?" "Aztlán," he answered. Ritch added that no one knew exactly where Aztlán actually was" (p. 173, 174). In spite of admitting that no one knew where Aztlán was, he went to great lengths to strongly suggest that it was originally in today's city of Santa Fe. "In the opening pages of *Aztlán*, Ritch warned his readers that what he was presenting as a coherent Montezuma legend had in fact been "gathered from various sources and connected." Ritch said that the Pueblo Indians of New Mexico and Arizona then believed that the great chief and emperor Montezuma had been born at the Pueblo of Santa Fe…" (p. 181).

It is interesting to note that he makes no mention of the 1848 Treaty of Guadalupe map. If he knew of it, he purposely ignored it. Why then? Possibly because the map would not have suggested or put Aztlán in Santa Fe. "Antigua Residencia" as a notation on the map is far removed geographically from the city of Santa Fe. "Ruinas de los Aztecas" another map notation is even further away. The number two is also notated to indicate it was the second stop for the Aztecas who historically headed south into central Mexico.

I find Ritch's use of the Montezuma myths as quasi proof to be use of a double standard. In the section on Adolph Bandolier I quote an author. "While doing research and residing at the New Mexican Nambe Pueblo Bandolier came upon an important discovery. He "…became intrigued by a newly found "campaign document" that related to the Montezuma Legend. It had been concocted in Mexico in 1846 in an effort to win support among the Pueblos in the fight against the United States. Bandolier borrowed the manuscript from a friend at the historical society and made a copy of it." This is especially interesting because Adolph Bandelier was used as a main source by this book's author. Both emperors Montezuma I and II could not have possibly led their people from Aztlán where ever it was unless they are speaking of an earlier and completely different Montezuma by the same name.

Rather than debate this specific issue or the presence of a Montezuma in the southwest as a culture hero in general, the point to make here is how the contents of a document as mentioned above is earlier discredited as a hoax and later that same content is used as proof that Montezuma and the Aztecs originated in the southwest. For a fascinating discussion of Montezuma and the Aztecs in the southwest in general and amongst the Pueblos specifically, I would suggest the book: *Handbook of North American Indians*, Volume 9, The Southwest. In the chapter by Richard J. Parmentier entitled, *The Mythological Triangle: Poseyemu, Montezuma, and Jesus in the Pueblos*, the Montezuma phenomenon is dealt with in detail and its many variations.

Here, the author poses four main questions about Montezuma, he writes: "There are four central questions about the Montezuma legend of the Pueblo Southwest. First, who was Montezuma historically? Second, how did the legend of Montezuma arrive in the southwest? Third, when did the legend become popular among the Pueblos? And fourth, why does Montezuma become associated with the Pueblo culture hero?" (loc. cit.)

On the second question, he further explores it in detail. "The question of how the story of Montezuma arrived in the southwest has at least three possible solutions. First, the legends about Montezuma I, having become popular among the Indians of central Mexico before the time of Cortés, may have diffused along well-established trade routes in to the Pueblos. Secondly, the legends may have been present aboriginally in the southwest before the Aztec migration into the valley of Mexico. Third, the legends may have arrived with the Indians who accompanied Francisco Vasquez de Coronado and Juan de Oñate on their expeditions." The author seriously challenges and disrespectfully dismantles William G. Ritchs' attempt to locate Monetzuma's birthplace near or in Santa Fe, New Mexico. He writes: "The absurdity of the second possibility is not seen by Ritch (1882:11) who confuses "A written report which is to be found in some of the Pueblos… that Pecos Pueblo was the birthplace of Montezuma" with the documentation of some legend." In this chapter, its author uses several examples of Bandolier's findings and his research showing the myth of Montezuma in the southwest was obviously pre-Hispanic, not to mention pre-American.[115]

So why is it important that the author Ritch tries to convince the reader that both Aztlán and Montezuma originated in the Santa Fe area? After all, there is not an island on a lake as indicated in Aztec origination and migration mythology. And why is it that he makes direct connections between the original Aztecs of Santa Fe and the glorious Aztecs of Mexico City? But first let's hear what author Ramon Gutierrez establishes as the motive for the book *Aztlán* by Ritch. Gutierrez writes, "For New Mexico's native Hispanos, the politics of statehood were clear. The sooner New Mexico became a state the better. So long as they were the numerically predominant population in the territory, they would control their own destinies. New Mexico would continue as an official bilingual state. The divinity of God would be taught in Roman Catholic schools. The communal land grants, which over the centuries the Spanish kings and the Mexican government had given them, would be held sacred. The profits from mining coal, iron, and other precious metals would be theirs. In short, there would be native rule."[116]

I recall reading a Xicano New Mexican author whom had written that the New Mexico territory had been turned down for statehood 24 times and the reason he sited was "too many Mexicans!" Now I understand why as is explained here.

"The movement to delay statehood came primarily from Anglo settlers. They feared the creation of a state ruled and dominated by Hispanos:... this "territorial machine," as the historian Howard R. Lamar has called the coalition, wanted New Mexico to wait for its statehood until Americans were the numerically dominant group" (p. 176).

Finally, the gringo politicos figured out an angle to promote New Mexico. "The Anglo proponents of statehood to move gringos knew that they needed American immigrant bodies. But how could they attract others of their kind, given the fact that early Anglo travel accounts had depicted New Mexico as a wasteland inhabited by superstitious racial inferiors who lacked a strong work ethic?" (loc. cit.)

To create a new image for New Mexico, one, which the territorial legislature hoped, would attract American businessmen and farmers to the area, on February 15, 1880, the legislature created the New Mexico Bureau of Immigration. The Bureau's mission was "to 'prepare and disseminate accurate information as to the soil, climate, minerals, resources, production and business of New Mexico, with special references to its opportunities for development, and the inducements and advantages which it presents to desirable immigration and for the investment of capital." Gutierrez continues, "What was never mentioned in the bureau's enabling legislation was the pivotal political role it ultimately would play in the statehood movement. If Anglos were to wrest control over New Mexico from the native Hispano elites, American immigrants were needed.

From 1880 to 1912, when the activities of the bureau essentially ceased-statehood for New Mexico having been accomplished – the bureau published and distributed 124 known titles, totaling some 500,000 items. The most popular of these promotional publications, was William G. Ritch's book, *Aztlán: the History, Resources and Attractions of New Mexico.* (pp. 176, 177)

Again, and again, and again as stated at the very beginning of my book and this section, over the centuries different people for different reasons have been looking for Aztlán. In reality, it is not Aztlán they are looking for but what Aztlán can do for them. The Spaniards used the promise of finding Aztlán in its many name variants to explore, expand, settle, convert, conquer, and control vast regions adding to their already vast empire simply by looking for it. Even after they felt they might never find it or for those who felt they had found Aztlán, but it was not what they expected it to be, it was still good for the empire even to its dying days to continue to go Looking 4 Aztlán because of its many positive by-products. Here we have seen another use, which found greater wealth in the *image* of Aztlán, rather than Aztlán itself. It reminds me of a historian who said the Spaniards sought the wealth of gold in Cuba's land mass but Cuba's great wealth a million times over became its production and distribution of tobacco and its many by-products.

As we transition to the section on Xicanos, looking 4 Aztlán we will see ourselves in the mirror that is created in this section. First is the eerie similarity between the gringo's New Mexican Bureau, "To prepare and disseminate accurate information…" and that of Aztlánahuac: Origins and migration Institute of Albuquerque, New Mexico.

Secondly, how the author Rich connected the original Aztecs of Santa Fe, New Mexico with those of Mexico-Tenochtitlan. The reasons are very obvious. There are no better documented, celebrated, and glorified Indians of the western hemisphere than the Aztecs (Mexica). Because of the shock and amazement the invading Spaniards, experiences when witnessing the governmental, architectural, military and agricultural achievements by as they wrote the most advanced nation on earth this gave them a special place in history forever. It is only because of this glorious greatness in central Mexico as witnesses in 1519 that the original Aztecs become important at all; glory always brings company.

W.G. Ritch by making Santa Fe, the original homeland of the Aztecs mythologically or hypothetically created a connection to magnificent Mexico-Tenochtitlan (Mexico City) and was able to draw sap from the tree of the glorious Aztecs.

Xicanos are repeating this scenario by claiming to be descendants of the Mexico city Aztecs therefore bathing in their glory and also claim to be indigenous to the United States because as descendants of Mexico City Aztecs who themselves descended from Aztecs who originated in the southwest United States they can claim to be indigenous to the

United States without giving up their Mexican identity. In both cases, it is the *best of both worlds*!

Further supporting my opinion on Ritch's intent is this paragraph from Gutierrez. "William G. Ritch concluded the "Legend of Montezuma" by noting that the eagle perched on a prickly pear cactus with a serpent in its beak had become the New Mexican territorial seal, the only difference being wrote Rich, "That the Mexican eagle is nestled confidently under the shadowing wing of the emblem of our own nationality" (p. 182).

Gutierrez closes his chapter with these words, which can be said of Xicanos today in *using* Aztlán to serve their own purposes. "*Aztlán*, then stands as a particularly poignant example of how a mythic complex was selectively appropriated, reinterpreted, and selectively transformed, in order to achieve concrete political gain. In 1885, William G. Ritch, as the territorial secretary, wanted to attract immigrants to New Mexico so that Anglos would outnumber Hispanos, his goal being an Anglo-dominated state. Ritch used all the energy and money he had, to project representations of an El Dorado that would appeal to capitalists and landless farmers, and to enlist the memories, hallucinations, and dreams of those spiritual refugees from industrial America who wanted to return to nature. Ritch and later witting and unwitting allies created their "Land of Enchantment," their caricatures of "Indians, " and their quaint Hispano peasants, which the tourists still flock to New Mexico to see. And indeed, the myths became so powerful that now even the natives utter them as truth" (p. 187). This is the constant historical pattern of peoples looking 4 Aztlán. Today, because the Gringos of New Mexico or southwest do not need an Aztlán to help it achieve any political, economic or historical goals, the discussion or presence of Aztlán in this state has completely disappeared. The only group of people discussing Aztlán in the southwest as the original homeland of the Aztecas is Xicanos. As we shall see in the next section once again, the search for *Aztlán* is a stepping-stone to something else.

We just witnessed how gringos weaved Aztlán into the history and geography of Santa Fe area, which has no *island* as is necessary and indicated by the Codice Boturini. We will now see Xicanos weave Aztlán with a map into a particular corner of the southwest, which also has no *island*.

1933
AZTLÁN IN WISCONSIN ?

"There was even a book published in 1933 entitled *Aztalán*, trying to prove that Aztlán, can be found in the lakes of Wisconsin."[117]

I wonder if Xicanos have been searching in Wisconsin for Aztlán or even China, which was suggested as another theory of its possible location.

1969
XICANO RESURRECTION OF AZTLAN

"It is necessary to point out the fact that before March 1969, the date of the Denver conference, no one talked about Aztlán. In fact, the first time that it was mentioned in a Chicano document was in *"El Plan Espiritual de Aztlán,"* which was presented in Denver at that time. Apparently, it owes its creation to the Poet Allurista who already, during the autumn of 1968, had spoken about Aztlán in a class held for Chicanos at San Diego State University."[118]

Allurista planted the seed; it germinated and exploded throughout the Xicano community in the United States for a people with a "landless" and "homeless" psyche. It made it convenient not to have to research and understand our diverse histories and identities. By simply saying, *"this is our land and our home,"* because this is ancient Aztlán home of our ancestors the Aztecs, we felt entitled to feel comfortably at home. The poem's author admitted in a documentary that it was meant to be simply a poem and he was shocked at the overwhelming response. I see it as a preamble in hibernation looking for a Xicano declaration of independence.

AZTLANAHUAC:
XICANOS GO LOOKING 4 AZTLÁN

In October of 1998, I received a letter in the mail from Ernesto Vigil of Denver Colorado. Actually, it was just a note with a newspaper article attached to it. It read, "Thought you might find this article interesting for your research on Aztlán." The title of the article was "1847 Map Ends Immigration Debate," written by Patricia Gonzales and Roberto Rodriguez and printed in the *El Semanario* newspaper from Denver, Colorado.

I have kept it, highlighted it, and am using this article for three major reasons.

1) It is reflective, I believe of the misinterpreted value of the 1847 Disturnell map.
2) Its' authors have created machinery to specifically promote this 1847 map and the false value that this and other archaic documents have.
3) The article reveals the Aztec *tunnel vision* Xicanos suffer from.

They write:

> The map which is housed in the National Archives in Washington, D.C., indisputably shows a site – "Antigua Residencia de los Aztecas," or ancient homeland of the Aztecs – somewhere in the four corners region of the U.S. southwest." In fact, the authors have since produced and marketed copies of this 1847 map for distribution throughout the country. I do not believe that financial profit is a motive, but the genuine belief that this document has value as indicated here. "This map incontrovertibly proves that rather than being foreigners, Mexicans (and Central Americans, who were also Nahautl-speaking peoples) are indigenous to Arizona, New Mexico, Colorado and Utah.

It continues,

> To us its as if the map has lifted an oppressive aura of "suspicion" from the psyche of Mexicans/Central Americans- populations that have been deemed to be illegitimate by some in the U.S. society."
>
> "The moral argument used against Mexicans in the immigration debate – that they are invading aliens – has been rendered completely baseless by Orozco's research and the map."

First of all the oppressor does not *debate* with the oppressed. That is why we honor the white founding fathers, Columbus Day and the fourth of July. White America has no maps or other documents to show their ancestors are indigenous to America but they do have a powerful government. *Their* government is rigidly supported by the selectively implemented rules of law, which is backed by the threat of force.

As we have chronologically followed the history of map making and mapmakers, I have specifically worked my way diligently toward the 1847 Disturnell map and the notation "Antigua Residencia de los Aztecas." I also could have had a section, "Apaxu goes looking for Aztlán," because I did. My first book took over seven years on the said notation and the location of the confluence, which I later found was wrong.

After, I first publicly presented what I thought was an accurate and complete description of this area and its historical residents, I was told at the end of my speech by Roberto Rodriguez that I had done my research in the wrong area. I did my research in Arizona along the lower Colorado River at the confluence of the lower Colorado River and the Bill Williams River. Mr. Rodriguez, himself also initially made this same mistake in his research, so we must have been looking at the same map which had written above it: "This section of the 1847 Disturnell Map of the United Mexican States, official map of the Treaty of Guadalupe Hidalgo, shows the area now known as the state of Arizona. The notation clearly shows two historical and legal facts: the area was recognized as an ancient homeland of the Mexican (i.e. Azteca) people."

1847 DISTURNELL
OFFICIAL MAP OF THE TREATY OF GUADALUPE-HILDAGO

My mindset had been placed in Arizona by this description. Mr. Rodriguez told me that the confluences of rivers are the upper Colorado River and the Green River placing the notation in Utah. "But," he said, "It doesn't matter where it was like you said!" That took some of the sting out of my mistake. I did, however, go back to the drawing board and research and rewrite the first part of my book. What I found as I have presented here is that Mr. Rodriguez was inaccurate also. The confluence on the maps is not the upper Colorado River and the Green River in Utah, but the Animas and San Juan Rivers in New Mexico. All of us keeping each other accountable in the Xicano community should be our version of "checks and balances."

The 1847 Disturnell map and its author as you have read have been shredded to pieces and found valueless not by me, but by cartographers, historians and politicians. The role I have played is to rediscover and display this fact. If we continue to move forward with this map as the cornerstone of our argument and "proof" then as a people Xicanos will be embarrassed and dispirited. The map as a whole is pathetic and the notations pointing to Aztec ancestry is from over a hundred years of underdeveloped and inaccurate cartography.

So convinced is the author, Roberto Rodriguez of the map's value that he stated in a speech at Eastern Michigan University that, "this is the most important document in the Xicano movement." Additionally, he has played a key role in creating the Aztlánahuac: Origins and Migration Institute.

The brochure reads, "People of Mexican/Central American origin in the U.S. have long been considered foreigners and unwanted populations in this country. Recently uncovered maps and other evidence, dating from 1847 to the 1500's show that the ancestral homes of Uto-Náhuatl peoples (also known as Toltecas-Chichimecas) appear to be in the U.S. four corners region. Some documents posit that people from Central and South America at one point also came from this region."

Here we go again: "Xicanos go looking for Aztlán." And what are they going to use to find Aztlán? — Archaic *documents*. We have seen the historic evolution of these archaic documents.

The brochure states in part as a strategy of the Institutes mission: "Its purpose is antithetical to traditional anthropology and archeology. The objective of all those associated with the Institute is to document "our" – not "their"—history and oral traditions—to document what we as a people have been building as opposed to simply a study of rocks or who passed through here." Isn't using the white man's map and his codices anti-antithetical??? It further states, "We cannot overstate the importance of this epic work. It has the potential to flip history upside down." Our problem is not history; our problem is we need to flip the white man's oppressive ass upside down! "You cannot make a revolution with flowers," Agosto Sandino.

Lastly, I want to comment on the name of their institute, Aztlánahuac, which reveals under the surface our real issues and their real objective.

At the very beginning, I spoke of how Mexica historians destroyed and rewove a neatly packed history for their nation to carefully incorporate the rugged Chichimec attributes and their Tolteca culturally refined attributes, *the best of both worlds.*

In the section Gringo Politicos go looking for Aztlán, we saw how the President of the New Mexico Bureau of Immigration used the duality of the Aztecs to also receive the *best of both worlds.* First, there is the glorious image of the Mexico-Tenochtitlan Aztecs to reap. The vehicle to that objective is via the proposed primitive Aztecs of Santa Fe. He both said his belief was not proven but possible that they the original Aztecs were indigenous to the Santa Fe area. If the Aztecs of Mexico had not been highly achieved, powerful, and glorious enjoying worldwide popularity there would not have been any desire on his part or anyone else to emphasize and capitalize on this claim. The duality of the glorious Aztecs was his vehicle to make New Mexico <u>attractive</u>. He made these connections between Santa Fe and Mexico City, between primitive Aztecs and the conquered Aztecs. Both the territorial flag of New Mexico and the artistic cover of his book have an image that is designed to emphasize this dual connection. The Aztec mystique radiated the promise of gold, silver, glory, and adventure.

It is eerie to say that Aztlánahuac and Xicanos in general have done the same thing. We want the glory of the Mexica (Azteca) of yesterday in Mexico, but we also want to stake our claim in the United States. That claim and reward is that we are an indigenous people here in the United States. Our vehicle again is via the primitive Aztecs of Aztlán.

Aztlán has been scholarly pointed to in other directions and other countries, but we only search here in the southwest. Because we want the original Aztecs to be indigenous to the United States. The brochure leans toward this by stating: "Ancient codices say the ancient ancestors of Mexicans (Mexica) left Aztlán to found Tenochtitlan in Anahuac. Aztlánahuac represents the joining of the two." In other words; *the best of both worlds*. The *Codice Boturini* itself shows Aztlán to be an island but there are no islands in the 4 corners area.

Why is it important that we prove Aztlán was originally in the United States? The newspaper article states what the map represents: "It shows definitively that Raza are not foreigners to what is now the United States. It confirms what Raza youth have said these past few years: "We didn't cross the border, the border crossed us." Actually, the usage of this map proves that we have crossed the border, by *acknowledging* this imperial border. Otherwise, we would not be using a map to "prove" to the real foreigners who systematically and historically made us (the real indigenous people) the modern foreigners.

"We believe," says the brochure, "this work will allow the descendants of the Uto-Náhuatl peoples to reclaim our rightful place in these lands, and to also reclaim our humanity as full human beings." Again, no map or documents would do this. But, this is what the United States Constitution and the promises of the 1848 Treaty of Peace embedded in this constitution are supposed to do. Remember, treaties are the supreme law of the land.

Ask the *enrolled* or federally recognized Indians how good life is in this country when your indigenous status is not questioned. Don't they lead all minority groups in the severity of their oppression?

Aztec tunnel vision is an issue I deal with later in the book.

I considered writing my opinion where I thought original Aztlán may have been, but I have decided not to at this point. When I wrote the first book on Looking 4 Aztlán, I concluded two things. One, it doesn't matter where Aztlán existed. And more importantly, two *it does not matter* if Aztlán ever existed at all! If you want respect, justice, and equality then you need power. History does not make power, power makes history. The best example I can give you is the American Revolution.

If your appetite for finding Aztlán has not dissipated as mine has then you might want to investigate the great Salt Lake area including Paradise Valley because you can hear "Echoes of Aztlán." There are archaic maps that point to this area as the Mexica homeland. But this is not the basis for my own personal suspicion. The reality is Aztlán; the place may never match up to our expectations or theories. It has joined the company of the Garden of Eden, El Dorado, Atlantis, the Fountain of Youth, King Arthur of Camelot and the Holy Grail in its mysticism, and unstable location.

THE MAKING OF AZTLÁN

THE CONCEPT

BIRTHRIGHT

NATURAL INHERITANCE
OR
DESCENT AND DISTRIBUTION

Let us suppose for the purpose of discussion and making a point that I, Apaxu Maiz have beyond a reasonable doubt, proven that Antigua Residencia de Los Aztecas as notated on the Treaty of Guadalupe map is in fact Aztlán. What does this really mean and what are the real rewards for this fact?

Many Xicanos believe that this map is proof of our birthright. In the dictionary, birthright is defined as: *the rights belonging to a person because he is the oldest son, or because he was born in a certain country, or because of any other facts about his birth.* In other words an INHERITANCE. That which you receive or inherit because of someone's death such as your parents or in this case, our blood ancestors. Based on this principle many Xicanos suggest or demand the inheritance is the land. Not only the island of *itty bitty* Aztlán but the entire southwest which is commonly defined as the southwest United States or the same land area taken by force in the Mexican-American War of 1846-48. Many Xicanos actually promote the idea that Aztlán was an ancient nation-state* or empire that was made up area wise of today's southwestern states which *ironically* was the very territory forcibly stolen by the imperialistic European-Americans through the War of 1846-48. *This is yet another neat package* movement Xicanos have put together in this case for geographic and political simplicity. However, we must ask ourselves, are these boundaries motivated by *logic* or greed or fantasy?

---

*"Before European colonization, the area that is now the southwestern United States and northern Mexico was called Aztlán as named by the Aztecs who built a powerful empire in central Mexico. After the Mexican-American War, from 1846 to 1848, the northern part of Aztlán became the southwestern United States." <u>Native North American Almanac</u>, ed. Synthia Ruse and Duane Champagne, (U-X-L an imprint of Gale Research, Inc., 1994) p. 54. I don't present this particular documentation as esablishing fact but somewhere along the line it has and may be used in the future by some as fact, simply because it is documented. It is very reminiscent of how stories become maps which become facts.

150

Are we now going to take the 1848 treaty map along with this document of mine to the southwest state legislatures, U.S. National Congress and or United Nations expecting return of our "inheritance," the lands of the southwest??? Keep in mind that the State of California and the Colorado River make the southwest the most powerful agricultural sector in the world not to mention the southwest's mineral wealth, tourism and the abundant resource of poor people (Mexicans, Xicanos, and Enrolled Indians) for menial jobs. Therefore, it is absolutely critical to the foundation of the economy and stability of the United States. There are Xicanos who suggest on the other hand, the modest and polite motive and advantage is that we demonstrate to the European-American that we have *proof* that we are *not* foreigners as they suggest but indigenous. What is wrong with this psychology???

Examine this scenario. A very long time ago, maybe as long as six or seven hundred years, a small group of *butt-naked* Indians we now call Aztecs left an area in the southwest we now call New Mexico and headed southward taking approximately one hundred years plus to settle on an island and lake area we now call Mexico City. Within a period of one hundred years they built, an amazing empire based from this island city (Mexico-Tenochtitlan) and dominated their surrounding city-states or all of what is now central Mexico. Approximately two hundred years later a white European named Hernando Cortez invades the Aztecs, conquers and dismantles the Aztec (Mexica) Empire in 2 years. Over the last five centuries, many of the descendants of the conquered Aztecs and other city-states who are now generically called Mexicans returned to the southwest or Aztlán (which is historically truly only a very small part of the southwest) as migrant workers. Today, these descendants of the earlier descending migrant workers and or indigenous Xicanos are demanding their birthright or the entire southwest United States, the land area taken by violent force by American *foreigners* who by the way have absolutely no birthright. (There is nothing on this map that states "Antigua Residencia de Los European-Americans"!) If modern Aztlán or the southwest would be granted to us today because of this logic and these two documents it would go down in history as an *"immaculate conception"*, of a nation-state or a *birth without bloodshed* or effort. A phenomenon unheard of in the birth of nation-states anywhere in the world.

It is also pertinent to ask these questions. Why is the land area or southwest taken by the American in the war designated as Aztlán, since Aztlán is historically according to a codice and oral history only an island? Was the Mexican government prior to losing this area acting as an *incubator* for Aztlán intending to surrender this land base to its future citizenry, Xicanos? If the southwest had remained intact as part of Mexico would, Xicanos be calling for Aztlán still? Better yet, why aren't the Mexican government and particularly the citizenry of Mexico City, the more likely direct descendants of the Aztecs filing land claims with the United States Congress and United Nations based upon this notation "Antigua Residencia de los Aztecas"? If we sincerely do believe this area to be our sacred ancestral beginnings then why don't we have an annual Mecca to the area (Antigua Residencia de Los Aztecas) to strengthen our emotional and historical reconnection? And, why haven't Xicanos made any efforts to investigate and appreciate the present inhabitants, who may possibly be descendants of the original Aztecs as well?

Why? Because it is non-sensible and fantasy. Yet, the promise of this fantasy self-evolving into a reality based upon these migration stories to and from Aztlán and or the southwest dominates the psyche of *movimiento* Xicanos. The word Aztlán has become the mythological "open sesame" of Xicanos. Believing, if we say and sing it often enough it will magically happen. I speak from experience since from an early age I inherited this intoxicating and seductive illusion from my *movimiento* predecessors. Aztlán is an imagined place and we are an imagined citizenry. Worst, we are in a *frozen* state of imagination. We have restricted ourselves to the safe and polite efforts of writing, reading, discussion, poetry, song and dance, and wishful thinking.

The other part of Aztlán* is the Aztecs or Azteca (Mexica). A name that was reportedly not used to identify themselves but a name introduced or at least reintroduced 300 years after the conquest of the Mexica by a German-national historian, a *foreigner*. For the purpose of

---

**The name of this place was Aztlán, meaning the "place of the cranes," from which the archaic name Aztec was taken. It was not until later during the migration that these peoples assumed the name Mexica by which they were known by the Spaniards. The original term "Aztec" reappeared again in scholarly studies of the 18th and 19th centuries, and is now accepted as a generic name for the people of the valley of Mexico at the time of the Spanish conquest. Richard F. Townsend, <u>The Aztecs</u>, p. 55.*

simplification, he used the name Aztec to classify all the Indians of central Mexico regardless of their true indigenous national identity. He called them Aztec because the Mexica or dominating Indians came from a place called Aztlán or Aztatlan. His intent as a historian evidently was to *unify* in order to *simplify* for non-Indian and non-Mexican readers. Just as all the diverse national African slaves were classified together irrespective of their original separate political identities as Negroes, or Blacks. It sure made things a lot easier for American white folks.

Michael D. Coe in *Mexico* writes, "Some may be disappointed to find the Aztec empire confined to a single chapter. "Aztec" and "Mexico" seem almost synonymous, but we now know that in the total span of man's occupation of that country the Aztecs were late upstarts, their empire but a final and brilliant flicker before the light of native civilization was put out once and for all." Still in spite of this reality, the Aztecs have become the beginning, the end, and the <u>only</u> connection that Xicanos make to the Indians of the southwest and all of former colonial New Spain or the medium from which Mexicanos were initially bred politically. Racially speaking all these peoples regardless of indigenous groups were homogenous. Their descendants or *we* are also homogenous.

The land boundaries created by the Spanish Conquistadores or the "Colony of New Spain" incorporated all of today's Mexico, a part of Guatemala and the southwest United States. Literally hundreds of bands, tribes, nations, languages, cultures, and indigenous physical national boundaries existed in pre-Columbian or pre-Conquest times. We as Mexicans, as Xicanos and Chichimecos (today's southwest enrolled Indians) have evolved from these many combinations; <u>not</u> genetically separate but politically separated, deconstructed, then reconstructed and historically re-identified and as a result psychologically separated by foreigners. The idea that if you are a Mexican national or a Xicano (a demexicanized national) you are a direct and only descendant of the Aztecs is very distorting and self-destructive. Granted the Azteca represented a fascinating people and era during their imperial centuries; and I embrace the pride that radiates from the genetic and cultural connection I have with these once amazing people. However, I do not limit myself to or define myself by their legacy.

David Weber author of *Foreigners in Their Own Land* writes: "Most Mexican-Americans are not descended from Aztecs. Rather, Mexican American ancestry lies in the diverse aboriginal population of Mexico, including such groups as Tlascalans, enemies of the Aztecs who cooperated with the Spanish Conquerors, and Indians of Northern Mexico such as Seris, Yaquis, and Tarahumaras."[119]

Even though Mr. David Weber is also a *foreigner* he does make a point that in my opinion is accurate and must be dealt with. It is this Xicano craving to identify solely with the glory of the Aztecs that we become myopic with tunnel vision when viewing Indigenous histories. By restricting our ancestry to the Aztecs we also restrict our modern ability to understand, embrace and benefit from all the peoples and elements that make up our identity. Yes we are indigenous to the southwest but not because of some map which was produced by *foreigners*; originally Spaniards, then Creoles and finally European-Americans. In fact, you give credibility to the map by recognizing it as a legitimate document. This document is the result of invasion, imperialism, and genocide directed against people who preceded and looked like us, our ancestors. Whether it is the physical boundaries of Colonial New Spain starting from 1521, to independent Mexico born in 1821, to Mexico reduced in 1848 and the southwest acquired through yet another European (American) invasion and imperialism. They were all in violation of their own rules of international law, which originated in Europe.

The Aztecs were not a separate and unique race from all other Indians of the American southwest, Mexico, Central America or North and South America. They were somewhat politically, linguistically, geographically and culturally different from these other indigenous (Indians) groupings. Genes can automatically be transmitted from generation to generation. But culture, politics, identity and language must be transferred by an organized cohesive grouping. That organized cohesive group, i.e. the Aztecs is extinct and fossilized. What remains beyond language and residual culture is their glory and connection possibly to the American southwest. If a bunch of English and Spanish-speaking Xicanos with European names want to reconnect with the Aztecs then start with something bold yet simple and revolutionary; change your Romanized names to Aztec names. Stop looking 4 Aztlán under the auspices of our white masters, the real un-indigenous people. Think and act Indigenous without permission and stop pimping the Aztecs!

Also and most importantly, *natural law, which is human rights*, and <u>land rights</u> granted by birth from the creator. The word natural means not man-made or artificial. The word natural is a cognate of the Latin word *natura*, which means *birth*. Natura comes from the Latin root word *nasci*, which means *to be born*. (Recall in your mind the Spanish phrase, ¿Donde nacistes?)

Thomas Paine an English national who immigrated (wetback!) to the American colonies and became a founding father of the American nation promoted *natural rights* as the foundation of revolutionary principles that is incorporated in this country's written constitution.

The dictionary of Thorndike-Barnhardt defines *natural law* as: "1) law based upon nature or the natural tendency of human beings to exercise right reason in dealings with others. Natural law PRECEDES and is regarded as the basis of common law; 2) A law or the laws of nature." Human rights and land rights both derivatives of natural law are not *gifts* from government but natural rights that come with birth from *God*.

In Thomas Paine's *Political Writings*, the author explains Thomas Paine's articulation of natural rights. "Natural rights are those which appertain to man in right of his existance. Of this kind are all the intellectual rights, or rights of the mind, and also all those rights of acting as an individual for his own comfort and happiness *which are not injurious to the natural rights of others*." Invasion, military conquest, land theft, intellectual theft (our natural inheritance) genocide against indigenous peoples, destruction and reconstruction of indigenous identities and enslavement all qualify as *injurious to the natural rights of others*. The European nations as a whole and Spanish and American (founding fathers included) whites in particular have all violated this principle. Further the author presents Paine's philosophy stating, "an inquiry into the origin of rights will demonstrate to us that *rights* are not *gifts* from one man to another, nor from one class of men to another; for who is he who could be the first giver, or by what principle or on what authority could he possess the right of giving?" These beautiful principles obviously have been selectively implemented and on a racial basis. Thomas Paine's first pamphlet written when arriving in America was entitled "Slavery in America" revealing the hypocrisy of freedom fighters enslaving blacks. Furthermore, the glorious constitution forbade people of color, even white women, and white non-property owners to vote. Slavery of Africans, genocide against indigenous peoples and discrimination amongst themselves hardly qualifies these people or this era as the benchmark or source of fairness, truth, and ultimate authority.

Are we expecting Aztlán to be our "gift" from white America? It is our ancestors' skeletons and artifacts dug up throughout the southwest for recreational study by *foreign* archaeologists.* It is the pre-American centuries of blood of our ancestors saturating the mountains, deserts, forests, plains, lakes, and rivers. The petroglyphs they attempt to interpret are from the hands of our ancestors not theirs. The foods which European-Americans today call Mexican food was being eaten in the southwest at least 5,000 years before the birth of Mexico or Amerigo Vespucci, the source of the name America.

Don't allow yourself to be confused by the foreigner's maze of archaeological terms such as basket makers, Cochise culture, Desert Culture, Patayan, Sinagua, Hohokam, Mogollon and especially Anasazi. These are all synthetically created vague cultures for the purpose of simplistic and uniform classifications serving professional insiders only. It has nothing to do with the issues of physical, indigenous or national boundaries and especially race. White scholars have through this scientific maze succeeded in separating us from our historical, geographical, racial and emotional connection to our ancestry and natural inheritance. The circle of inheritance has been broken and now we are disconnected.

Archaeologists were and are successful in confusing themselves when it comes to classifying and naming prehistoric and historic indigenous cultures. For example, the confusion became such a mess that in 1927 renowned archaeologist Earl Morris received a letter from another famous archaeologist named Ted Kidder calling for a conference hoping to solve this problem. The letter read in part:

---

*Archarology means the excavation, collection, and interpretation of vanished cultures from historic times back to prehistoric times. C.W. Ceram, <u>The First American, a Story of North American Archaeology</u>, p. 107

>...Roberts and Judd and I are planning to have a get-together of many field workers in southwestern archaeology as possible at Pecos for two or three days, beginning August 29th, in order to thrash out at leisure the various questions of problems, method, and nomenclature which we discussed in a preliminary way in Judd's office this autumn.
>
>Along with about forty workers from widely separated digs all over the four states comprising the southwest, Earl and his party arrived at the Rocky Pecos mesa. In its shadow, after evaluating past accomplishments, they set about charting the future course of southwestern archaeology. Their names were the cornerstones upon which the discipline had been founded...
>
>Three days had been set aside, as an account in science stated, "To bring about contacts between workers in the southwestern field; to discuss fundamental problems of southwestern history, and to formulate plans for coordinated attack upon them; to pool knowledge of facts and techniques, and to lay foundations for a unified system of nomenclature."[120]

Standardized nomenclature was intended to eliminate or reduce confusion but continued subdivisions began and continue to cause even more confusion among archaeologists. "In more recent years it has been found necessary to subdivide both the basket maker and cliff dweller periods even further. Basket makers have been classified as I, II, and III, and by this time the subdivisions are seeming to become even more minute, for one often hears the terms "early," "middle," or "late basket maker III," for instance. How much further this process will go in the future is problematical."[121]

According to Ruth Benedict in *Race: Science and Politics*: "...Race and culture are distinct. In world history, those who have helped to build the same culture are not necessarily of one race, and those of the same race have not all participated in one culture. In scientific language, culture is not a function of race."[122] Additionally she states, ".Culture is the sociological term for *learned* behavior, behavior which in man is not given at birth, which is not determined by his germ cells as in the behavior of wasps or the social ants, but must be learned anew from grown people by each new generation." (Loc. cit.) Yet, gringos have managed to convince Spanish-speaking Indians that they are Hispanic while not calling English-speaking Indians, Englishmen. This is why sadly we use issues like maps to convince white people we are indigenous. It is our disconnection with our Indian identity, the land, and the belief that as Spanish-speaking Indians (Hispanics) somehow we are a different race from enrolled Indians.

Because the indigenous cultures of Patayan, Hohokam or Anasazi for example of the southwest are classified by and for white foreign archaeologists and do not mention specifically *Aztec* (another white classification); Xicanos cannot decipher and emotionally, racially and historically connect themselves to the southwest as indigenous people. However, for some of us, now we have a *permission slip* we call a map notating "Antigua Residencia de Los Aztecas" and validated by the white man himself so we can "exhale"; we are now officially indigenous. This map has become the *Holy Grail* for Xicanos. However, it is fantasy to believe anything positive will come of it simply because it is in existence.

A right cannot be anymore basic or reduced than at birth and from the creator. When man's synthetic rules, laws, or policy violate this natural principle, then they must be challenged and eliminated. They then should be replaced with laws that honor natural laws, which honor natural rights.

IDENTITY
THE DOORWAY TO NATURAL INHERITANCE
(Indian – Pre-American – Chichimeca – Xicano)

This brings me to the issue of identity. I will give a definition of the word identity, which you will not find in any dictionary. Dictionaries do not create words or their definitions. They simply in an organized and documented fashion report how the public is using words. Therefore, they are not the ultimate authority on the meanings of a word. Consequently, the absence of this following definition should not serve in our minds to disqualify the definition I give it. After having given so much thought and observance to the uses and abuses of identity, I have developed this definition when identity is being referred to people. *The artificial and temporary boundaries created by people to restrict people's entry into or exist out of the defined (identified) grouping.* Identity you can see is not only what you are but also what you are not. As you will realize here, identity determines boundaries and boundaries are used to determine rightful inheritance.

Identity has at least four major components. It is (1) **artificial**: all identities (or groupings) are man-made. Even in the natural sciences, though humankind attempts to contour identities to natural and similar characteristics in the end they use a synthetic* system of classification; (2) **temporary**: all identities are temporary. For example, the Romans, Vikings, Etruscans and Vandals to name a few no longer exist. Eventually the identity of Americans will be a thing of the past. People will romantically dispute this fact. Remember, however that the Romans existed for close to a thousand years and they disappeared or merged or emerged as something else; (3) **multiple**: all identities are multiple. For example, as Xicanos we have at least 4 major levels of identity starting with the most basic: 1) *Indian*, 2) Pre-American, 3) Chichimeca, and 4) Xicano. As Xicanos (a rejected people) we are first and foremost

---

Currently, there is a world-wide movement by some scientist to dismantle and replace the centuries old binominal system for naming plants. It is claimed the present system is to unnatural and inaccurate thus limiting its effectiveness.

generically (1) Indians or descriptively, indigenous Pan-Americans. That is the highest and most general level of our layers of identities.

Throughout the Americas, the indigenous peoples or Indians now serve as landless peasants relegated and regulated to the lowest levels of society. This unfortunate reality forces or should force us to recreate our own levels and layers of identity. Within the geopolitical boundaries of the United States, we are not American Indians or Native Americans as defined by the federal government. However, we are in fact native to America and Indians. In other words, we are in *reality* Native Americans and or American Indians. In a legal sense, we are not de jure American Indians or Native Americans, but we are *de facto** American Indians or Native Americans. The terms Native American and American Indians are viewed by the many whom this term legally covers as insensitive, mandatory. and inaccurate. Like the inappropriate terms, Hispanic and Latino it serves to unify and simplify for better manipulation and management by *foreigners*. These gringo identification labels also serve to restrict, to reduce and to eventually dissolve the number of so-called "real" or federally recognized Indians instead of encouraging or allowing the other *generic* (greater in numbers) unrecognized Indians to address themselves, or think of themselves or act as indigenous peoples. What we are not as Indians is "Enrolled Indians" or legally recognized Indians under the *Federal Indian Identification Policy,* developer of the "Certificate of degree of Indian Blood" or commonly called *blood quantum.*

Some of us would incorporate the misnomer and colonial negative identity of Hispanic or Latino, which is usually nothing more than a Spanish-speaking Indian. The beauty of this title or identity for gringos is that it de-Indianizes Spanish-speaking people and takes away their land base and therefore natural inheritance. This identity leaves us to drift in a gaseous state because we are unanchored by a homeland. Imagine this, we have gone from the rightful and natural indigenous

---

Word Origin: de facto is Latin for "from the fact," hence existing in fact with or without legal sanction. In law, *de facto* is the opposite of *de jure*, "by right, according to law". Thus if both an owner of a piece of land and a squatter who lives on that land claim it, the owner may claim it *de jure*, according to law, but the squatter may claim it *de facto*, from the fact that he actually lived on it. [Reader's Digest Family Word Finder, p. 208]

peoples of the southwest to millions of homeless people. This de-Indianization is now occurring for indigenous people on a hemispheric level. A prime example of hemispheric *de-Indianization* of indigenous Pan-Americans is an article in the July 2, 1999 edition of Newsweek magazine entitled, Latino Americans: The face to the future. It states: "Latinos can't be neatly pigeonholed. They come from 22 different countries of origin, including every hybrid possible. Many are white, some are black, but most are somewhere in between." Not only are we classified as mulattos or a racial mixture of black and white, but there is no mention of brown-skinned Indian people, whether *puro Indio* or *mestizo*. Of the seven young ladies in the picture, six have very dominant Indian features.

Whites are originally from Europe and Blacks are originally from Africa. So where and better yet, who are the indigenous people? Yet, Indios make up the majority population of the entire Western Hemisphere*. The country of Mexico alone social scientists overwhelmingly estimate is Indian. Driver estimates that "more than 80 percent of the genes of the entire [modern Mexican] population are probably Indian, with the remainder divided equally between Negroes and Europeans." This would make the Mexican population less than 10 percent white, as compared to the Census Bureau's 90+ percent white categorization.[123]

Further supporting this fact is a quote from author Paul Radin: "The Winning of the West meant the annihilation of the Indian. True, their annihilation had begun much earlier, with the first landing of the Spaniards. Yet, strange as it may seem, the Spaniards, in spite of all their cruelty and lust for gold, did not eradicate the native population so completely as did the Anglo-Saxons. With the exception of the West Indies, Indians are today still living in large numbers throughout Spanish America and although they are nominally Catholics, many of their old cultural possessions have been incorporated in the new civilizations that have arisen there. In fact, Argentine and Brazil excepted, Spanish America is racially Indian."[124]

---

*That includes the invaders sythetic and dissolving caste classification of Mestizos.

Scientific author Ruth Benedict writes, "The fundamental reason why language cannot be equated with race is that language is learned behavior, and race is a classification based on hereditary traits."[125] So, I ask you, if Indians who speak Spanish are called Hispanics or Latinos then why are not Indians who speak English called Englishmen or Black people who speak English also called Englishmen? We are not Hispanics. We were victimized by Hispanics. If you are identified after those who have victimized you then why aren't Jews called Germanics? By calling Indigenous people erroneously yet purposefully Latino or Hispanic, European-Americans are successful in removing us from a land base or *birthright*. Latino is a simple reference to one whose spoken language is a derivation of the Latin language and this speaker could reside any place in the world. That is not a reference to a specific race area or country. Latinos are also Europeans in Spain, Portugal, Italy, and even Romania, all white nations. Latino Americano is a reference to countries or areas and or peoples in the American hemisphere who speak a Latin language. This includes Brazil, Argentina, Peru, Cuba, Mexico and the Spanish-speaking population of the southwest, for examples. Not only can it embrace members of the mentioned countries but also in fact French-Canadians, and the Mission Indians of California. The term Latino leaves you *floating* and powerless in limbo without the benefit of an accurate identity, land base, or homeland. But then again that is the whole point, to make us confused and homeless. Enrolled Indian author Jack D. Forbes writes in *Aztecas del Norte, the Chicanos of Aztlán*: "Regardless of mythology, however, the fact remains that perhaps eighty percent of the genetic makeup of the Mexican people is Indian or Native American and only about ten percent is Spanish-European. For practical reasons, then, the typical Mexican can be considered, racially, as if he were a pureblood Indian, since his non-native racial heritage is relatively insignificant. The typical Mexican would correspond to a United States Indian of one-eighth or one-sixteenth Caucasian ancestry."[126] (p. 151)

To encompass the indigenous peoples of the present U.S.A. boundaries, I utilize the term (2) *pre-American**. This disallows outside

---

*I use the term "pre-American" which supercedes and bypasses European-American standards and authority.

interference in our identities by European-Americans and embraces all descendants of pre-American ancestry' to share in our common land and ancestry. (3) *Chichimeca* is a reference to all indigenous Indians of the southwest in particular including Xicanos. The term is indigenous and had been in use over 600 years before its use was discontinued by the invading European-Americans. It is time to reintroduce and utilize it once again. I will deal in greater depth with this identity in a separate chapter.

The most rigid and localized level is that of (4) *Xicano*. Spanish-speaking Indians whose birthplace and birthright as a people is in the southwest. Now we have become re-Indianized with a land base and homeland! Now we can enjoy the psychological and territorial benefits of natural inheritance. Now we go from visitor to homeowner which is what we are; we go from a pathetic attitude to a powerful altitude. I call Xicano our cellular identity because it is capable of standing alone in distinction but must combine with other levels of identity to strengthen and survive. For example and comparison, in biology you have one of the most basic levels of identity which is cellular (*Xicano*), followed by tissue (*Chichimeca*) all southwestern Indians followed by organ (*pre American*) of U.S.A. and lastly the human body or (*Indian*), the most generic level Indigenous Pan-American. All these are levels separate but not independent of each other. Our racial victimization over the centuries by European invaders has necessitated that we initiate, expand, and utilize as necessary our multiple identities.

As for the identity of an American, there are those who would place this part of their identity at the very top of the spectrum, somewhere in the middle at the very end or not at all. Depending on how successfully you have been externally manipulated or how well you have internally self-manipulated and demystified the foreigner's clouded maze. The occasion and or the individual personality will dictate or allow the dictation of their identity or levels, layers and order of identities at the time of its use. In the end, the identity must serve you in a positive sense. Speaking for myself and from my lifelong experience at the mercy of White Americans, I do not embrace the term American.

We are not truly Americans in that we fully enjoy the rights and advantages of citizenship as white-Americans do. We are Americans in the words of European-Americans only when we unite in force and respond successfully to injustices against us by White-Americans; also, when we dress in military uniforms and leave for foreign lands to support the imperialistic agenda of this country. When we are at home and everyday citizens, however, we are not truly Americans but Americans with an <u>apologetic</u> "hyphen" – Cuban-Americans, Mexican-Americans, Puerto Rican-American, etc.

The fourth component of identity is its use as a **power block** or **block to power**. As a block to power, your identity can be used to confuse and therefore diffuse your efforts and ability to either create, congregate or participate in a larger or dominant grouping. Simply put, it disturbs your ability to unify, strengthen, and utilize the grouping (identity) you are part of. It is beneficial for the U.S. Government to restrict and separate generic Indians and "federally recognized" Indians by keeping this already scattered and diminished and diminishing population to a manageable low number and eventually dissolving them altogether. All natural rights to natural inheritance will therefore be dissolved.

As long as Xicanos are convinced we came *from* Mexico and are not the descendants of the original Indians of the southwest and/or arrivals from Mexico prior to the founding of the thirteen original European colonies then we possess an apologetic and weakened attitude of being a *foreigner* or *visitor* instead of one of the rightful* owner's of our house; the southwest.

A *power blocked* identity or grouping that is of seemingly different people who actually share a common origin and whose victims (in this case) share a common history of genocide and massive displacement by a common conqueror. While their descendants (European Americans) on the other hand continue today through the manipulation of discrimination, segregation, isolation, incarceration, and intimidation do benefit from the brutal conquests of *their* founding fathers. These very negative *common* characteristics can be the foundation to reverse the negative momentum against us to create a positive momentum for us. In

---

*Chichimecos or southwestern "Enrolled Indians, our genetic, cultural, historical and territorial brothers and sisters are also rightful, natural owners.

other words, we move from a *block to power* to a *power block*. We ourselves determine the criterion for our new identity group to respond as a power block.

If it is the color of our skin, and/or the language we speak, and/or the economic status we are restricted to that is used against us for example then these very characteristics should be our cement and building blocks of the power we need to respond to, demand compensation and discontinuation. We must recreate our identity on our terms for our benefit and not those of *foreigners* for their benefit.

The definition of identity can be reduced to one pivotal word and that word is boundary. A dictionary defines boundary as *something that restricts entry or exit – tangible or intangible*. Tangible boundaries are very obvious boundaries and can be seen or touched, such as rivers, mountains, deserts, oceans, fences, extreme cold, extreme heat and so forth. In ancient times, these types of boundaries or natural boundaries as they are called were very vivid. Today with the modern technology of flight, automobiles, trains, and watercraft, these boundaries are not necessarily as vivid because they are not as insurmountable as they once were. The root word of boundary is *bound* which means primarily to tie down or restrict.

Skin color is another example of an obvious boundary. Right? Wrong! It is any combination of social, political, moral, or legal enforcement that uses color as a demarcation line or boundary. Interracial dating or marriage once had obvious severe penalties and today in some places still does. Race scientist Ruth Benedict writes: "The inescapable conclusion from a consideration of its history is that these racist claims are a *front* designed to hide self-seeking aggressions and alliances. THEY ARE CAMOUFLAGE."[127] She further states, "…In order to understand race persecution, we do not need to investigate race; we need to investigate *persecution*. Persecution was an old story before racism was thought of." (loc. cit.) For example, it is not the difference in color (race) that physically prevents or hinders sexual intercourse, dating or interracial love, it is dominant society's enforcement of racism. Intangible boundaries are non-physical and usually unseen boundaries. There are a vast array and potential of these kinds of boundaries. They can be political, legal, economic, intellectual or social to name the basics.

Men don't go into women's public bathrooms and women don't go into men's public bathrooms. Why? There are no armed guards to prevent you nor would you probably be arrested if you did. It would be considered rude, and against customs to do so and would leave you open to ridicule and negative publicity. Examples of other intangible boundaries are ethics, customs, morals, attitudes, and traditions. All learned behavior. When driving if there is no one around when we come to a street light which is red we stop and wait for the color to change to green for fear of the penalty of law; yet another example of an intangible boundary. When we claim a map will help us overcome a boundary such as the 1847 map then the boundary is in *our* mind, not the gringos. He is the one who put it there!

Let's examine a white racist boundary being created and designated without making a reference to race. Years ago when Pat Buchanan was traveling the presidential campaign circuit he was fond of making this statement. "What we have to do is *take* this country back and *return* it to the *true* sons and daughters of the founding fathers." Using a combination of historical, political and biological boundaries Mr. Buchanan is able to promote racism. Who are the *official* founding fathers? They're white slave owners who also practiced genocide and forced relocation against indigenous peoples. Since the founding fathers are white then the true sons and daughters would be white. We are *restricted* entry into this select grouping by the boundaries of identity: "Founding fathers." In addition, the benchmark or standards of when and what the definition of *native*, of course is decided by *foreigners*. "Enrolled Indians" are called Native American when in fact the more accurate descriptive identity should be "pre-Americans." How can "Enrolled Indians" be Native American if the concept, nation-state boundaries, and words were brought over by the Europeans – the true Native Americans. A nationally organized and recognized White-American society refers to its members by the call letters P.R.D. or Plymouth Rock Descendants. Having studied indiscriminately Indigenous peoples and eras of the southwest and Mexico; not just the Aztecs or the Aztec period I found that archaeologists referred to the earliest cultures and peoples of the southwest (and Mexico) as that of the **Basketmakers**. They were here at least 30,000 to 70,000 or more years before the arrival of Europeans (if Indians did *arrive*). Because they made artifacts of basketry and had no pottery, a later development, they were called basket makers. Where are our preAmerican societies of B.M.D. or Basket Maker Descendants? We and not the people of P.R.D. are first in line for our natural inheritance. Here the benefits are pride in being first, comfort in being indigenous and in knowledge if not in fact knowing the land we have been detached from is actually ours by natural inheritance or NATURAL LAW. In Texas, they have the Daughters of the Texas Revolution. They truly enjoy their inheritance that is really ours.

The English only movement and immigration policies suggest the same *acquiescence* or unspoken understanding. Though English only and immigration policies suggest patriotism and concern of American social, cultural, and economic stability their selective enforcement is actually reflections of racism, targeted against the basket maker descendants. This sneaky strategy is called *social engineering*.

My favorite example of a racist boundary is that of the identity/definition of *pioneer*. We all know that a pioneer is someone or some group of people who does something first or arrives at some previously unoccupied area first. I was motivated to investigate the meaning of this word because of an article I read in a newspaper some years ago. The article dated July 27, 1990 was under the title of *"Indian's History in Genes."* It makes two major points. One, almost all Indians throughout the Americas are genetically derived from the same racial group. Two, Indians are the pioneers of the American hemisphere.

> "Nearly all American Indians are descendants of a single small band of PIONEERS who walked across what's now the Bering Strait from Asia, 15,000 to 30,000 years ago a geneticist researcher said Thursday.
>
> The descendants of this hardy group make up 95 percent of American Indians, including the Mayans, Incas and many others spread throughout North, Central and South America".

Out of curiosity and habit, I sought out the Barnhardt-Thorndike Dictionary description of Pioneer: 1. *A person who settles in a part of the country that has not been occupied before* EXCEPT *by primitive tribes.* 2. Figurative: *A person who goes first, or does something first, and so prepares a way for others.*

In other words, *except* means not only are we not eligible to be pioneers but we are not really a person or the plural people. This identity or boundary or definition is not only racist but so beautifully acquiescent and even *harmless* you would think, so what's the big deal?

Not only have European-Americans once again reestablished the benchmark or standard for who is a pioneer they have intellectually stolen our natural inheritance: the rights of original occupation; the land and the ancestry. Pioneer is in fact a racist term as defined in this instance.

As the original peoples with natural rights originating from natural law, we are entitled to our inheritance – the land. The natural cycle of inheritance from our ancestors has been sabotaged, disconnected, and redefined. The lands and ancestry where the blood, bones and artifacts of our ancestors has been stolen (reindentified) and placed beyond reach not only of our hands but of our *minds* and even worst our *hearts*, for today *not only has our land been taken from us but we have been taken from the land.*

Another definition I looked up was the word *Chicano: a person living in the United States who was BORN in Mexico or DESCENDS from persons BORN in Mexico: A Mexican-American.*

I put emphasis on the words born and descends because it is important that this racist definition make an inference to Chicanos not being eligible for natural inheritance and that they create a detachment between Xicanos and the southwest. It is important to the true foreigner that Xicanos not be allowed to be thought of or to think of themselves as indigenous. In Michigan state law, they have what is called *descent* and *distribution*. This principle indicates that unless the maker of the will otherwise indicates it then descent will dictate distribution. This is an example of common sense or natural law. That is why in the white man's definition of Chicano the word *descends* is crucial. It is their way of disqualifying you for your natural inheritance and that is being indigenous.

Returning to the map and the point that it proves we are not foreigners let me remind you it was the European-Americans who *made* us foreigners as is indicated here. Read for example the titles of these two history books very closely:

(1) *Foreigners in Their Own Land,* by David J. Weber.

(2) *Strangers in Their Own Land,* by Albert Prago.

The implication here is that they *became* or were *made* foreigners or strangers in their **own** homeland.

While Chicanos are being defined out of the southwest and into Mexico or *foreigners*, Enrolled Indians are being defined out of existence. The eventual outcome of federal blood-quantum policies can be described as little other than genocidal in their final implications as historian Patricia Nelson Limerick recently summarized the process: "Set the blood quantum at one-quarter, hold to it as a rigid definition of Indians, let intermarriage proceed as it had for centuries, and eventually Indians will be defined out of existence. When that happens the federal government will be freed of its persistent 'Indian Problem'[128] (or treaty responsibilities)." Along the same lines Shoshone activist Josephine C. Mills put it in 1964, "There is no longer any need to shoot down Indians in order to take away their rights and land (or to wipe them out)... legislation is sufficient to do the trick legally." (loc. cit.) Both quotes come from the book *The State of Native America*.

Author Jack Forbes writes:

> The Bureau of Indian Affairs (The United State's Colonial Office for Indians) at a later date became (and still is) the governments' most ancestry-oriented agency. The bureau keeps records on every Indian, recording the supposed exact degree of blood in a detailed manner undreamed of even by the Spaniards. Furthermore, the bureau decides who is an Indian and who is not an Indian and which Indians are eligible for Indian services.
>
> One can well ask if there is any significant reason for keeping records of five-eighths Indians, one-quarter Indian, one-tenth Indian, "full bloods," half-bloods" and so on. What purpose does it serve? The categorization of Anishinabe* by degree of blood

---

Jack Forbes used the word Anishinabe to mean all Indians of the western hemisphere including Xicanos. He defines Anishinabe to mean first peoples (indigenous) of this hemisphere.

serves to transform the Anishinabe People from a group of nationalities into a series of castes.

The overall objective of United States native policy has been to liquidate the Anishinabe people entirely. One step in liquidation is to prevent Indians from assimilating (absorbing) outsiders and even to prevent them from retaining the loyalty of their own racially mixed children or grandchildren.[129]

Again, identity or boundaries created by foreigners are at work to *confuse, diffuse,* and *dissolve* the possibility of power blocking by indigenous peoples, so gringos can refuse us our natural inheritance.

In Carey McWilliams' classic *North From Mexico* he states very clearly and strongly: "Migration from Mexico is deeply rooted in the past. It follows trails that are among the most ancient on the North American continent. Psychologically and culturally, Mexicans have never immigrated to the southwest: THEY HAVE RETURNED."[130] (emphasis added) Like the little red book of Mao was elevated to bible-like status among the Chinese this book should be owned, coveted and referred to often by Mexicanos, Xicanos and Enrolled Indians.

Again, in *North from Mexico,* Carey McWilliams provides us with a powerful and truthful quote: "The Spanish-speaking have an identification with the southwest which can never be broken. They are not interlopers or immigrants but an INDIGENOUS people. As a consequence they resent any designation which implies a hyphenated (Mexican-American) relationship to their native environment and particularly so when this designation is applied by Anglo-American **interlopers** and **immigrants**."[131] As a white American who made this statement around 1950, it took considerable courage and commitment. For you as a Xicano to realize, embrace, and utilize the title status, attitude, and resulting *altitude* of *indigenous* to the southwest empowers you dramatically.

When we as Xicanos strictly stereotype ourselves as descendants of the Aztecs and Aztecs only we, *self restrict* our boundaries leaving little need for the European-American to restrict us with his definitions. On the one hand we tell European-Americans we are indigenous to the southwest yet when we as Xicanos tell our history to him we immediately emigrate over a thousand miles south and talk about the Aztecs of Mexico City (Mexico-Tenochtitlan). The only connection to the southwest with the Aztecs is the migration story of Aztecs from the itty-bitty island of Aztlán that took place about 700 years ago. That's our interpretation of indigenous? That is birthright? No, that is ridiculous!

When the Spaniards arrived in the southwest, they began and continued as in the lower half of the colony of New Spain the process of what I call the four C's, which they called *reduccíon*. First, they would militarily <u>Conquer</u> the Indians of the targeted territory. Then they would <u>Congregate</u> them together into missions*, visitas or rancherias irrespective of their differing languages and nationalities. (In sedentary and densely populated central Mexico they were congregated primarily into what was then called pueblos). Then they would <u>Convert</u> them to the Christian religion, Spanish language, Spanish customs, holidays, dress and so forth. Then as a result they were <u>Controlled</u> or enslaved by these institutions of missions or rancherias.

Theoretically and eventually, they were to be released with an allotment of land and the skills to farm or ranch them. Also, they were eventually allowed (with limitations) to be mainstreamed into the lower levels of new Spanish society. These southwestern Indians who like central Mexican Indians were once independent tribes or nations had become Hispanized to become the future Mexicanos and eventually Xicanos (with Mexican separation resulting from American expansion) of the southwest. In other words, our initial Xicano ancestors were manufactured or carved out of the southwest; they did not entirely or substantially immigrate from Mexico!

With the end of colonial New Spain and the birth of Mexico there was the 1827 legal elimination of the missionization of so-called wild Indians. All these remaining missionized and Hispanized once independent or wild Indians were turned free by the tens of thousands throughout the southwest.** Unable to live in the wild, unaccepted by their wild and free brethren, and detached from their tribal or national

---

*In Mexico the victims of the 4 C's were rounded up by force into newly created PUEBLOS designed for just that purpose. For details of the tactics, strategies, and methodologies read Robert Richard's The Spiritual Conquest of Mexico. He does not use the phrase 4 C's, that's my phrase to simplify the process used.

**30,000 from the missions of California alone.

identity they were absorbed and melted into mainstream second-class Mexican citizenship and became Mexicanos.

Secularization expedited the process of Mexicanization in the southwest of now landless indigenous people. And, even though it may have seemed at the surface intended to benefit Indians it was really a camouflaged tactic of again stealing our natural inheritance. We were first missionized to detach us from our stolen lands and eventually demissionized resulting in indigenous Indians who became detribalized, deIndianized and Mexicanized (civilized Indians).

The Mexicanized Indians of northern Mexico would then be geographically split from southern Mexico or deMexicanized as a result of the 1846-1848 Mexican-American War. These Mexicanized and deMexicanized Indians would continue, even to this day, to be thought of and treated as deIndianized. Instead of thinking of ourselves as Spanish-speaking Indians, we are thought of and think of ourselves as Hispanics, Latinos or Mexican-Americans as if we in fact are a different race from other Indians in general and especially in the southwest.

> Secularization of the missions – transferring control of mission properties from the friars to civil authorities – had been considered and repeatedly recommended. Many of the missions were wealthy, owning great herds of livestock and controlling thousands of acres of choice land. Civilians, looking with covetous eyes upon these fields and herds, advocated secularization. Political theorists, with a passion for democracy, recommended that the mission Indians be liberated from the practicle slavery in which they lived. Finally, the Mexican Government responded with the decree of August 17, 1833, ordering secularization for the California missions… A plan of gradual emancipation. Hoping thus to ease the way for the mission Indians and protect their interests. Half the land and livestock was to be distributed among these Indians. The remainder was to be placed under civil administrators…

Between 1834 and 1836, secularization was accomplished at all of the missions. The results were highly disappointing. Few administrators were honestly interested in the red men's welfare; and the property they controlled was soon dissipated. Large grants of land formerly occupied by Indians were given to politically influential civilians... The Indian, in whose interest, presumably, the plan was devised were more harmed than helped by the process.[132]

This land thievery would return in the twentieth century disguising itself as democratic and called the Allotment Act (Dawes Act) and the Termination Act victimizing this time, instead of mission Indians, reservation Indians. In fact, this was one of the purposes for the birth of "enrollment." Each enrolled Indian individual would be allotted a specific amount of acreage. Once all enrolled Indians were granted land, the remaining "surplus" was put up for private purchase by whites and National Parks reducing previous reservation areas by over one-half their original acreage. Additionally, the great majority of land distributed to Indians was not arable. Those that had arable land did not have the knowledge, skills, machinery or market to establish, develop and distribute their would be products. So, what did they do in most cases as a result? They sold it, just as planned by the white sponsors (Bureau of Indian Affairs (BIA) and Congress) who secretly predicted this would happen. Our national inheritance is continuously being stolen in different and ingenious ways.

These reservation Indians or gotta-way* Indians are the descendants of Chichimeca also. These initially unconquered Indians or Chichimecos as they were called (under Spaniard and Mexican administrations) would later be defeated and placed on reservations by a new invading people called Americans. They would call these Chichimecos or Indios in English *Indians* and they would become today's "Enrolled Indians" made possible and necessary by their being incarcerated onto reservations. Not all Chichimecos or independent Indian Nations were

---

Gotta way from the process of the 4 C's which Mexicanized or colonized Indians into mainstream society..

placed on reservations; however, it was primarily those Indian nations who presented the greatest military threat with few exceptions. Those other independent Indian nations of the southwest would gradually melt or merge into the Hispanized or Mexicanized communities losing their distinct identities and become Mexicanos. For example: those less rebellious Apache nations not placed on reservations were allowed to live around the outskirts of Tucson and Phoenix only to eventually melt into Mexican society. Those nations that were placed on reservations were documented therefore ironically allowing them in most cases to keep their tribal or national identity in tact: Today they are called "Enrolled Indians." Really, they are Indians who escaped the Spaniards and Mexicans policy of the 4 C's. They did not however escape the European-American policy of extermination or relocation for those who survived inevitably were forcibly placed on reservations.

Author William B. Griffen writes on this phenomenon.

> In the twentieth century, all the original Indian groups of the area are culturally extinct. For a time in the later colonial period and into the Mexican national period, there existed two different kinds of people called Indians or Indios. One consisted of people occupying marginal places in the Spanish social system and generally the lowest stratum. They were partly or largely Hispanicized and basically Spanish-speaking, forming part of the less skilled labor force. People of lower socioeconomic status were still on occasion referred to as Indios in the 1970's.
>
> The other kind of Indian was those groups not incorporated into Spanish society who continued to dwell in the hinterland in direct continuity with their earlier native way of life. These often became the specialized, wide-ranging, and hard hitting raiders of Spanish colonial settlements who, mounted on horseback, adopted a number of Spanish material culture (such as knives, clothing) into their way of life. A number of different peoples, such as the Cuachichil, Toboso, and Coahuileños, evolved into this type of society before they became extinct. The best remembered are the Apache, the last of a long line of colonial raiding specialists…[133]

Kidnapping and slave trade had gone on before, during, and after pre-Columbian times between indigenous nations and groups far north and south of the current Mexican-American border. You only have to read southwestern Indian history to find that Mexicans extensively kidnapped Apaches for example and Apaches extensively kidnapped Mexicans (detribalized & Hispanized Indians). Mexicans kidnapped Apaches to place them into servitude or citizenry and Apaches kidnapped Mexicans especially those 5 years old and below to become citizens of their nations. The famous Apache Chief Chihuahua (a kidnapped Mexican) is a prime example of this. Geronimo himself married kidnapped Mexican women, a common practice among the Apache. Mexico was the permanent home for many Apache nations and winter home of many southwestern Apache nations and even today; Apaches live on both sides of the border.

Another way of deIndianizing, by definition or description, Xicanos and other hemispheric Indians are with the synthetic and externally (European-Americans) placed racial concept and label of *Mestizo*. Mestizo comes from the Spanish world *mezcla* meaning mixed. The truth is when you hear Xicanos and other Indians apologetically saying, "I'm Mestizo or I'm mixed," what they are really saying is "I'm mixed up."

Jack D. Forbes writes:

> The colonial policies of Spain, Britain, and the United States have invented the concept of Mestizo and given reality to the concept through racist, caste-oriented policies that favor white persons over nonwhites while distinguishing grades of people within the nonwhite world.

Isn't it time that this grading system is halted forever?

The Plan to Liquidate the Anishinabe Peoples

In Mexico an Indio who puts on shoes, learns Spanish, and moves to a larger city becomes a non-Indian (he becomes a Mestizo or a Mexicano).

In Peru an Anishinabe woman who sets up a small shop becomes a chola. She is not longer an India.

In Guatemala, a Cakchiquel who learns Spanish and moves to the city becomes a ladino. He is no longer Indio.

In Peru, Bolivia, Mexico, and elsewhere, millions of people who were Indios just a few years ago are now officially campesinos. Bolivia has no more Anishinabes, only peasants.

In Brazil an Indian who takes up farming away from a tribal village becomes a caboclo or perhaps a mestizo or simply a Brazilian peasant.

In the United States, an Indian whose reservation is terminated becomes officially a non-Indian.

In Canada, an Indian whose group never signed a treaty or received a reservation is a metis.

In the United States, many Chicanos of unmixed physical appearance are classified as whites with Spanish surnames.

In Mexico, a man of complete Indian appearance who wears a suit, has a college education, and speaks Spanish has to be a Mestizo, since he could never be an indio.

Throughout the Americas a strange phenomena exists. Almost every country in the hemisphere is doing away with Indians, either by genocide (as in Brazil, Colombia, and Ecuador) or by legislation and custom. The computers of the minds who dominate Anishinabe-waki have decided that the Anishinabe is programmed to disappear, but, of course, this disappearance is completely imaginary and exists only in the minds of the European-oriented ruling class.

The plan to liquidate the native people originated with the Spanish, English, and Portuguese imperialists. It involved several components: (1) killing Anishinabe in wars of conquest; (2) forcibly destroying native identity and culture in programs of missionization or "civilizing"; (3) transforming economically independent natives into serfs, slaves, or urban proletariat and thereby making them part of the imperial economy; (4) making native (indio) ways of life a bad thing and encouraging, via racism, everyone to try to become español, white portuguesa or at least mestizo; (5) discouraging the association of mixed-bloods with people still identified as Indian and developing jealousy and shame on the part of the various castes; and (6) doing everything possible to be sure that all people, whether of European ancestry, mixed ancestry, or native ancestry, regard everything European as good (civilized) and everything Anishinabe as bad (uncivilized or, at best, rustic).[134]

Why liquidate indigenous people nationally and hemispherically? It is all about the LAND baby or DETACH and SNATCH. Detach the original intended natural inheritors from the land in their minds and snatch it up by claiming the Indians or indigenous peoples are no longer in existence. Since the indigenous people no longer exist in their own minds, the land no longer exists in their hearts. There is no threat of once-indigenous people taking back what is rightfully theirs based on natural inheritance.

EXTINCTION & ABSORPTION
(DETRIBALIZATION/DENATIONALIZATION) OR THE SAME DIFFERENCE

Extinction and absorption is a sociological process by which a group of people loses their original identity (extinction) and are merged (absorption) usually into a larger group or identity.

"Most groups lost their identities as free-moving units during the seventeenth and eighteenth centuries. Their distinctive names, one by one, disappearing from written records. Their decline was the result of prolonged attrition: deaths in periodic epidemics, deaths in warfare (early rebellion against Spanish control, disputes with other local groups, and attacks by intrusive Apaches), migration of remnants to other regions, punitive dispersion by Spaniards to work at distant plantations and mines, high infant mortality and general demoralization… Small remnants of some groups lost their identities by merging with larger remnants of other groups. By 1800, the names of very few ethnic units were noted in documents and by 1900, the names of all Indian groups native to the region had disappeared.

The last bastions of ethnic identity were Spanish missions and small, unstable refugee communities near a few Spanish or Mexican towns. The communities were tolerated because the Indians caused little trouble and the communities were convenient reservoirs of unskilled labor. In both missions and refugee communities the original ethnic names ceased to be important because of intermarriages. By the close of the eighteenth century, most missions had been terminated and Indian families were given small parcels of mission land. **Eventually all surviving Indians passed into the lower economic levels of Mexican society.**"[135]

Author Jack Forbes speaks of how Mexican Indians were created then used by the Spanish entradas to Hispanize and eventually Mexicanize the indigenous Indians of the southwest. He writes: "The mixture of Mexicans, Taracans and so on, with the northern tribes was a continual process, stimulated by the placement of the former in most of the missions of northern Mexico. Eventually, the smaller semi-nomadic groups were entirely absorbed by the Mexicans."[136] From here the onslaught of Mexicanization (detribalization and deIndianization) gather forces and steam to enter into northern New Spain (southwest United States). "Perhaps the most significant result of the Hispano-Mexican northward movement was, however, the process of unification, whereby many tribes were amalgamated into the hispanized Mexican community" (p. 27). Once again, I say Xicanos didn't primarily migrate to the southwest; they were carved out of the southwest.

As Xicanos who are Aztec myopic and practice *history a la carte*, we have overlooked this historical phenomenon. That is why we keep going a thousand miles south of the border to collect and reflect our history.

The area we call the southwest and Mexico has for thousands of years figuratively been like a bumper pool table with thousands of groups, languages and cultures criss-crossing back and forth. Even today in the face of the most powerful military nation in history, that criss-crossing of the so-called border cannot be stopped, hindered maybe, but not stopped. Harriet Tubman would have developed a deep appreciation if she saw this Underground Railroad in action. A great part of the modern credit goes to the European-American business community and U.S. government also, since they encourage the demand for cheap Mexican and other Spanish-speaking Indian laborers from Latin America. This country's government and economy simultaneously contributes to the instability of Latin American nations and their citizen's constant dislocation.

Che Guevara of Argentina, Fidel Castro of Cuba, Agosto Sandino of Nicaragua, Pancho Villa and Emiliano Zapata of Mexico all studied the Apache Indians to perfect their guerilla science of making war. They all considered the Apache their ancestors. However, because they didn't build temples, monuments and palaces and didn't call themselves Aztecs, Xicanos who not only live in the southwest but are indigenous to the southwest cannot identify with their powerful and beautiful ancestral brethren. There may have been no greater warrior in the history of mankind. No one could match up with the Apache or Apachu* as they were called by their victims. They called themselves Indeh and they did and do reside on both sides of the modern Mexican border. Today the most technologically advanced helicopter as a war machine is called Apache ironically by the very nation that sent them into near extinction. On the other hand, Xicanos because of their Aztec mindset cannot tap the Apache mother lode of pride, beauty, motivation, power, glory, and southwestern homeland!

The letter X in Xicano has many political and historical meanings and one of them is the many centuries of the *criss-crossing* of the Mexican-American border as written by Paul Radin in *The Story of the North American Indian*; "Tribes of marauding barbarians, akin to the lowly Comanche and Ute, were to feel the impact of the Toltec culture, and moving southward to become the famous Nahuas and Aztecs of history. After the year 600 A.D. this criss-crossing was never to cease."

Ironically after they moved southward as tribes, then generations and centuries later some of their descendants would return northward as Mexicanos or detribalized, renationalized and deIndianized Indians under a different identity in a different era or generation. Same race but different identity. For example, as Wallace and Hoebel write in their book *The Commanches*: "The shift from the Shoshone norm may quite possibly be the result of extensive admixture with Mexican captives. Since their arrival in the south plains, the Commanches have incorporated great numbers of Mexican captives into their tribe, and Mexican infiltration continues today at a rapid pace."[137] The previous paragraph elaborates on how groups like the Comanche became the Aztec (Mexica) and now this paragraph speaks of how Mexicans (Mexica or Aztec) became Comanche or criss-crossed.

Texas was dominated militarily by Commanche Indians when the European-Americans arrived. They were the only warriors of any nation white or non-white who were successful against the Apaches. In fact, even today the western boundary of the Mexican state of Cuahuila

---

Apachu is the Zuni Indian word meaning "enemy."

(though its named after Indians who resided in Texas and northeast Mexico) is the exact trail used by Apaches and Commanches among others going deep into northern Mexico and vice-versa to kidnap and raid. It was so obvious a highway from centuries of foot and hoof travel that it made a convenient natural state demarcation or boundary.

The state name of Texas (Teks-us) is a cognate of an Indian term as notated here in the publication *World of the American Indian* by the National Geographic society. "Attempts by explorers and settlers to spell Indian words could lead to surprising results. The caddo term *Taysa* (pronounced roughly "tie-shah") meant "friend" or "ally"; it often referred to people of the Caddo confederacy of what is now Louisiana and Texas. The Spaniards at the time spelled the *sh* sound as *x*; Adding the plural yielding *Texas*. We have reinterpreted the X by English conventions and produced a word that sounds quite remote from its origin."[138] The Texa (Te-shah) through use of the 4 C's were systematically melted into Spanish-speaking Texas like other distinct indigenous nations. In other words, they *came* (Europeans) and we *became* as they chose to *name*.

Yet, another form of *criss-crossing* (*Xriss-crossing*) was that of importation and deportation of Indians by invading Europeans over the centuries. "…The importation of Indians from distant areas was a regular practice. Often nomadic Indians were captured, given a criminal sentence that legalized their enslavement, and then sent to mines at Parral or Zacatecas. Natives from the Mexican west coast and from New Mexico were regularly taken to mining areas of northern New Spain."[139] People are unaware that after the complete genocidal elimination of indigenous Carribbean Indians they were not only replaced by black African slaves but also Indians from throughout Spanish America, with special emphasis on Mexican Indians due to its proximity.

Only by viewing Aztec history before, during, after, under, over, and around do we see what truly makes us indigenous to the southwest. The Aztecs are a brilliant and proud "flicker" of light but they are not the sun or sum of our identity or existence. We as Xicanos have many "uncles" (figuratively), the Aztecs are but one of the them however, so are the Apaches, Mojave's, Texa, Pueblos, Mission Indians of California,

Commanches, Toboso, Shoshone, Pima, Yavapai and on and on. Terms like *pioneer* and *foreigner* as you see can be very racist with specific and negative intent. Ruth Benedict points out, "Racial slogans serve the same purpose in the present century that religious slogans served before, that is, they are used to justify persecution in the interests of some class or nation." (Ruth Benedict) My oldest son when in his teens taught me this jingle which I have never forgotten and it becomes more meaningful as I age. It is, "*sticks and stones may break my bones, but names will scar me forever.*"

FROM CHICHIMECA TO CHICHIMECOS TO MECOS

In closing this section on Birthright, I want to briefly mention the word, people, and concept of the Chichimeca. In our four levels of identity, I have labeled it number (3). It is not my intent individually and egotistically to set the standards for identity but I believe powerfully that our identities must be *standardized*. My intent primarily has been to show its possible uses and present abuses.

Some scholars believe prior to calling themselves Aztecs (if they did) they may have called themselves Chichimeca. There are many interpretations of the meaning of this word such as *people of the dog*, or *people of the eagle* and as some historians suggest *barbarians*. Many historians writing of the period just before the birth of Mexico-Tenochtitlan and just after gave this word a generic interpretation meaning any of the northern, nomadic invaders who entered into the central Mexican valley. The word and identity of Chichimeca therefore caused much confusion when referring to the Aztecs specifically or some other group of Indians.

For examples, Mixcoatl who led the Tolteca into the central valley of Mexico centuries before the Mexica arrived. Xolotl who is often referred to as "Attila on foot" appeared in the central valley of Mexico as an invading conqueror approximately 100 years *before* the Azteca (Mexica). Like the Aztecs who came after him, he also came from the north but spoke an entirely different language (Pame) than that of the Mexica. However, though they were genetically (racially) the same they were tribally (or nationally) different.

It is known however that *after* the Aztecs did establish themselves as an empire they along with other sedentary city-states generically referred to all northern, nomadic, and barbaric (uncivilized) Indians as Chichimeca. Geographically this area would be the *southwest* or the area encompassing today the U.S. southwest and northern Mexico. The geographic and topographic similarities of these desert-like areas, which also shared climatic similarities, made it very homogenous. With the exception of the four corners area and its sedentary and advanced cultures which would eventually collapse from the lack of available water the archaeological and general classification of culture of this vast area was called a "desert culture". Indians primarily were hunters, gatherers, minimally horticultural, nomadic, and less developed in terms of culture when compared to the sedentary and civilized city-states of central Mexico.

This explains how – culture came north and military invasions went south creating the *criss-crossing* effect for century after century. Cultural influences even among the nomadic Indians of the southwest from Mexico are well documented and established. As for the four corners area it was culturally, architecturally and linguistically a satellite of central Mexico. The occupants over its entire existence as a whole are archaeologically referred to as the Anasazi. This is a Navajo (Dine) word meaning "Ancient" or "Ancient Ones." This very inappropriate scientific misnomer differentiates, separates, isolates, and insulates this area from indigenous peoples of the southwest and Mexico. It prevents these peoples from connecting to their natural inheritance of this area and the mysteriously beautiful histories and lands.

Whereas this area should be another MECCA for Indigenous peoples (especially Xicanos) to proudly and vigorously flood and dominate in numbers yearly, unfortunately it serves as an educational and recreational playground for European-American and Europeans only. Talk about stolen inheritance!

Using the word and process called "*science*" and scientific terminology and phrases our ancestry has been severed from under our eyes. Ruth Benedict writes of the potential trickery of the word, science. "A manufacturer of cosmetics conducted not long ago an investigation of various advertisements of his wares. He found that the two words which had most sales-appeal were "immediately" and "scientific" uniqueness and by this ballyhoo millions are impressed. It was the same with fake medicines, with drug-store drinks, and with health foods until it became necessary to defend the public by federal supervision of manufacturer's claims. The slogan of "science" will sell most things today, and it sells persecution as easily as it sells rouge." Scientific terminology and phraseology in this case is nothing more than the language of an in-crowd who have scientifically severed our historical, cultural and genetic connections to our ancestors' natural museums.

You cannot name <u>any</u> southwestern Indian nation that annually returns in large numbers to the four corners to recapture their ancestral history and re-energize themselves with great pride. The four corners have been scholarly and scientifically severed from all peoples of Mexico and the southwest.

There is overwhelming scientific evidence of the cultural, political, and genetic ties and similarities between the southwest and central Mexico. So why don't we *feel* or actively seek to *feel* the connections and benefits from these realities? C.W. Ceram in his book *A Story of North American Archaeology* writes of this strange incident. "In contrast to Cushing, Bandeliers' investigations were aimed for more at establishing cultural relationships, which at this period meant beginning to uncover historical developments. In Pecos he drew comparisons with the Mexican architecture of Uxmal, although J.W. Powell had counseled him "not to attempt to trace relationship." – a strange piece of advice for what was more natural?"[140]

Bandelier strongly felt that both the Azteca and the Toltec made their homes in Arizona and/or New Mexico prior to their migration into the central Mexican valley. But why would findings and information of this sort be discouraged and kept away from the public by scientists? The answer again, is *natural inheritance*.

Even after the arrival and occupation by the Spanish conquistadores the word Chichimeca continued to be used but Hispanized. "Soon the area of Spanish occupation extended northward into regions occupied by natives representing a relatively primitive peoples whom the Spanish designated by the word **Chichimecos**, a term which became descriptive of non-sedentary tribes as distinguished from the advanced peoples of central and southern Mexico. Beginning on the eastern coast north of Vera Cruz, the line separating the *two types* of natives indicated ran westward, passing a short distance above Mexico City and Guadalajara to Compostela and Tepic."[141] (emphasis added)

This area even had a name to identify it. "Since the 1960's archaeological research in northern Mexico has produced a mass of explicit data that necessitate redrawing the southern boundary of the "North American Southwest" to include all of the northern Mexico as far south as the Tropic of cancer. This additional expanse includes a very substantial part of what has been called, following colonial Spanish usage, the **Gran Chichimeca** – *Chichimeca being the names applied by the Aztecs to the barbarian tribes north of the area of Mesoamerican civilizations. This vast, semi-arid region of over a million square kilometers has been defined both as the northern periphery of Mesoamerica and as the southern periphery of the American southwest. In a very real sense it was both, as on the one hand it was the homeland of the Cochise-like desert dwellers, and on the other hand it was an exploitable frontier to the Mesoamericans who from time to time sponsored various mercantile ventures into this northern borderlands.*[142] (emphasis added).

Isn't it ironic how Xicanos claim the Aztecs came from the southwest (**Gran Chichimeca**) but they cannot identify with any other Indian nations who came from, went to or reside in the southwest, past or present??? That is myopic tunnel vision and that is "identity self-incarceration," and self-robbery believing you are only a descendant of the Aztecs. Still some of the greatest Apache Chichimeca were no doubt Mexican. The great Apache Chief Chihuahua was kidnapped as a young Mexican boy and so was the great Victorio. As writes author Angie Debo, "Geronimo" also was very likely Mexican born. "It should be noted... that some of the older Fort Sill Apaches believe that Geronimo was born in old Mexico. They remember that he spoke with an accent different than that of their own people."[143] Like many Apaches, Geronimo also spoke Spanish. By today's white standards, he would be called an Hispanic.

Europeans will have you believe that Mexico was conquered in two years, but consider this passage by George C. Valiant in *Aztecs of Mexico*: "It took almost four hundred years to conquer and pacify the north, a process in which Spanish, French, British and other nationals participated. This largely explained by the fact that most of this region was inhabited by nomadic hunting – gathering groups who loved their liberty and tenaciously opposed subjugation."[144]

So, the truth is since Spain's occupation started from 1519 and ended in 1821 with Mexican Independence then the reality is that in the end the Mexican **Chichimeca** defeated these Spanish invaders!!! So militarily inept and frightened of the Chichimeca were the Spaniards that they nicknamed the area of the Gran Chichimeca, **Tierra de Guerra**.

Antonio Haas in his book *Mexico* writes, "In Mexico the last of the Chichimeca on the Mexican side of the border finally surrendered. The conquest and settlement of the northern states constituted the last, painfully prolonged stage of the **Chichimeca War**. The Sonora Yaqui War for example signed its most recent armistice with President Cardenas as late as 1937."[145] (emphasis added)

On the **American** side the Chichimeca Wars ended with the Apache (Geronimo) and lastly with the Mojave; but some 40 to 50 years later they finally surrendered in Mexico! But wait the Yaqui's were not the last to surrender. The Chichimeca War was still not over. In *Desert, the American Southwest*, Ruth Kirk discusses evidence of their continued struggle. "The Spanish repeatedly sought to "tame" them and resettle them at inland missions for transformation from fishermen and desert hunters to farmers of corn and squash. They failed. Nor could the Mexicans who succeeded the Spanish as rulers manage to subdue the Seris. As late as the 1940's the government of Mexico acknowledged the tribe still controlled about 1000 square miles. Determining their own lives and thinking their own thoughts. Frontier Indians holding their culture intact and dealing with modern realities only on their own terms. The Seri fished and sold the catch; they hunted sea turtles with spears, and deer with bow and arrows. They painted their faces and sang their songs and lived their lives."[146] The collapse of these Chichimeca began to occur with the advent of protestant missionaries and commercial interest in the guise of fishermen. "A final, blow came in 1965 when Tiburon Island, the largest island in Mexican waters and most beloved stronghold of the Seri Indians, was decreed as a preserve for wildlife and closed to hunting."(loc. cit.)

Some colonial Spanish historians from their interviews with indigenous informants further subdivided the generic Chichimeca. The **Teo**chichimeca were considered "complete barbarians." The **Zaca**chichimeca were "wild men of the woods." The Mexican city of Zacatecas was named after the Chichimeca who originally resided there calling themselves, the Zacateca (people of the "woods" or "wild"). What do we call grass in Spanish? *Zacate*, no doubt a Hispanized Náhuatl word that is a cognate with the word Zacateca. Chichimeca fishermen who lived and worked along the water were called **Atl**chichimeca meaning "barbarians of the water." Let me caution you on the Spaniards interpretation of Chichimeca to mean barbarian for it was in their interest to demonize the indigenous people they were out to destroy.

Going back to the earlier figurative description of all our ancestoral nations as being a collection of uncles, my favorite is that of the Apache... As a result, I *discarded my* Roman name. My indigenous name now is Apaxu, which is a cognate of Apache or Apachu. It is the name I chose to pay them respect for their military success against the invading white Europeans. They stimulate me with great energy and pride that should be the objective of history and not confusion and disillusion.

I've yet to speak to one graduate or participant of Xicano Studies who has changed their Roman name for an Indigenous name. Why promote and participate in Xicano Studies if it doesn't free and activate the caged Indian in you?

"Chichimeca is a Náhuatl term of uncertain meaning that was used by the Spaniards in the Spanish forms of Chichimecas or Chichimecos as a generic label for the unsettled peoples of northern Mexico and the southwest. An example of Chichimecos that certainly includes Apaches is found in Diego Pérez de Luxán's account of the Espejo expedition."[147] When I came across this quotation, it convinced me that some time in the future I must write a monograph. Its' title will be, *Chichimeca: Forgotten Ancestors*. In a speech I gave at California State University, Fullerton, I compared my ancestors the Azteca and the Apache, I remember saying: "When I read about the Aztecs I feel motivated to build pyramids, temples and monuments, but when I read about the Apache-Chichimeca I feel like kickin' some ass and taking back some land!" I was given a standing ovation.

The purpose of history can be reduced to one word, "energy." It can *energize* you or it can *anesthetize* you. History as it is taught to us institutionally de-energizes us. We must take the reins of history and not *reconstruct* but truthfully *reveal* our history so we can be energized.

You have to admit that the generic identity of the Chichimeca provide us with a greater land base, greater numbers of people, histories, pride and motivation contrary to Aztec *history a la carte*. However, the identity of this word (Chichimeca) has many modern incorrect and distorted interpretations and usages detrimental to our psyche. Today, especially in

Mexico Chichimecos means "a person without education and having indecent bad manners and language."[148] It became a term to insult and disrespect people or peoples especially Indios. It evolved from the Spaniards use and definition to signify uncivilized people even though it did not originally mean this. Here in the United States in the slang form mecos, its' clipped version means "sperm."* Just think about this. On the one hand, we boast of the Aztecs who were originally called Chichimeca but on the other hand, we defame them specifically and all the other beautiful people represented by our Chichimeca ancestors by utilizing the definition propagandized by foreign invaders of Europe. Because we do not know our HISTORIES and allow others to identify us, they are able to take our language and concepts to redefine and degrade.

The *vandals* a nomadic people of pre-modern Europe no longer in existence but who paralleled the Chichimeca in many ways they are another example of how and when Indigenous peoples are conquered their identities become degraded by the conquerors and adopted in definition by the conquered themselves. "*Vandalism* became a vernacular word for wanton destruction of everything fine and precious."[149]

Let us take back this pre-Columbian indigenous word and identity, reconstruct and reintroduce its definition, modernize, utilize, and personalize it. Let us call all the indigenous peoples of the southwest United States Chichimeca. Mysteriously it serves as a beautiful acronym, since it incorporates all the indigenous groups that make-up the southwest.

---

*Meco/meca-lower class person; person in a bad mood; mecos npl. (vulg.) semen, seminal fluid "Mecos- (popular abbreviation of Chichimeco, Chichimecos)... someone who in his bowel movements has dark grooves or lines." Robelo, p. 78).

CHI.CHI.ME.C.A. or XI.XI.ME.C.A.

CHIcanos (Xicanos)	XIcanos
CHIchimecos (today's southwestern enrolled Indians)	XIximecos
ME (Mexicanos)	MExicanos
C (Ciudadanos)	Ciudadanos
A (Anasazi)	Anasazi

That is right, we are all Anasazi or ancient *citizens* of the southwest map or no map. Mexicanos are the descendants of a multitude of Indigenous nations throughout former New Spain (Mexico and United States southwest) that were detribalized and systematically over centuries Mexicanized (Mexicanos). Xicanos were de-Mexicanized Mexicanos as a result of the 1846-1848 Mexican-American War and its aftermath. Enrolled Indians of the southwest are the Indians that survived Spanish and Mexican detribalization into Mexicanization. The American warring with and placing them on reservations maintained their tribal identity.

President Nelson Mandela while a nationalist revolutionary member of the African National Congress (A.N.C.) symbolically burned his "pass book" which was used to identify individuals of color and regulate their legal movement throughout South Africa. Whites, the minority invaders, and people in power were not required to carry such *"pass books."* Organized gatherings of tens of thousands of indigenous Black South Africans would repeat Mandela's burning of the "pass book", a document introduced by foreign invaders to simplify and better control indigenous peoples. Do not let this map that we treasure so much become our "pass book"! Like Nelson Mandela implied, indigenous people do not need permission from foreigners! No, as Indios, tambien; *We don't need to enroll, we need to overthrow his externally imposed identities and control our self-imposed identities.*

Lastly, I feel reinstituting the term and concept Chichimeca will heal the scars of separation and act as a bridge to understanding and unity between enrolled and unenrolled Indians in the southwest.

RIGHT 4 BIRTH
NATION BUILIDING
(DOORWAY TO POWER)

During the course of looking 4 Aztlán, I came to this realization. It is not a question of birthright, but an issue of Aztlán being right 4 birth. In any combination of political, social, archaeological, linguistic, or racial logic and honesty, it can be clearly established that Xicanos are indigenous to the southwest (not to mention the Gran Chichimeca). The difference is that today indigenous authors are willing, able and actually articulating this fact which we have not done or been allowed to do to any great degree in the past.

This now moves us to the next challenge of the making of Aztlán or *nation building*.

There are many of those who will say Aztlán is in the making. I strongly disagree and at the risk of being labeled a pessimist or even the classic vendido I will further state Aztlán has not even been born, not to mention developing and crystallizing. Nations are not born spontaneously with wishful thinking; they are built from the ground up one brick at a time. The basic and critical tool used to build a nation is nationalism or "the idea (ism) of building a nation." No nation as a state (territory) or as a people has been born without the tool of nationalism. Nationalism is *value neutral* meaning that it is neither good nor bad but simply a tool. The person or group of people who harness and utilize its properties will determine whether it is righteous or evil.

Since it is my objective only to introduce the idea of nationalism and not thoroughly define, defend, analyze and promote it I will only briefly discuss it.

How do oppressed people go about nation building?

RESEARCH. The first step is research. Each and every one of us must take the personal responsibility of researching successful nation builders of the past and modern era; both inside and outside of the United States. I say inside of the United States because there are several powerful nations within the United States. Such groups as the Amish, Mormons, and American Jews. Historically, the American founding fathers provide an excellent example. Nation builders outside of the United States such as the Israeli Jews, Palestinians, the French, and the Zapatistas of the 1910 Mexican Revolution should be closely examined as to how and to what extent they successfully used nationalism. You may or may not like one or any of these groups or identities but there is a wise Chinese saying that is applicable here: "You can learn from those you admire, and you can learn from those you love; but you can also learn from those you hate". Yassir Arafat's Palestinian Nation operates under the belief that they have no permanent enemies or permanent friends, only permanent goals. In the Zapatistas' declaration of independence or Plan de Ayala it is written, "…We are not personalists, we are partisans of principles and not of men!" The pre-Israeli Jews while land-less, without a common language and in worldwide Diaspora extracted most of their knowledge about nationalism from their two worst oppressors; the Germans and the Russians. Today they have a nation of their own more powerful than those two combined. It is the infrastructure of nationalism that we should seek, examine, and apply.

NATIONAL DISCUSSION. Once we begin to study and understand nationalism, we must introduce and discuss this concept with our families, circle of friends, barrios, regional grassroots political groups, and national conferences. There has never been a national conference that has focused intensively and extensively on the issue of nationalism as a vehicle to improving our living conditions or outright autonomy or even independence. I heard the term mentioned very often but never have I heard anyone define its properties. There are many myths and misunderstandings of the word and concept. It is important to realize that unless you understand it then you cannot intelligently comment on its worth or worthlessness. It is all "around" you camouflaged in many colors, shapes, words, and forms. If these bodies of people use it successfully then why shouldn't we? I have repeatedly pointed out in my lectures that if I would return to college I would enroll in Jewish-Studies instead of Xicano or Native American Studies. Xicano Studies has become a compilation of *contributions* by Xicanos to this nation rather than works of how Xicanos can empower themselves through nation building. Our contributions or lack of contributions are not the source of our problems or solutions. The lack of power is our fundamental problem, and the gathering of power is our solution.

The study of Zionism in my opinion offers the very best model of the intricacies and infrastructure of nationalism. Their documented struggles of inventing, developing and crystallizing the idea of Zionism is the most prolific and informative of any case of nation building in the world. Israel is often referred to as a warrior-nation but they are also a nation of authors. Comparatively speaking they may have the most authors per capita than any nation. They have a great concentration of writing about the Holocaust and the making of their nation whose vehicle was a nationalism they called Zionism.

NATIONAL BODY. It will be found that in utilizing nationalism successfully it is necessary to create a national body made-up of Xicanos with Congress-like responsibilities to represent and mobilize in unison a people who desire to become a nation. This national body fundamentally will act to *centralize* (1) leadership (not power); (2) policy; (3) activities.

For nearly two thousand years, Jews were landless, nation less, scattered, and victimized throughout the world. In the 1800's, a single European Jew invented the idea of religious Zionism or the return of Jews throughout the world to Mt. Zion (a hill) to await the arrival of the true Messiah. Decades later another European Jew in another part of Europe deviated from religious Zionism and created political Zionism. It was his belief that not only must Jews return to Israel (then Palestine) but that Israel itself must be returned to the Jews. Its founder Theodor Herzl helped formulate the *World Zionist Congress*, used to centralize leadership, policy, and activities for Jews from throughout the world to act in unison. Their main objective after some time became the massive infiltration (immigration) occupation, development, and eventual liberation of Palestine (Eretz Israel) into modern Israel in 1949. Prior to the birth of Israel but during their systematic world-wide Jewish infiltration of then Palestine the Jewish-Palestine population was voluntarily self-directed by an unofficial Congress-like body called the *National Council of Eretz Israel*. Even though this land prior to the birth of modern Israel was called Palestine, the incoming Jews called it Eretz Israel meaning the land of Israel. This is similar to Xicanos calling the southwest Aztlán instead of (or in addition to) by the name of its states.

Today the World Zionist Congress since it served its main purpose has disappeared. However, Jews from throughout the world do have the benefit of a world congress-like body, which is even more powerful called the *World Jewish Congress*. This is the organization, which brought Switzerland to its economic knees for their country's role in conspiring with Nazi Germany of WW II to steal Jewish gold and savings.

Today the Palestinians, the victims of Zionism have studied, emulated, and even copied much of the infrastructure of Jewish Nationalism. They have had for several decades a congress-like body they call the P.N.C. or Palestinian National Council. The semi-autonomous mini-state or *Palestinian Authority* is a direct result of the existence of the P.N.C. Apartheid of South Africa owes its current collapse to the A.N.C. or African national Congress. I can envision a legitimate and mature Xicano National Congress taking on the issue of the Spanish land grants, for example, as a numerous gigantic Xicano nation and having much more leverage and success instead of our present impoverished and fragmented groups attempting to seek legal justice individually.

There are more Palestinian refugees in exile than reside within the Palestinian authority. In spite of the fact that they are a people in Diaspora and a nation in exile, they among all other Arab peoples are the best educated (per capita) and most cohesive. Nationalism provides their rigid boundaries. They are not only fighting against the warrior-nation of Israel, the worlds fourth largest militia, but the greatest military nation (U.S.A.) in history and nearly all of Europe as well. Where as other peoples would have submitted and submerged they are a vivid people or nation to be reckoned with.

The Amish reside within the United States. Though they number less than a quarter-million and are scattered throughout the Midwest and utilize limited technology they are also benefactors of nationalism. Their national community is made up of designated districts made up of Amish families. Each district is provided leadership by a bishop who with other bishops throughout the nation occasionally meet to function as an unofficial congressional body. From the bishop down to the individual of each family is guided by a written religious* doctrine created in Europe several hundreds of years ago. Though they are probably less than 1/50

---

*The original doctrine is called "Dotre-Tua Confession of Fatta" – 1683 in Doretre Tua Holland.

the population of Xicanos they have hundreds of schools, medical facilities, economic autonomy, control and develop agricultural lands and produce, speak three languages, refuse outside interference or aid, and do not under any circumstances spill blood for this country. They are a nation within a nation. They do all this without breaking any laws or conducting themselves violently, unethically, or immorally.

The Jews spoke and speak of *Biblical entitlement* in founding, justifying, and maintaining their nation of Israel. Now Xicanos speak of *Map Entitlement* in dreaming of Aztlán (or the southwest). Are these both the same strategies: using documents as *silly putty* to say what they wish it to say? If it is or is not the difference is the Jews got real, got busy and got nationalistic. Xicanos on the other hand only *got conferences*, more conferences, and more conferences. Conferences unfortunately have lost their vigor and sincerity resulting in a carnival like atmosphere. There is no sense of panic, urgency, or mission among its participants only excitement and recreation.

In comparison to the Zionist Jews of yesteryear, we have many advantages:

1) We do not have to have a massive and expensive campaign to emigrate and immigrate to infiltrate. We are already here and in great numbers.

2) We have greater cultural cohesion than the Diaspora Jews had when arriving in Palestine (Eretz-Israel). We share common foods, language, religion, political, historical, economic and social status. These are all potential building blocks for nationalism.

3) Though "Antigua Residencia de los Aztecas" does not give us birthright per se or the land, we do have a name for the birth of our nation – AZTLÁN. Lets stop trying to find it and start to define and develop its nationalistic boundaries, territorially, culturally, and politically.

4) We have a name for the citizenry of Aztlán – XICANOS; Another great advantage since this creates rigidness in our identity and population.

5) We have been and are the economic backbone of the southwestern economy. We now have to harness our group membership or become like ants: organize, cooperate, coexist, and give supreme loyalty to our newly selected group or nation.

Another element though that turned the momentum in favor of the World Zionist Congress was the World War II holocaust. I hope we do not have to have a similar catastrophe to realize we must nationalize. That is what the ghost dance movement was in a nutshell. The realization that unless indigenous nations united and dropped their psuedo differences the end or extinction at the hands of European invaders was inevitable. Indians did begin in a panic to unite through the ghost dance phenomenon. That realization and response, however, came too late.

In the case of the Holocaust the World Zionist congress fortunately had in operation already the framework or infrastructure of a congress to accommodate the building of a nation and Israel was born. Will we be ready should we need to encounter a similar fate to activate? There are those that argue that *ethnic cleansing* has quietly but violently continued in this country and in our community since the military acquisition of the southwest some 150 years ago. We are disproportionately represented in the prison populations, die in greater numbers of aids, tuberculosis, alcoholism, diabetes and other diseases. We have the lowest paying jobs which means the most impoverished neighborhoods which means the least effective schools and academic achievements and on and on. This may not be as obvious and vivid as the Jewish Holocaust and the images of millions of skeleton-thin defenseless people being gassed to death, however, it is just as vicious in its' eventual wholesale destruction of an indigenous people. Is this enough to mobilize a people to large-scale action?

There should be in place in advance an infrastructure or Congress that Xicanos can resort to should living conditions worsen, which they undoubtedly will. I believe it was the revolutionary Jose Martí who once accurately stated, "People are not motivated by ideas but by conditions."

NATION OR STATE

You can have a nation without having a state but you cannot have a state without having a nation. Nation building or nationalism is a prerequisite to a nation-state.

A state requires specific territorial boundaries and the acting of the highest civil authority. Calling for the territorial state or nation-state of Aztlán would be a direct challenge and confrontation with the United States Congress, or simply put: a declaration of war. Is this what you or we want? This is what the First American Congress did in their Declaration of Independence. Is the Plan de Aztlán a document to be taken seriously or poetically (really the Poem de Aztlán)? There is a saying that goes, "The victors of war write history and the losers write poetry." Are we poets pretending to be revolutionaries?

Or are we committed to the idea of observing, utilizing and implementing what American Jews, Mormons, and the Amish for example have done in this country. They have created nations within a nation. They utilize and enjoy a dual citizenship with their primary loyalty belonging to members of their grouping or nation. In developing and crystallizing social nationalism only, you do not need territory but the cooperation, coexistence, consolidation and supreme loyalty of its' group's membership or citizenry. That is the challenge, which is Aztlán, which is being indigenous and not the notation on the map: "Antigua Residencia de los Aztecas."

We will always be a part of the southwest as history has shown. The question is however, **are we to be here as masters of our destiny or as the destiny of our masters**? We can have a say and nationalism is the way.

Michael D. Coe in *Mexico* writes:

"ODD THOUGH IT MAY SEEM, DURING THE HYPSITHERMAL, MEN CONTINUED TO LIVE THROUGHOUT EVEN THE MOST DESICATED ZONES OF NORTH AMERICA. SPECIES AFTER SPECIES OF LARGE GAME ANIMALS PERISHED NOT LONG AFTER ITS ONSET – MASTADON, MAMMOTH, HORSE, CAMEL, GIANT BISON, GROUND SLOTH, DIRE WOLF, ETC. – **BUT THE INDIAN SURVIVED.**"

WE AIN'T GOING NO WHERE, THIS IS HOME, **OUR** HOME!

ENDNOTES

1. Richard F. Townsend, *The Aztecs* (London: Thames and Hudson, Ltd., 1992), pp. 55, 56.
2. Michael Pina, "The Archaic, Historical and Mythicized Dimensions of Aztlán," in *Aztlán, Essays on the Chicano Homeland*, ed. Rudolfo Anaya and Francisco A. Lomelí (Albuquerque: University of New Mexico Press, 1989), p. 29.
3. Pina, p. 30.
4. Jacques Soustelle, *Daily Life of the Aztecs*, on the Eve of the Spanish Conquest (New York: The MacMillan Company, 1962), p. 217.
5. Pina, p. 30.
6. Pina, (italics added), p. 20.
7. Henry P. Walker and Don Bufkin, *Historical Atlas of Arizona*, 2nd Ed., (Oklahoma: University of Oklahoma Press, 1986), p. 16A.
8. Seymour E. Ehrenberg, *The Mapping of America*, (New York: Harry N. Abrams, Inc., Publishers, 1980), p. 287.
9. Jack Utter, *American Indians, Answers to Today's Questions*, (Michigan: National Woodlands Publishing Co., 1993), pp 6-8.
10. C.W. Ceram, *A story of American Archaeology*, (New York: Harcourt Brace Jonavich, Inc., N.Y.), p. 32.
11. David Greenhood, *Down to Earth: Mapping for Everybody*, (New York: Holiday House, 1951)
12. Greenwood, p. 5.
13. Greenhood, p. 6.
14. Luis F. Hernandez, *Aztlán, the Southwest and its Peoples*, (New Jersey: Hayden Book Company, Inc., 1975), p. 7.
15. Wilfred Funk, Litt. D., *Word Origins and their Romantic Stories*, (New York: Bell Publishing Company, 1978), p. 250.
16. Marshall Trimble, *Arizona, A Cavalcade of History*, (Arizona: Treasure Chest Publications, 1990), p. 54.
17. John R. Chávez, "Aztlán, Cibola, and Frontier New Spain" in *Aztlán, Essays on the Chicano Homeland*, ed. Rudolfo Anaya and Francisco A. Lomelí (Albuquerque: University of New Mexico Press, 1989), p. 56.
18. Trimble, p. 54.
19. Hernandez, p. 10.
20. Chávez, pp. 56, 57.
21. Richard Townsend, *The Aztecs*, (Thames and Hudson, 1992), p. 57.
22. Trimble, p. 57.
23. Chávez, p. 59.
24. Hernandez, p.13.
25. Edwin Corle, *The Gila, River of the Southwest*, (Lincoln: University of Nebraska Press, 1951), pp. 38-39.

26 Robert Julyan, *The Place Names of New Mexico*, (Albuquerque: University of New Mexico Press, 1998), p. 27.
27 Greenwood.
28 Julyan, pp. 83, 84.
29 Hernandez, p. 16.
30 Trimble, p. 57.
31 Chavez, p. 61.
32 New Spain's Far Northern Frontier, *Essays on Spain in the American West, 1540-1821*, ed. David J. Weber (Albuquerque: University of New Mexico Press, 1979), p. 22.
33 Hernandez, p. 13.
34 Carl I. Wheat, *Mapping the Transmississippi West*, (Martino Publishing, 1995), Vol. I, p. 21.
35 Weber, p. 29.
36 Wheat, vol. I, p. 25.
37 Joseph P. Sanchez, *Explorers, Traders, and Slavers, Forging the Old Spanish Trail, 1678-1850*, (Salt Lake City: University of Utah Press, 1997), p. 5.
38 Wheat, vol. I, p. 27.
39 Trimble, p. 60.
40 Wheat, vol. I, p. 26.
41 Trimble, p. 60.
42 Chavez, p. 63.
43 Weber, p. 26.
44 Seymour E. Ehrenberg, *The Mapping of America*, (New York: Harry N. Abrams, Inc., Publishers, 1980), p. 112.
45 Chavez, p. 62.
46 Sanchez, p. 5.
47 Carey McWilliams, *North from Mexico*, (1949).
48 Weber, p. 29.
49 Sanchez, p. 7.
50 Weber.
51 Charles W. Polzer, *Kino, a Legacy, his Life, his Works, his Monuments*, (Tucson: S. J. Jesuit Fathers of Arizona, 1998), p. 49.
52 Sanchez, p. 11.
53 Ehrenberg, p. 110.
54 Sanchez, p. 11.
55 Wheat, vol. I, pp. 80.
56 Sanchez, p. x.
57 Pina, p. 20.
58 Sanchez, p. 6.
59 *The Dominguez-Escalante Journal*, their Expedition through Colorado, Utah, Arizona and New Mexico in 1776, ed. Ted J. Warner, translated by Fray Angelico Chavez, (Salt Lake: University of Utah Press, 1995), p. 31.

60 Sanchez, p. 38.
61 Wheat, vol. I, p. 87.
62 Wheat, vol. I, p. 83.
63 Sanchez, p. 44.
64 *The Route of the Dominguez-Escalante Expedition, 1776-77*, ed. David E. Miller, (A report of trail research conducted under the auspices of the Dominguez-Escalante state/federal Bicentennial committee and the Four Corners regional commission, 1976), p.v.
65 Warner, ed., p. 52.
66 Sanchez, p. 12.
67 Miller, ed., p. 1.
68 Warner, p. 33.
69 Sanchez, p. 15.
    *Miera was schooled in the use of the modern astrolabe – a crude ancestor of the modern sextant – and could make maps and chart locations and route for the expedition. Miller, ed., david miller]
70 Warner, p. 53.
71 Herbert E. Bolton, *Pageant in the Wilderness, the story of the Escalante Expedition to the Interior Basin, 1776* (Utah: Salt Lake City, 1951 (Historical Quarterly, Vol XVIII, 1951, pp. 243-250).
72 Wheat, I, p. 102. Miera doubtless erred as to the smelting of metals. But extraordinary ruins of these ancient peoples still distinguish this general area, the best known being probably those of Mesa Verde.
73 Stephen Metzger, *New Mexico Handbook*, (Moon Publications, 1991) p. 68.
74 Wheat, vol. I, p. 105.
75 Warner, p. 63.
76 Sanchez, p. 46.
77 Sanchez, p. 66.
78 Wheat, vol. I, p. 98.
79 Sanchez.
80 Bolton, p. 244.
81 Warner, p.22.
82 *The Missions of New Mexico, 1776*, a description by Fray Francisco Atanasio Dominguez, with other contemporary documents, translated and annotated by Eleanor B. Adams & Fray Angelico Chavez, (Albuquerque: The Unveristy of New Mexico Press, 1956) p. 287.
83 Warner, p. 32.
84 Bolton, p. 44.
85 Warner, p. 73.
86 Sanchez, p. 14.
87 Sanchez, p. 15.
88 Warner, p. 72.

89 Helmut de Tierra, *Humboldt the Life and Times of Alexander Von Humboldt, 1769-1859*, (New York: Alfred A. Knopf, Inc., 1955), p. 84.
90 L. Kellner, *Alexander Von Humboldt*, (Friedrich Wilhelm Heinrich), (London: Oxford University Press, 1963), p. 61.
91 Wheat, vol. I, p. 132.
92 Wheat, vol I, p. 137.
93 Kellner, p. 66.
94 de Tierra, p. 203.
95 Richard F. Townsend, *The Aztecs*, (Thames and Hudson, 1992), p. 55.
96 C. A. Burland, *Montezuma*, (New York: G.P. Putnam's Sons, 1973)
97 Carl I. Wheat, *Mapping the Transmississippi West*, (Martino Publishing, 1995), vol 2, p. 96.
98 Jack Rittenhouse, *Disturnell's Treaty Map, the map that was part of the Guadalupe Hidalgo Treaty on Southwestern Boundaries, 1848*, (Santa Fe: Stagecoach Press, 1965), p.5.
99 Carl I. Wheat, *Mapping the Transmississippi West*, (Martino Publishing, 1995), vol. 3, p. 37.
100 Rittenhouse, p. 12.
101 Rittenhouse, p. 13.
102 Wheat, vol I, p. 36.
103 Rittenhouse, p. 35.
104 Wheat, vol. 3, p. 7.
105 Rittenhouse, p. 7.
106 Wheat, vol. 2, p. 24.
107 Wheat, vol. 1, p. 25.
108 Wheat, vol. 3, p. 37.
109 Warner, p. 120.
110 Sanchez, p. 16.
111 Charles H. Lange and Carroll L. Riley, *Bandelier, the Life and Adventures of Adolph Bandelier*, (Salt Lake City, University of Utah Press, 1996), p. 2.
112 Lange and Riley, p. 204.
113 Sanchez, p. 33.
114 Ramón A. Gutiérrez, "Aztlán, Montezuma, and New Mexico: The Political Uses of American Indian Mythology" in *Aztlán, Essays on the Chicano Homeland*, ed. Rudolfo Anaya and Francisco A. Lomelí (Albuquerque: University of New Mexico Press, 1989), p. 172.
115 *Handbook of North American Indians*, ed. William C. Sturtevart, Volume 9, the Southwest, (Smithsonian Institution, 1979), p. 617.
116 Gutierrez, pp. 175, 176.
117 Luis Leal, "In Search of Aztlán" in *Aztlán, Essays on the Chicano Homeland*, ed. Rudolfo Anaya and Francisco A. Lomelí (Albuquerque: University of New Mexico Press, 1989), p. 10.
118 Leal, p. 11.

119 David Weber, *Foreigners in Their Own Land*,
120 *Earl Morris and Southwestern Archaeology*, University of New Mexico Press, reprinted by Southwest Parks and Monuments Association, p. 85.
121 Ann Axtell Morris, *Digging in the Southwest*, (Chicago: E.M. Hale & Co., 1933), p. 48.
122 Ruth Benedict, *Race: Science and Politics, The State of Native America, Genocide, Colonization, and Resistance*, ed. M. Annette Jaimes (Boston: South End Press, 1992), p. 53; fn 123.
123 Paul Radin, *Story of the American Indian*, (Liveright Pub. Corp., 1962), p. 364.
124 Benedict,
125 Jack Forbes, *Aztecas del Norte*, the Chicanos of Aztlán, (Greenwich: Fawcett Publications, Inc., 1973), p. 151.
126 Benedict, p. .
127 Jaimes, p.
128 Forbes, p. 195.
129 Carey McWilliams, *North from Mexico, 1949*.
130 McWilliams, p.
131 LeRoy R. Hafen and Ann W. Hafen, *Old Spanish Trail, Santa Fe to Los Angeles*, p. 233-234.
132 William B. Griffen, *Handbook of North American Indians*, (Smithsonian Institution), p.341.
133 Forbes, p. 197.
134 *Handbook of North American Indians, Vol. 10*. ed. Alfonso Ortiz (Smithsonian Institution, 1979), p. 347.
135 Forbes, p. 31.
136 Ernest Wallace and E. Adamson Hoebel, *The Comanches, Lords of the South Plains*, (Norman: University of Oklahoma Press, 1958), p. 18.
137 National Geographic Society, *World of the American Indian*, p. 154.
138 *Handbook of North American Indians Vol. 10*, ed. Alfonso Ortiz (Smithsonian Institution, 1979), p. 340.
139 C.W. Ceram, *A Story of North American Archaeology*, p. 73.
140 *Bolton and the Spanish Borderlands*, ed. John Francis Banon, (Oklahoma: University of Oklahoma Press).
141 Ortiz, vol. 10, p. 329.
142 Geronimo p.9.
143 George C. Vaillant, *Aztecs of Mexico,Origin, Rise and Fall of the Aztec Nation*, (New York: Doubleday & Co., 1950).
144 Antonio Haas, Mexico.
145 Ruth Kirk, *Desert, the American Southwest*, p. 104.
146 Ortiz, vol. 10, "Southwest."
147 Cecilio A. Robelo, *Diccionario de Aztequismos* (Mexico Press).
148 Benedict.

BIBLIOGRAPHY

Benedict, Ruth. *Race: Science and Politics.*

Bolton, Herbert E. *Pageant in the Wilderness, the story of the Escalante Expedition to the Interior Basin, 1776.* Historical Quarterly, Vol XVIII. Utah: Salt Lake City, 1951

Bolton and the Spanish Borderlands. ed. John Francis Banon. Oklahoma: University of Oklahoma Press.

Burland, C. A. *Montezuma.* New York: G.P. Putnam's Sons, 1973.

Ceram, C. W. *A Story of American Archaeology.* New York: Harcourt Brace Jonavich, Inc., N.Y.

Chávez, John R. "Aztlán, Cibola, and Frontier New Spain" in *Aztlán, Essays on the Chicano Homeland,* ed. Rudolfo Anaya and Francisco A. Lomelí. Albuquerque: University of New Mexico Press, 1989.

Corle, Edwin. *The Gila, River of the Southwest.* Lincoln: University of Nebraska Press, 1951.

de Tierra, Helmut. *Humboldt, the Life and Times of Alexander Von Humboldt, 1769-1859.* New York: Alfred A. Knopf, Inc., 1955.

Ehrenberg, Seymour E. *The Mapping of America.* New York: Harry N. Abrams, Inc., Publishers, 1980.

Forbes, Jack. *Aztecas del Norte, the Chicanos of Aztlán.* Greenwich: Fawcett Publications, Inc., 1973.

Greenwood, David. *Down to Earth: Mapping for Everybody.* New York: Holiday House, 1951.

Griffen, William B. *Handbook of North American Indians.* Smithsonian Institution.

Gutiérrez, Ramón A. "Aztlán, Montezuma, and New Mexico: The Political Uses of American Indian Mythology" in *Aztlán, Essays on the Chicano Homeland,* ed. Rudolfo Anaya and Francisco A. Lomelí. Albuquerque: University of New Mexico Press, 1989.

Haas, Antonio. *Mexico.*

Hafen, LeRoy R., and Hafen, Ann W. *Old Spanish Trail, Santa Fe to Los Angeles.*

Handbook of North American Indians, Vol. 9, the Southwest. ed. William C. Sturtevart. Smithsonian Institution, 1979.

Handbook of North American Indians, Vol. 10. ed. Alfonso Ortiz. Smithsonian Institution, 1979.

Hernandez, Luis F. *Aztlán, the Southwest and its Peoples.* New Jersey: Hayden Book Company, Inc., 1975.

Julyan, Robert. *The Place Names of New Mexico.* Albuquerque: University of New Mexico Press, 1998.

Kellner, L. *Alexander Von Humboldt, (Friedrich Wilhelm Heinrich).* London: Oxford University Press, 1963.

Kirk, Ruth. *Desert, the American Southwest.*

Lange, Charles H., and Riley,Carroll L. *Bandelier, the Life and Adventures of Adolph Bandelier.* Salt Lake City, University of Utah Press, 1996.

Leal, Luis. "In Search of Aztlán" in *Aztlán, Essays on the Chicano Homeland,* ed. Rudolfo Anaya and Francisco A. Lomelí. Albuquerque: University of New Mexico Press, 1989.

Metzger, Stephen. *New Mexico Handbook.* Moon Publications, 1991.

Miller, David E. *The Route of the Dominguez-Escalante Expedition, 1776-77,* (A report of trail research conducted under the auspices of the Dominguez-Escalante state/federal Bicentennial committee and the Four Corners regional commission), ed. 1976.

The Missions of New Mexico, 1776, a description by Fray Francisco Atanasio Dominguez, with other contemporary documents, translated and annotated by Eleanor B. Adams & Fray Angelico Chavez. Albuquerque: The Unveristy of New Mexico Press, 1956.

Morris, Anne Axtel. *Digging in the Southwest.* Chicago: E.M. Hale & Co., 1933.

Morris, Earl and Southwestern Archaeology, University of New Mexico Press, reprinted by Southwest Parks and Monuments Association, p. 85.

McWilliams, Carey. *North from Mexico.* 1949.

National Geographic Society, *World of the American Indian*.

Pina, Michael. "The Archaic, Historical and Mythicized Dimensions of Aztlán," in *Aztlán, Essays on the Chicano Homeland*, ed. Rudolfo Anaya and Francisco A. Lomelí. Albuquerque: University of New Mexico Press, 1989.

Polzer, Charles W. *Kino, a Legacy, his Life, his Works, his Monuments*. Tucson: S. J. Jesuit Fathers of Arizona, 1998.

Radin, Paul. *Story of the American Indian*. Liveright Pub. Corp., 1962.

Rittenhouse, Jack. *Disturnell's Treaty Map, the map that was part of the Guadalupe Hidalgo Treaty on Southwestern Boundaries, 1848*. Santa Fe: Stagecoach Press, 1965.

Robelo, Cecilio A. *Diccionario de Aztequismos*. Mexico Press.

Sanchez, Joseph P. *Explorers, Traders, and Slavers, Forging the Old Spanish Trail, 1678-1850*. Salt Lake City: University of Utah Press, 1997.

Soustelle, Jacques. *Daily Life of the Aztecs, on the Eve of the Spanish Conquest*. New York: The MacMillan Company, 1962.

The State of Native America, Genocide, Colonization, and Resistance, ed. M. Annette Jaimes. Boston: South End Press, 1992.

Trimble, Marshall. *Arizona, A Cavalcade of History*. Arizona: Treasure Chest Publications, 1990.

Townsend, Richard F. Townsend. *The Aztecs*. London: Thames and Hudson, Ltd., 1992.

Utter, Jack. *American Indians, Answers to Today's Questions*. Michigan: National Woodlands Publishing Co., 1993.

Vaillant, George C. *Aztecs of Mexico, Origin, Rise and Fall of the Aztec Nation*. New York: Doubleday & Co., 1950.

Walker, Henry P. and Bufkin, Don. *Historical Atlas of Arizona*, 2nd Ed. Oklahoma: University of Oklahoma Press, 1986.

Wallace, Ernest and Hoebel, E. Adamson. *The Comanches, Lords of the South Plains*. Norman: University of Oklahoma Press, 1958.

Warner, Ted J. *The Dominguez-Escalante Journal, their Expedition through Colorado, Utah, Arizona and New Mexico in 1776,* ed. with translation by Fray Angelico Chavez. Salt Lake: University of Utah Press, 1995.

Weber, David J. *New Spain's Far Northern Frontier, Essays on Spain in the American West, 1540-1821,* ed. Albuquerque: University of New Mexico Press, 1979.

Wheat, Carl I. *Mapping the Transmississippi West,* Vol. I, III. Martino Publishing, 1995.

Weber, David. *Foreigners in Their Own Land.*